AL-KINDĪ

GREAT MEDIEVAL THINKERS

Series Editor
Brian Davies
Blackfriars College, University of Oxford,
and Fordham University

DUNS SCOTUS
Richard Cross

BERNARD OF CLAIRVAUX
Gillian R. Evans

JOHN SCOTTUS ERIUGENA
Deirdre Carabine

ROBERT GROSSETESTE
James McEvoy

BOETHIUS
John Marenbon

PETER LOMBARD
Philipp W. Rosemann

BONAVENTURE
Christopher M. Cullen

AL-KINDĪ
Peter Adamson

AL-KINDĪ

Peter Adamson

OXFORD
UNIVERSITY PRESS
2007

OXFORD
UNIVERSITY PRESS

Oxford University Press, Inc., publishes works that further
Oxford University's objective of excellence
in research, scholarship, and education.

Oxford New York
Auckland Cape Town Dar es Salaam Hong Kong Karachi
Kuala Lumpur Madrid Melbourne Mexico City Nairobi
New Delhi Shanghai Taipei Toronto

With offices in
Argentina Austria Brazil Chile Czech Republic France Greece
Guatemala Hungary Italy Japan Poland Portugal Singapore
South Korea Switzerland Thailand Turkey Ukraine Vietnam

Published by Oxford University Press, Inc.
198 Madison Avenue, New York, New York 10016

www.oup.com

Library of Congress Cataloging-in-Publication Data
Adamson, Peter, 1972–
Al-Kindi / Peter Adamson.
p. cm.—(Great medieval thinkers)
Includes bibliographical references and index.
ISBN-13 978-0-19-518142-5; 978-0-19-518143-2 (pbk.)
1. Kindi, d. ca. 873. 2. Philosophy, Islamic.
I. Title. II. Title: Kindi. III. Series.
B753.K54A53 2006
181'.6—dc21 2006046401

3 5 7 9 8 6 4 2
Printed in the United States of America
on acid-free paper

SERIES FOREWORD

Many people would be surprised to be told that there *were* any great medieval thinkers. If a *great* thinker is one from whom we can learn today, and if "medieval" serves as an adjective for describing anything which existed from (roughly) the years 600 to 1500 A.D., then, so it is often supposed, medieval thinkers cannot be called "great."

Why not? One answer often given appeals to ways in which medieval authors with a taste for argument and speculation tend to invoke "authorities," especially religious ones. Such invocation of authority is not the stuff of which great thought is made—so it is often said today. It is also frequently said that greatness is not to be found in the thinking of those who lived before the rise of modern science, not to mention that of modern philosophy and theology. Students of science are nowadays hardly ever referred to literature earlier than the seventeenth century. Students of philosophy in the twentieth century have often been taught nothing about the history of ideas between Aristotle (384–322 B.C.) and Descartes (1596–1650). Contemporary students of theology are often encouraged to believe that significant theological thinking is a product of the nineteenth century.

Yet the origins of modern science lie in the conviction that the world is open to rational investigation and is orderly rather than chaotic—a conviction which came fully to birth, and was systematically explored and developed, during the middle ages. And it is in medieval thinking that we find some of the most sophisticated and rigorous discussions in the areas of philosophy and theology ever offered for human consumption—not surprisingly, perhaps, if we note that medieval philosophers and theologians, like their contemporary counterparts, were often university teachers (or something like that) who participated in an ongoing world-wide debate and were not (like many seventeenth-, eighteenth-, and even nineteenth-century philosophers and theologians), people working in relative isolation from a large community of teachers and students with whom they were regularly involved. As for the question of appeal to authority: it is certainly true that many medieval thinkers believed in authority (especially religious authority) as a serious court of appeal; and it is true that many people today would say that they cannot do this. But as contemporary philosophers are increasingly reminding us, authority is as much an ingredient in our thinking as it was for medieval thinkers (albeit that, because of differences between thinkers, one might reasonably say that there is no such thing as "medieval thought"). For most of what we take ourselves to know derives from the trust we have reposed in our various teachers, colleagues, friends, and general contacts. When it comes to reliance on authority, the main difference between us and medieval thinkers lies in the fact that their reliance on authority (insofar as they had it) was often more focused and explicitly acknowledged than it is for us. It does not lie in the fact that it was uncritical and naive in a way that our reliance on authority is not.

In recent years, such truths have come to be recognized at what we might call the "academic" level. No longer disposed to think of the Middle Ages as "dark" (meaning "lacking in intellectual richness"), many university departments (and many publishers of books and journals) now devote a lot of their energy to the study of medieval thinking. And they do so not simply on the assumption that it is historically significant but also in the light of the increasingly developing insight that it is full of things with which to dialogue and from which to learn. Following a long period in which medieval thinking was thought to be of only antiquarian interest, we are now witnessing its revival as a contemporary voice—one with which to converse, one from which we might learn.

The *Great Medieval Thinkers* series reflects and is part of this exciting revival. Written by a distinguished team of experts, it aims to provide substantial introductions to a range of medieval authors. And it does so on the assumption that they are as worth reading today as they were when they wrote. Students of medieval "literature" (e.g. the writings of Chaucer) are currently well supplied (if not over-supplied) with secondary works to aid them when reading the objects of their concern. But those with an interest in medieval philosophy and theology are by no means so fortunate when it comes to reliable and accessible volumes to help them. The *Great Medieval Thinkers* series therefore aspires to remedy that deficiency by concentrating on medieval philosophers and theologians, and by offering solid overviews of their lives and thought coupled with contemporary reflection on what they had to say. Taken individually, volumes in the series will provide valuable treatments of single thinkers many of whom are not currently covered by any comparable volumes. Taken together, they will constitute a rich and distinguished history and discussion of medieval philosophy and theology considered as a whole. With an eye on college and university students, and with an eye on the general reader, authors of volumes in the series strive to write in a clear and accessible manner so that each of the thinkers they write on can be learned about by those who have no previous knowledge about them. But each contributor to the series also intends to inform, engage, and generally entertain even those with specialist knowledge in the area of medieval thinking. So, as well as surveying and introducing, volumes in the series seek to advance the state of medieval studies both at the historical and the speculative level.

The subject to which the present volume is devoted is the first medieval Islamic thinker to which a volume in the series has been devoted. It is appropriate that this should be so since, as Peter Adamson observes, al-Kindī (born c. 800 A.D.) was the first philosopher in the Arabic tradition (as Thales of Milesia was the first philosopher of ancient Greece). Al-Kindī's surviving writings constitute a substantial corpus and display a great range of interests. Possibly born in Baṣra, he wrote on what we would now recognize as philosophical and theological topics. He also wrote about medicine and astrology. As a commentator, he had things to say about figures such as Aristotle, Euclid, and Ptolemy. Concerned to use newly translated Greek philosophical works to speak philosophically to an Arabic-speaking audience, al-Kindī delivered an inheritance to later Arabic thinkers (e.g., Avicenna and Averroes), an inheritance which filtered through to Christian philosophers and theologians working in Europe from the early thirteenth century and onwards.

Does al-Kindī have sensible things to say to us? Are his arguments for the positions he adopts good ones? Is he, though long dead, a figure with whom to engage intellectually now? As well as documenting al-Kindī's thought with great scholarly rigor, the present volume also seeks to engage with it so as to treat al-Kindī as someone worth talking to today. Peter Adamson, as well as knowing a lot about al-Kindī's writings, is also someone who can reflect on them in detail. You shall see what I mean as you read through what follows.

BRIAN DAVIES

PREFACE

A couple of years ago, when I was beginning to think about putting my thoughts about al-Kindī together into a book, I happened to read John Marenbon's superb contribution to this series on Boethius. Here, I thought, was exactly the sort of book I hoped to write. While giving a scholarly and thorough treatment of all Boethius' writings, Marenbon concentrated above all on the ideas in these writings, addressing a philosophical audience. This book aims to follow suit, by subjecting al-Kindī to a more explicitly philosophical analysis than he has usually received. I was also struck, while reading Prof. Marenbon's book, by similarities between al-Kindī and Boethius: both were involved in the translation of Greek works, and both applied Greek philosophical tools to problems of their respective religions. (In fact, some of the ideas that Boethius had used to explicate the doctrine of the Trinity are used by al-Kindī in order to attack the same doctrine.) Thus encouraged, I offered to contribute a volume on al-Kindī to the present series.

I did so with slight trepidation, since I had a similar worry to the one addressed by Prof. Marenbon in the introduction to his volume: was al-Kindī really a "great medieval thinker"? Whether or not he was a "great thinker, " I suppose readers of this book will judge for themselves. More delicate is the question of whether he was "medieval." He lived in the ninth century, which is, I suppose, as medieval a century as one could ask for. But in standard usage the term describes a certain period of European history, not Islamic history, and its connotations are misleading with regard to the Muslim world. In general I would prefer to speak of the first few centuries of philosophy in Arabic as the "classical" or "formative" period. On the other hand one must be practical about these things, and admit that when al-Kindī is read by philosophers, he will most often be read by people who are taking courses about, or doing research on, the medieval period. In any case I am in favor of anything that will lead to a wider readership for al-Kindī and subsequent philosophers who wrote in Arabic. If this means calling them "medieval, " so be it.

This book was written with the generous support of the Leverhulme Trust, for which I am very grateful. I have also received help and encouragement from many friends and colleagues. I should begin by thanking the members of an Arabic reading group at the Warburg Institute, especially Charles Burnett and Fritz Zimmermann. Thanks to this reading group I learned a great deal about Arabic and al-Kindī himself, and I also first met Peter Pormann, my collaborator on a forthcoming volume of translations of al-Kindī's works. Without his input my grasp of these texts, on all levels, would be much shakier. I have had very useful advice from other Arabists in and around London, especially Anna Akasoy, Rotraud Hansberger, Tony Street, and Sophia Vasalou. In the wider community of scholars of Arabic philosophy, my work on the Kindī circle has benefitted from years of wise counsel from David Burrell, Cristina D'Ancona, Dimitri Gutas, and Richard Taylor. I owe a particularly large debt to Jon McGinnis, who kindly read through a manuscript of the book and made many useful comments. I am very grateful also to my colleagues in the Philosophy Department at King's College London, and especially to Verity Harte, MM McCabe and Richard Sorabji for making King's such a stimulating and congenial place to work on Greek philosophy. Finally I would like to thank my family for their support: my grandfather, my parents and brother. Above all, I am grateful to my wife, Ursula, and our daughters, Sophia and Johanna, for being such delightful company while I was writing this book.

CONTENTS

CITATION AND TRANSLITERATION CONVENTIONS

This study is meant to be a companion volume with *The Philosophical Works of al-Kindī*, translated by myself and Peter E. Pormann (Oxford University Press, forthcoming). The translations in quotations from al-Kindī's works are mine, most often in conjunction with Peter Pormann. All other translations are mine unless otherwise noted.

When citing works by al-Kindī that appear in our translation, I give the section number from that translation. I also give page references, which are usually to the main editions of al-Kindī's works, as follows:

AR	M.'A. H. Abū Rīda, ed., al-Kindī, *Rasā'il al-Kindī al Falsafiyya* (Cairo; Dār al-Fikr al-'Arabī, 1950), vol. 1.
AR[2]	M.'A.H. Abū Rīda, ed., al-Kindī, *Rasā'il al-Kindī al Falsafiyya* (Cairo; Dār al-Fikr al-'Arabī, 1953), vol. 2.
RJ	R. Rashed and J. Jolivet, eds. and trans., *Oeuvres Philosophiques et Scientifiques d'al-Kindī*, vol. 2, *Métaphysique et cosmologie* (Leiden; Brill, 1998)

Thus, for instance, *On First Philosophy* §XIX.1 (AR 153, RJ 83), refers first to the section XIX.1 in the translation in Adamson and Pormann (forthcoming), and then the page numbers of the Abū Rīda edition and the Rashed and Jolivet edition. For references to other editions, see the note where the work is first cited in this book. Some citations include a line number, given after page number and separated with a full stop (e.g., 10.11 means page 10, line 11).

This book does not assume knowledge of Greek, Arabic, or Latin on the part of the reader, but I have frequently given terms and phrases from the original languages. For Arabic transliteration I have generally followed the conventions used in the *International Journal of Middle Eastern Studies*. The feminine ending *tāʾ marbūṭa* is written -a, even in *idāfa*, and the definite article is written al- or ʾl-.

AL-KINDĪ

I

LIFE, WORKS, AND INFLUENCE

The history of philosophy is a competition, in which mostly long-dead thinkers vie for the attention of the historian. In this competition, there is nothing quite like the advantage of having been first. Thales of Milesia exerts a powerful attraction for historians—even though we know almost nothing about him—because he was the first philosopher of ancient Greece. At the same time, historians of philosophy are interested in the transmission of ideas: in the way that one philosopher reads, adapts, and transforms the thought of his or her predecessors. Of course the two sorts of interest usually coincide. With the possible exception of Thales, the first thinker in any tradition must come to grips with previous traditions, if only to reject them. Few philosophers, though, invite both sorts of interest as much as al-Kindī. He was the first philosopher in the Arabic tradition, and his thought was defined in large part by his engagement with the Greek tradition that preceded him. Thus al-Kindī has had a fair amount of attention from historians of ideas and scholars of the Graeco-Arabic translation movement. For readers with these interests, the reasons to study al-Kindī speak for themselves. This book, however, is aimed equally at readers who are primarily interested in a philosophical approach to the history of philosophy. By this I mean that I will spend most of my time analyzing al-Kindī's ideas and arguments, rather than identifying his sources or discussing his later influence. The philosophical analysis of his works takes up the bulk of the book, beginning with chapter 3. This chapter and the next are devoted more to placing al-Kindī within his historical and intellectual context.

Life and Historical Context

Though we do not know a great deal about al-Kindī's life, we know perhaps more than we would have any right to expect, thanks to several biographical reports about him in later Arabic literature.[1] We can also reach a fairly reliable estimate of his dates, thanks to an astrological work he wrote on the duration of the reign of the Arabs.[2] This mentions an uprising that occurred in 866, which means he must have died later than this; his death date is usually estimated at about 870 A.D. As we will see, his career peaked under the caliphate of al-Mu'taṣim (reigned 833–842 A.D.), and he was already active under al-Ma'mūn (reigned 813–833 A.D.). Since he was still alive in the late 860s, if he was an active scholar already around 830, then we must put his birth date at about 800 A.D.

His name was Abū Yūsuf Ya'qūb b. Isḥāq al-Kindī, and he is said to have been born in Baṣra, though his father Isḥāq b. al-Ṣabbāḥ was the emir of Kūfa. His family was a particularly noble one within the important Arab tribe of Kinda. (For this reason he is sometimes called the "philosopher of the Arabs.") As the biographers stress, our al-Kindī was a direct descendant of al-Ash'ath b. Qays, the king of Kinda and a companion of the Prophet. Al-Kindī seems to have moved to Baghdad early in his life, because he received his education there. Ibn Abī Uṣaybi'a claims that he was "of great standing under al-Ma'mūn and al-Mu'taṣim." Our evidence indicates that his career peaked under the caliphate of al-Mu'taṣim, but one of his works is addressed to al-Ma'mūn,[3] which reinforces the idea that he was already a highly placed (albeit fairly young) scholar under the earlier caliph. It was however under al-Mu'taṣim that al-Kindī wrote most of the philosophical works to be considered in this book, including *On First Philosophy*, addressed to the caliph himself. Al-Kindī was also the tutor to al-Mu'taṣim's son Aḥmad, who was the recipient of numerous Kindian treatises.

We have no evidence as to how al-Kindī fared for the next couple of decades, but there is an intriguing report about an episode that occurred at the end of the caliphate of al-Mutawakkil (reigned 847–861 A.D.). Again, our source is Ibn Abī Uṣaybiʿa. He tells us that al-Kindī was victimized by the plotting of the two famous mathematicians and scientists, Muḥammad and Aḥmad b. Mūsā. The Banū Mūsā persuaded al-Mutawakkil to seize al-Kindī's library, which at this stage of his career was no doubt considerable, and to have him beaten. This may have been out of jealousy or at least professional competition, since they also schemed to remove another scholar, Sind b. ʿAlī, from the caliphal court. But the Banū Mūsā soon had problems of their own. They appointed an engineer to build a canal, and he incompetently made the mouth of the canal lower than the rest of the channel, so that water would not flow through it. The Banū Mūsā had to beg Sind b. ʿAlī to save them from the caliph's wrath, and as a condition for his assistance Sind made them return al-Kindī's books. This story, which mostly has the ring of truth,[4] is our last biographical information about al-Kindī apart from a report of how he died. This is found in al-Qifṭī, who takes his account from al-Kindī's associate, the astrologer Abū Maʿshar:

> He had a buildup of phlegm in his knee, and to treat it he drank aged wine. Then he repented of this, and instead drank honey juice. But the mouth of his veins did not open, and nothing of its heat managed to reach deep down into his body. Thus the infection spread, and made his nerves cause him extreme pain, until this pain reached into his head and brain. Then the man died, because the nerves are rooted in the brain.

The most important feature of al-Kindī's wider historical context is that he worked during the massive translation effort that took place under the ʿAbbāsids. A good deal of excellent scholarship has been devoted to the translation movement, and al-Kindī's part in it, in the past several decades.[5] To give the briefest of summaries: the translation movement began already under the caliph al-Manṣūr (reigned 754–775 A.D.) and by the time of al-Kindī had reached its peak. Al-Kindī is indeed an almost exact contemporary of the great translator Ḥunayn b. Isḥāq. Building on earlier Syriac translations from the Greek, translators sponsored by the ʿAbbāsids rendered a startling amount of Greek scientific and philosophical literature into Arabic, sometimes by way of a new Syriac version. Gutas has shown that this was intended to support a variety of ʿAbbāsid political objectives, such as competition with the Byzantines and trumping the claims of Persian culture with a new, learned Arabic culture.[6] The texts translated were chosen for practical purposes. For instance the *Sophistical Refutations* was translated early on for use in theological dispute, and much effort was put into translating medical literature. The translators themselves tended to be Christians who spoke both Greek and Arabic. Ḥunayn was an example, as were several translators who worked closely with al-Kindī. Thanks to the pioneering work of Gerhard Endress,[7] we now know that a family of translations of Greek philosophical works, by Aristotle, Alexander of Aphrodisias, Plotinus, and Proclus, were all produced by a circle of translators led by al-Kindī. These provided the immediate inspiration for al-Kindī's own writings.

Though the translation movement is naturally the feature of 'Abbāsid life that has drawn the most attention from historians of philosophy, it is important to realize that philhellenism was only one strand of this vibrant intellectual period.[8] The ninth century saw an explosion in Islamic theological speculation, or *'ilm al-kalām*; as we will see al-Kindī responded directly to this development.[9] This was related to the study of *ḥadīth*, that is, reports about the sayings and actions of the Prophet. The ninth century was a peak time for scholarship in this area, collecting reports and evaluating their authenticity, and theologians appealed to *ḥadīth* along with the Koran in their disputations. At this time we also have the emergence of refined Arabic literature, or *adab*; yet another almost exact contemporary of al-Kindī's was the greatest literary figure (*adīb*) of them all, al-Jāḥiẓ. In short, al-Kindī was competing against many other burgeoning fields of inquiry when he put forth his own synthesis and adaptation of Greek thought. His works had the dual function of expounding the newly translated texts, and of promoting them and arguing that they were of unique importance for his erudite ninth century, Arabic-speaking audience.[10]

Works

Our knowledge of al-Kindī's corpus is dependent on two strokes of good fortune. First, there is the fact that his philosophical writings have survived at all. For most of the treatises that will be discussed in this book, there is only a single manuscript, which is held in Istanbul and was discovered by Helmut Ritter.[11] Had this manuscript not come down to us, we would know far less about al-Kindī's thought than we do, too little, indeed, to write a philosophy book about him. Less fortunate is that even this manuscript, and the other scattered textual evidence for al-Kindī, preserve for us only a small fraction of al-Kindī's corpus. On the other hand, we know the size of this original corpus only thanks to a second stroke of good luck, which is that we have an extensive list of al-Kindī's writings contained in the invaluable *Fihrist* (meaning "list") of the tenth-century book merchant Ibn al-Nadīm, and repeated in later authors.[12]

This list, which contains almost 300 titles, shows the astonishing range of al-Kindī's interests. It would seem that strictly philosophical research took up only a fraction of al-Kindī's energy and time. A mere 21 are devoted to what Ibn al-Nadīm calls "philosophical" topics,[13] with another 10 or so apiece on logic and practical philosophy (labelled here as "his books on governance [*kutubuhū al-siyāsiyyāt*]" but including titles on both ethics and politics). On the other hand, there is no firm line to be drawn within this list between philosophical topics and those we would now consider to be non-philosophical. For instance, some of the texts that will occupy our attention in this book are labelled as "cosmological" (more literally "his books on the celestial spheres [*kutubuhū al-falakiyyāt*]"). The list shows that al-Kindī also wrote many works on mathematics, in its various branches (Ibn al-Nadīm devotes sections to arithmetic, geometry, music, astronomy, spherics, and the measurement of distances),[14] as well as on medicine and astrology. These, along with philosophy proper, were his major areas of interest. Notice the inclusion of astrology in that list: al-Kindī was deeply involved in disciplines we would now consider to be "pseudo-science," and especially astrology and other methods of precognition, like scapulomancy (hence the sections "his books on astrology" and "his books on foretelling"). The *Fihrist* also tells us, though, that al-Kindī wrote a refutation of the deceptions (*khuda'*) of the alchemists. He was thus no uncritical enthusiast for every supposed scientific discipline, and as we will see (chapter 8) his belief in astrology is grounded in his philosophical cosmology.

Alchemy seems to be one of the few pursuits al-Kindī had no time for. The *Fihrist*'s inventory, especially a final section on miscellaneous topics, shows the diversity of his interests, including jewels, glass, dyes (we also know of a text on the removal of stains), swords, perfumes, zoology, tides, mirrors, meteorology, and earthquakes. The biographical accounts mentioned above also pay due homage to the breadth of his learning. Our initial impulse will no doubt be the same: to marvel at the sheer number of different topics al-Kindī took on. But a useful second reaction would be to note that his work on many of these topics must have grown out of al-Kindī's relationship to the caliph's family and other patrons. His keen interest in mathematics and astrology is representative of a general emphasis on these topics under the early 'Abbāsids.[15] Other topics just mentioned, like swords, jewels, and perfumes, would clearly have been of interest to al-Kindī's wealthy patrons. The *Fihrist* shows that al-Kindī strove, as Franz Rosenthal put it, to ensure that "he lacked no knowledge that an educated man of his time might need."[16] His wide-ranging virtuosity would have been a flattering ornament for the caliphal court.

If anything unified these many intellectual undertakings, it was the project of interpreting and promoting the Greek inheritance, as we would expect given al-Kindī's involvement with the translation movement. This is clear not only from the extant corpus, but from the *Fihrist*. It tells us that he wrote numerous commentaries on, and abridgements or clarifications of, works by Aristotle, Euclid, Ptolemy, and others. The influence of the Greeks seems to have been at least as strong regarding mathematical and scientific topics as regarding philosophical topics. (Again, this is borne out by the extant works on mathematics and science, as we will see in chapter 7.) But there is also a section on polemical works (*al-jadaliyyāt*), which shows that al-Kindī engaged in disputes with his contemporaries over controversial topics of the day. He wrote against the doctrines of other religions, such as the Manicheans. He also wrote on contemporary issues within Islamic theology such as atomism and the justice of God's actions. The loss of almost all of these works deprives us of a chance to see al-Kindī reacting directly to his immediate contemporaries. But what we do know suggests that even in these sorts of controversial works, he drew upon Greek materials.

Two final issues to be considered regarding the *Fihrist*'s report have to do with the relation of this list to the extant corpus as it has come down to us. First, there is the consideration of genre. Most of the entries on Ibn al-Nadīm's list are called "epistles [*rasā'il*]," and this corresponds to our textual evidence. The works preserved in the Istanbul manuscript and elsewhere are usually explicitly addressed to a patron, frequently the aforementioned Aḥmad, son of the caliph al-Mu'taṣim. These would mostly have been short works, often only a few pages long, which helps to explain how al-Kindī was able to write so many works on so many different topics.[17]

Second, there is the question of titles. In the cases of some extant works mentioned in the *Fihrist*'s account, we find that the titles of the texts in our manuscripts differ from those known to Ibn al-Nadīm. A good example is what the Istanbul manuscript calls *On First Philosophy* (*Fī 'l-Falsafa al-Ūlā*). Al-Kindī also refers back to it in later works using this title. The *Fihrist* has two distinct titles that might refer to the work, which are the first two entries; in both the phrase "*On First Philosophy*" is only the beginning of a longer title. Meanwhile, the later author Ibn Ḥazm quotes from this work but calls it *On Oneness* (*Kitāb al-Tawḥīd*). Finally, Sāʿid al-Andalusī is presumably referring to the same work when he says, "among [al-Kindī's] well-known works [is] a book on oneness (*tawḥīd*), known as *The Mouth of Gold* (*Fam al-Dhahab*), in which he followed the view of Plato in the discussion of the creation of the world without time." Most of the "titles" in the Istanbul manuscript and the *Fihrist* are in fact more like overviews of the contents of each epistle; the titles do not aspire to pithiness (consider for instance *On the Explanation That the Nature of the Celestial Sphere Is Different from the Natures of the Four Elements*, or *On the True, First, Complete Agent and the Deficient Agent That Is Metaphorically* [*an Agent*]). It seems likely that, in some cases at least, al-Kindī himself did not give his epistles titles, and that the titles that have come down to us simply represent others' attempts to summarize their contents.[18] In some cases we have to guess as to which titles in the *Fihrist* represent which extant works. For example two works preserved only in Latin, *On Rays* and *On Perspectives* (*De Radiis* and *De Aspectibus*), probably correspond to entries in the *Fihrist*, but it is impossible to be sure.[19] In other cases, Kindian works that have come down to us do not appear in the *Fihrist* inventory. Inclusion in Ibn al-Nadīm's list should not be taken to be a necessary condition for authenticity.

For all that has been lost, the extant Kindian corpus is rich and varied.[20] Obviously this book will deal chiefly with the philosophical works. Most of these, as mentioned above, survive only in one Istanbul manuscript, and were (mostly) edited in the 1950s by Muḥammad Abū Rīda.[21] Of these the most important and famous is *On First Philosophy*, which is in fact only partially extant. We have the first four sections, which deal most prominently with the eternity of the world and the problem of divine attributes. These are the two issues most commonly associated with al-Kindī by historians of Arabic philosophy, and they will occupy our attention in chapters 3 and 4. The Istanbul manuscript also includes one of a very few Arabic texts for a work known chiefly in Latin translation, *On Intellect*—probably al-Kindī's most famous work after *On First Philosophy*. Several other works on psychology are included as well, as will be discussed below in chapter 5. We have works on cosmology, in particular the nature of the heavens and how they relate to the sublunar world; on these see chapter 8. There is a lengthy ethical work, *On Dispelling Sadness*, which along with some supplementary materials will be considered in chapter 6. Two further works are aids to the study of philosophy. One version of *On Definitions*, which is transmitted in several very different redactions, appears in the Istanbul manuscript (in a different hand from the other treatises). And *On the Quantity of Aristotle's Books* gives a survey of the Aristotelian corpus, with a surprising digression in the middle on the nature of prophecy. Though *Quantity* and several other works give evidence of al-Kindī's engagement with Aristotle's logical writings, we do not have any Kindian treatises devoted specifically to logical issues.[22]

The rest of the Istanbul manuscript's treatises are on what we would consider to be scientific topics: meteorology (for instance a treatise explaining phenomena like snow, hail, and thunder), medicine (on coitus and on lisps), astronomy (on eclipses), measuring the height of mountains, the nature of color, and so on. But these represent only a small fraction of the extant scientific corpus. In other manuscripts we also have numerous works on optics and catoptrics (i.e. the study of mirrors).[23] One of the longest treatises is the aforementioned *On Rays*,[24] which explains magic and the influence of the stars. There are several extant medical works,[25] and *On Degrees* (*De Gradibus*)[26] deals with the administration of drugs. From his pharmacological works we also have a medical formulary, that is, a list of recipes for drugs.[27] And there are numerous works on astrology as well as several works on music.[28] The bulk of the extant corpus, then, deals with topics in the physical sciences. While these topics will not be at the center of attention in this book, they are of some philosophical interest and it would distort al-Kindī's thought to exclude them. Chapter 7 of this book is therefore devoted to mathematics and science, while chapter 8 will put al-Kindī's astrological interests in the context of his cosmology.

Before leaving the topic of the corpus, a word about the relative chronology of al-Kindī's writings. This is a problem that has been given no attention whatsoever by previous scholars, as far as I can tell, and with good reason. Apart from a very small number of cross-references within his works,[29] and the fact that some epistles can be roughly dated by the identity of their recipients, we have precious little hard evidence to go on here. I do however have a tentative suggestion to make, which I cannot defend in detail here. One way to establish the relative priority of al-Kindī's writings would be to determine which Greek sources he is using. That is, if in work A he does not seem to have access to a certain text, but then uses that text in work B, then A is prior to B. An example of this might be his use of an Arabic paraphrase of Aristotle's *De Anima*. As I have shown elsewhere, his optical work *On Perspectives* seems to draw on this paraphrase, as do several other treatises.[30] Yet as we will see later some psychological writings found in the Istanbul manuscript strikingly fail to make use of the *De Anima*. This suggests that the psychological works predate his access to the Arabic *De Anima* paraphrase, which in turn predates *On Perspectives*.

Such arguments from silence are notoriously weak. Yet this example among others makes me suspect that many of the philosophical works found in the Istanbul manuscript—which are dominated by concern with Neoplatonic metaphysics and psychology, the eternity of the world, and a cosmology deriving from Aristotelian sources—fall into a single period, during the caliphate of al-Muʿtaṣim. These works show an interest in an axiomatic methodology inspired by mathematics, as we will see in the next chapter. But they show at most a rudimentary use of mathematics itself, including geometry (though some of the cosmological treatises do have very simple geometrical diagrams). By contrast there are numerous other works that are dominated by their use of complex geometrical demonstrations and mathematics. These include al-Kindī's works on optics, his treatment of the proportions of drugs in *On Degrees*, and also the use of geometrical relations as a general theory of physical influence in *On Rays*. As we will see *On Rays* also makes major doctrinal departures from the works found in the Istanbul manuscript, which could be explained more easily on a developmental account, unless we reject its authenticity altogether (see chapter 8). A final point worth considering is that some of the more "mathematical" treatises explicitly criticize or go beyond ancient authorities. Al-Kindī begins *On Degrees* by saying that he is undertaking a project the ancients had not, namely the analysis of compound drugs. Even more strikingly, he is critical of Euclid in several works on optics, one of which is indeed titled *On the Rectification of Euclid's Errors*.[31] This contrasts sharply with the attitude he takes in the more "metaphysical" writings, where he is evidently concerned to promote and defend the Greek authors on whom he draws.

My tentative proposal, then, is that the philosophical works that will take up most of our attention in this book are earlier than the more technical, mathematicized treatises just mentioned.[32] If this proves to be the case, we might speculate that the beginning of al-Kindī's career was devoted to the metaphysical and cosmological concerns typical of late Greek, Neoplatonizing Aristotelians. Later, his interests evolved, and he became a practicing scientist and mathematician engaged in empirical research. He also became more willing to strike out on his own, and to engage in criticism of the ancients. Of course the change in his interests could have resulted in part from which Greek texts al-Kindī had been able to read in translation. Equally, his evolving interests may have guided his choices about which texts ought to be translated in his circle. Of course all of this remains speculation for now; hopefully further research will determine whether the speculation is well founded or not.

The "Kindian Tradition"

Al-Kindī's legacy within the Arabic philosophical tradition is in a sense pervasive and permanent, but in a sense narrow and temporary. In the first sense, his project of using the newly translated Greek philosophical works to produce philosophy for an Arabic-speaking audience becomes definitive of philosophy in the Islamic world. To this extent philosophers like al-Fārābī, Avicenna and Averroes may be thought of as heirs of al-Kindī. But of these three, only Averroes ever mentions al-Kindī, and then to criticize him (see the next section). On the other hand, he did have a more direct legacy, embodied by a philosophical tradition that engages directly with al-Kindī's own works and follows his lead on certain methodological and doctrinal points. This "Kindian tradition" was a significant force in the Islamic intellectual milieu for about two centuries following al-Kindī's death. In this section, I will quickly identify the main figures in this tradition and explain the common features that allow us to group them together.[33]

The core of the Kindian tradition is made up of al-Kindī's own students, and the students of those students. There are two figures we know about from the first generation of students: Abū Zayd al-Balkhī (died at an advanced age in 934) and Aḥmad b. al-Ṭayyib al-Sarakhsī (b. 833–837, d. 899).[34] Unfortunately no complete philosophical works have come down to us from either of them. We do have biographical information about both, though, including lists of titles and some fragments. Al-Sarakhsī was evidently a close follower of al-Kindī's thought. Many of the titles ascribed to him match those of works by al-Kindī and these may even have reproduced al-Kindī's own words to some extent. Al-Sarakhsī is also an intermediary source for a famous report about the Sabians of Ḥarrān attributed to al-Kindī.[35] We know even less about Abū Zayd's thought, but he is the most important conduit for a Kindian approach to philosophy, having passed it on to his own students, Abū 'l-Ḥasan Muḥammad b. Yūsuf al-'Āmirī (d. 992) and Ibn Farīghūn (tenth century).

Al-'Āmirī is the most significant figure with a direct link to al-Kindī, numerous of his philosophical works having survived.[36] As we will see he epitomizes many of the features of the Kindian tradition, no doubt because of the influence of Abū Zayd. We know far less about Ibn Farīghūn, the author of a fascinating work called the *Compendium of the Sciences* (*Jawāmi' al-'ulūm*), a treatise that uses branch diagrams to explain and subdivide every sort of human knowledge.[37] Ibn Farīghūn may or may not also be the author of a geographical treatise that has come down to us. But apart from that, we know nothing about him except that he was a student of Abū Zayd's (and even this is based only on a single note in a manuscript of the *Compendium*).

In addition, there are several authors who are directly influenced by al-Kindī and who quote his works, usually without naming him. These include an associate of al-Kindī's, Abū Ma'shar al-Balkhī (d. 886), the greatest astrologer of the Islamic world. Making his career possible was perhaps al-Kindī's most important contribution to astrology: the *Fihrist* tells us that Abū Ma'shar was a *ḥadīth* scholar until al-Kindī contrived to turn his attentions towards mathematics, and thence to astrology. Abū Ma'shar's *Great Introduction to Astrology* also makes some use of al-Kindī's cosmological writings.[38] But the figure whose extant corpus makes the most extensive use of al-Kindī's works is the Jewish thinker Isaac Israeli (ca. 855–ca. 907).[39] Unfortunately we don't know how Isaac came to have such an extensive knowledge of al-Kindī's writings, but he uses numerous Kindian treatises, especially *On Definitions*, which influenced his own work of definitions. Finally, we should mention Miskawayh (d. 1030), a famous historian and philosopher who quotes al-Kindī in one of his ethical treatises.[40] Though these are the figures with direct links to al-Kindī, the list of "Kindians" could be lengthened considerably by naming other tenth-century Neoplatonists who drew heavily on the same texts as these authors and shared some of their attitudes about how philosophy was to be integrated into Islamic culture.[41] Of course, these various figures did not agree about everything. For example, whereas al-Kindī and Abū Ma'shar were significant figures in the history of Arabic astrology, Abū Zayd rejected its validity.[42] But they may be loosely grouped together on doctrinal, and above all methodological, grounds.

What, then, are the defining features of this tradition, apart from the historical and textual links between its members and al-Kindī? Obviously all of them were practicioners of *falsafa*, that is, they wrote philosophical treatises inspired by and engaging with Greek philosophy. But this is true of other philosophers of the same time-period, in particular the Aristotelian philosophers who were based in Baghdad. The most famous of these is al-Fārābī. Many members of the Baghdad school were Christians, such as the relatively well-known Abū Bishr Mattā (who was the founder of the school) and Yaḥyā b. 'Adī (a student of al-Fārābī's).[43] These philosophers serve as a useful foil for our Kindians, since along with the figures we are interested in, they form the most significant philosophical tradition in the period before Avicenna.

The first and most striking contrast between the Kindians and the Baghdad Peripatetics is a geographical one. Though al-Kindī worked in Baghdad, his influence was chiefly on philosophers who hailed from the eastern reaches of the Islamic empire. (Hans Hinrich Biesterfeldt has thus suggested the slogan "from Baghdad to Bukhara" for the phenomenon I am calling the Kindian tradition.[44]) For example, as their names indicate, Abū Ma'shar and Abū Zayd were from Balkh and al-Sarakhsī from Sarakhs in Khurāsān. Others just mentioned hailed from, or spent significant parts of their careers, in places such as Rayy (south of the Caspian sea, in modern-day Iran) and Bukhara (north of the River Oxus, in modern-day Uzbekistan). Roughly, the Kindians tend to be found in Iran and Khurāsān, especially Transoxania, whereas the Peripatetic movement was strongest in Baghdad.

A second striking difference is that the two groups tended to focus on different texts from the Greek tradition. It is tempting to say that the Baghdad philosophers were simply much more interested in logical texts than the Kindians, since it is al-Fārābī's achievements in logic that are his greatest contribution to Arabic thought, whereas we have almost no extant works by Kindian authors devoted to logic. However, this is to some extent an illusion created by our incomplete textual evidence: we know that al-Kindī himself already wrote summaries, commentaries, or treatises on texts from Aristotle's *Organon*, and this is true for several other Kindian philosophers mentioned above. Less misleading would be to say that al-Kindī himself was more interested in the *early* parts of the *Organon*, in particular the *Isagoge* of Porphyry (which became the standard introduction to Aristotle's logic) and Aristotle's *Categories*. Later Kindians did engage with, for instance, the *Posterior Analytics*, which had not yet been translated in al-Kindī's time. But never do we find the Kindians showing much facility with the technicalities of the Aristotelian syllogistic. In other words, as far as we can tell the Kindian tradition failed to do anything with the *Prior Analytics*, whereas the Baghdad school's greatest triumph was in general their interpretation of the entire *Organon*, and in particular al-Fārābī's work on syllogistic. By the same token, there are texts that are central for the Kindians and of little import for the Baghdad school. Here I am thinking especially of Neoplatonic works in Arabic translation, like the Arabic Proclus (a version of which became the *Liber de Causis* in Latin translation) and Arabic Plotinus (the so-called *Theology of Aristotle*). As we will see the Neoplatonic metaphysics of these works are decisive for al-Kindī's thought, and we later find, for instance, al-ʿĀmirī writing a paraphrase of the *De Causis*.[45]

Another temptation is thus to say that the Kindians were "Neoplatonists" while the Baghdad school were, as I have called them, "Aristotelians" or "Peripatetics." This isn't a bad approximation of the truth, but it is misleading in several ways. The Baghdad school read Aristotle through the Neoplatonic commentators, though they were not much influenced by Plotinus and Proclus.[46] And conversely, the Kindians all drew heavily on Aristotle. To contrast the two schools, it is more useful to stick to specific intellectual commitments rather than broad philosophical allegiances. One such commitment amongst the Kindians is that they construe metaphysics first and foremost as *theology*: for them the Greek inheritance is a tool for studying the nature of God. And for them, theology is the topic of Aristotle's *Metaphysics*, something denied by al-Fārābī.[47] This is not unrelated to their interest in texts like the *Theology of Aristotle*, which have a lot more to say about God than the genuinely Aristotelian *Metaphysics*. By the same token, the Kindians are not mystics or proto-Sufis; they share a confidence that rational philosophy can be used to understand God's nature at least in part.

The Kindians' confident intellectualism is also manifest in their approach to ethics, which we already find in al-Kindī (see chapter 6). By this

I mean that the Kindians tend to see moral perfection as residing in or following on the attainment of theoretical wisdom, that is, turning away from the physical world in favor of the immaterial world of the intelligibles. Or, to put the point in a different way, Kindian ethics deals with the individual's quest for perfection, where this does not require that the individual act within the political sphere.[48] Here the contrast to al-Fārābī, above all, is very strong: several of his works join a theoretical or metaphysical section to a section exploring what is required of the philosopher within society as a whole.

Meanwhile the Kindians were much more open than the Baghdad school to indigenous Muslim theology, or *'ilm al-kalām*. While al-Fārābī and later Averroes spurn *kalām* as dialectical apologetics, in contrast to the demonstrative philosophy that is science, Kindians extol the value of *kalām* and engage in it themselves. Indeed, one of the most characteristic strategies that al-Kindī passes on to his successors is the use of Greek ideas to solve specifically Muslim theological dilemmas. Later in this book, we'll see examples of him doing so even in explicitly philosophical works. And we have already seen that several titles from the *Fihrist*'s report on al-Kindī seem to reflect disputes that fell more narrowly within contemporary *kalām*. These tendencies only increase among his followers. Two generations later, al-'Āmirī was even capable of arguing that the religious sciences, including *kalām*, are superior to the theoretical disciplines of *falsafa*.[49]

The Kindian tradition's irenic attitude towards *kalām* is part of their general eagerness to engage in all the intellectual activities of their culture. Many such activities fall under the notion of *adab*, Arabic "belles lettres." Al-Kindī and his student al-Sarakhsī both wrote (lost) works on the secretarial art of letter-writing, for instance. (In this book the work we will study that comes closest to *adab* is a collection of Socratic sayings ascribed to al-Kindī; see chapter 6.) Later Kindians, from al-Sarakhsī on, were even more engaged in a wide range of literary pursuits. Some of these seem to have been abiding interests of the Kindian tradition, for instance geography and the study of foreign religions and cultures. The Kindians, in short, were not so much professional philosophers as professional intellectuals, ready to write on a wide range of topics. They saw no tension between disciplines that came down to them from the Greeks, and the autochthonous pursuits of Arabic culture. Of course these "Arab" sciences developed considerably from the time of al-Kindī to that of the later

Kindians, just as the translation of Greek philosophical works continued after al-Kindī's death. But for over two centuries, we find Kindians combining the "foreign" and "Arab" sciences even as both of these evolved.[50]

Thus the Kindians at least aspired to be a mainstream intellectual tradition, in a way that the Baghdad Peripatetics did not. Yet for all their attempts to weave philosophy into a broader, usually explicitly Muslim, intellectual endeavor, the Kindians had little direct influence on later philosophy in the Islamic world. At least part of the explanation for this was Avicenna's preference for the Baghdad thinkers, or at least al-Fārābī, and his ignoring of the Kindians. After Avicenna, philosophy in Arabic is always "Avicennan" in the sense that it responds to his thought, either positively or critically. So Avicenna's failure to engage with the Kindians meant that the later tradition also tended not to engage with them. Still, as we have seen al-Kindī's own positive legacy was significant, though temporary. In the next section we will see that he also had a legacy among later thinkers who mention him only to criticize him.

Later Critiques

Let us begin with the two most entertaining such negative treatments, the first by the famous polymath al-Jāḥiẓ in his *Book of Misers*.[51] In this work someone named al-Kindī is presented as a notorious miser and cheat, especially in his role as a landlord. Unfortunately there is no consensus as to whether this al-Kindī is the philosopher or a different member of the same tribe—although several arguments in defense of "thrift" might be seen as a parody of our al-Kindī's philosophical arguments.[52] It is also worth noting that the introduction to Ibn al-Nadīm's list of al-Kindī's works (see above) mentions his miserliness.

A second parodic reference to al-Kindī is doubtless to the philosopher. It is to be found in the famous report of the debate between al-Sīrāfī and Abū Bishr Mattā over the relative merits of grammar and logic.[53] The grammarian al-Sīrāfī reduces Abū Bishr, founder of the aforementioned Baghdad Peripatetic tradition, to ineffectual fumbling as he debunks the claims of logic and philosophy in general. His rhetorical *tour de force* includes a viciously funny parody of al-Kindī and his writing style. He refers to al-Kindī as a "compatriot [*ṣāḥib*]" of Abū Bishr, which is interesting in its own right because it shows that opponents of *falsafa* at least sometimes failed to distinguish between the Baghdad school and those I have been calling the Kindians. In the story retailed by al-Sīrāfī, heartless wags mock al-Kindī by putting to him meaningless philosophical questions, which he takes seriously, mistakenly thinking they derive from "foreign philosophy [*al-falsafa al-dākhila*]" (127.8). The episode is told as a pastiche of philosophical terminology in the Kindian style; though the mock-philosophy is nonsense, many of the terms used are genuinely Kindian.[54] Al-Sīrāfī remarks that things are told of al-Kindī "that would make a bereaved mother laugh, that would make an enemy gloat and a friend grieve. He inherited all this from the blessings of Greece, and the benefits of philosophy and logic" (128.7–8).

While al-Kindī appears here as little more than a hapless representative of philhellenism and philosophy, other critics make more specific complaints about his methodology and doctrines. One biographical report mentioned above, that of Ṣā'id al-Andalūsī, concludes with the following remark:

> As for the art of synthesis [*tarkīb*] that Ya'qūb [i.e. al-Kindī] pursued in these books of his, this is of use only to someone who is already in possession of the principles. At that point synthesis is possible. But the premises of any object of inquiry are found only through the art of analysis [*taḥlīl*]. I don't know what led Ya'qūb to abstain from this important art—whether he was ignorant of its power, or whether he withheld its disclosure from the people. Either way he was deficient in this respect.[55]

Obviously understanding this criticism requires knowing what *tarkīb* and *taḥlīl* mean. If the complaint has any basis in al-Kindī's genuine methodology, then I suspect that what is meant is that al-Kindī tends to assume undefended axioms or premises, and argue from these, rather than first establishing the truth of these premises through "analysis" (on this see chapter 2). A later version of the criticism, in the report by al-Qifṭī, adds that "analysis" provides the "foundations of logic [*qawā'id al-manṭiq*]"—which I take to mean the axioms or first premises (368.2).[56]

Other authors were provoked into attacks on al-Kindī by specific philosophical and scientific works.[57] Here I will mention some of the most significant. Al-Kindī wrote a short work using Aristotelian logic to attack the Christian doctrine of the Trinity, which received a point-by-point refutation by Yaḥyā b. 'Adī, the Christian student of al-Fārābī mentioned above.[58] I have already mentioned al-Kindī's attack on alchemy. This also provoked a refutation, by the famous philosopher and physician Abū Bakr al-Rāzī.[59] Unfortunately neither document has survived, depriving us of what was no doubt one of the most interesting exchanges on the subject of alchemy in the Arabic tradition. Al-Kindī's greatest extant work, *On First Philosophy*, was attacked by the Andalusian thinker Ibn Ḥazm.[60] Ibn Ḥazm's attack includes references to parts of *On First Philosophy* that are no longer extant, which gives us important evidence for the scope of the original complete treatise. Also in Andalusia, Averroes explicitly mentions al-Kindī to criticize his views on compound drugs (on which see chapter 7).[61]

To these Arabic critics we can add the medieval Latin author Giles of Rome, whose work *On the Errors of the Philosophers* includes a section on al-Kindī.[62] Giles' treatment reflects the fact that the Latin tradition knew al-Kindī primarily through his works on science, and especially his teachings on astrology and magic.[63] The source for the ideas attacked by Giles is *On Rays*, which Giles refers to as *De Theorica Artium Magicarum* (*On the Theory of the Magical Arts*). Among other things, Giles complains that al-Kindī believes that all things happen of necessity, that al-Kindī denies the applicability of positive attributes to God, and that al-Kindī affirms the efficacy of various magical devices like sacrifices. Although this is the most striking engagement with al-Kindī in Latin, there is plentiful evidence that his works were translated and copied in the Latin West. Indeed a few Kindian works are extant only in Latin (like *On Rays*), while for others we have both a Latin translation and an Arabic text. *On Intellect* is particularly well represented in the Latin manuscript tradition, in two different translations, and there is a Latin version of *On Sleep and Dream*.[64] Al-Kindī is cited by numerous Latin authors, including Albert the Great,[65] and the influence especially of his scientific and mathematical works continues through the Renaissance.[66]

Overall, then, we can say that al-Kindī's direct impact on subsequent thinkers was significant. This is especially true of his students and his students' students, whose whole approach to philosophy seems to follow his in broad outline. And as the critiques just summarized show, he was a well-known figure both as a kind of symbol of philhellenism and as the author of specific treatises and doctrines. Yet he looms larger for the modern historian of philosophy than he did for his contemporaries, because of the inevitable interest for us in seeing the first extensive engagement with

Greek thought in the history of Arabic thought. There is a danger here, which is that al-Kindī's works are treated as little more than a repository of information about which Greek works were known in his time period. Of course *Quellenforschung*—the identification al-Kindī's sources—is crucial in understanding the thought of an author like al-Kindī, and has been a goal of much excellent scholarship about him. In the rest of this book, as I have said, I will instead focus on al-Kindī as a philosopher, attempting to understand his philosophical positions and why he held them, as well as to determine the extent to which these positions cohere into a single, systematic philosophy. But even this sort of approach cannot dispense with a discussion of the sources that shaped al-Kindī's thought. Which were the most decisive sources, and what overall conception of philosophy did al-Kindī take from them? These will be the issues taken up the next chapter.

2

FALSAFA

Sources and Structure

The word for "philosophy" in Arabic is *falsafa*, taken from the Greek *philosophia*. The fact that it is a loan-word from Greek is not insignificant: in al-Kindī's time and beyond, Arabic-speaking culture viewed philosophy as a foreign import. This is shown not just by the attitude of critics like al-Sīrāfī, whom we met at the end of chapter 1. It is shown also by more neutral authors like al-Khwārizmī, whose encyclopedic *Keys to the Sciences* (written about 977 A.D.) is divided into two sections: one on native Arabic disciplines, and one on foreign, that is, Greek, disciplines.[1] The latter consist essentially of the Aristotelian sciences as filtered through the late ancient and early Arabic traditions. Right up to and past the time of Avicenna, the importance and legitimacy of the Greek sciences would be hotly disputed. A debate about the relative merits of (Greek) logic and (Arabic) grammar served as a kind of microcosm of the wider dispute. But at least there was widespread agreement about the contents and structure of this imported knowledge.

More than 100 years earlier than al-Khwārizmī, al-Kindī could not yet rely on these assumptions. He had not only to defend and promote the value of the newly translated works against critics, but also to try to explain what Greek philosophy consisted of. On the other hand, al-Kindī had an advantage that tenth-century thinkers did not: the battle lines between Greek and Arabic thought had not yet been drawn. In the ninth century the translation movement received massive social and political support, from the highest levels of 'Abbāsid society. In this context al-Kindī could be optimistic about the prospects of bringing Greek ideas into Arabic intellectual discourse. The Greek ideas would not replace Arabic or Muslim ones, but would ultimately *become* Arabic and Muslim. As a result, polarized contrasts such as the one between *falsafa* and *kalām*—familiar to us from figures like al-Fārābī and Averroes—are to some extent anachronistic when applied to al-Kindī. Al-Kindī did have contemporary opponents who rejected Greek ideas for their foreignness, and as we will see shortly he passionately disagreed with them. But his concern was not merely to show that foreign truth and wisdom were truth and wisdom nonetheless; it was also to show how foreign truth and wisdom formed an integrated body of knowledge, and then to show how this knowledge could be integrated with the Arabic language and the teachings of Islam.[2]

The Defense of *Falsafa*

One of the most celebrated passages in al-Kindī comes at the end of the first part of his *On First Philosophy*. It follows on an introduction to the topic of the work, which is metaphysics or "first philosophy," here understood as the study of the first cause, God. Al-Kindī is not shy about the value of what he will offer in this work: "of the human arts, the highest in rank and the noblest in degree is the art of philosophy, which is defined as the knowledge of things in their true natures, insofar as this is possible for man" (§I.2, AR 95, RJ 9). And because of the eminence of its object, first philosophy is the noblest part of philosophy. Alluding to the Koranic epithet for God, *al-ḥaqq* ("the Truth"), al-Kindī asserts that "everything that has being has truth," and that God, the First Truth, is the cause of all truth insofar as He is the cause of all being. This leads him on to the meditation on truth that concerns us now.

The passage begins with an injunction to value any contribution made to the truth, whatever its provenance. Philosophy is a collective enterprise, so that even if every philosopher contributes only a little, "if one collects together the little that each one of these people has attained of the truth, the result is quite considerable." He then says:

> *On First Philosophy* §II.4 (AR 103, RJ 13): We must not be ashamed to admire the truth or to acquire it, from wherever it comes. Even if it should come from far-flung nations and foreign peoples, there is for the student of truth nothing more important than the truth, nor is the truth demeaned or diminished by the one who states or conveys it; no one is demeaned by the truth, rather all are ennobled by it.

An admirable sentiment to us, no doubt, but not an uncontroversial one among al-Kindī's contemporaries. In what follows al-Kindī says:

> *On First Philosophy* §III.1–2 (AR 103–4, RJ 13–15): [We must] be on guard against the evil of the interpretation of many in our own time who have made a name for themselves with speculation, people who are estranged from the truth. They crown themselves undeservedly with the crowns of truth, because of the narrowness of their understanding of the ways of truth . . . [and] because of the filth of the envy that has mastered their bestial souls, whose veil of darkness cloaks the vision of their thought from the light of truth.

This begins a long invective against a group of unnamed opponents, whom al-Kindī accuses of "trafficking in religion." Obviously one would like to know whom he has in mind.

The first clue is that these are people who have become known for "speculation [*naẓar*]," and as a result risen to positions of prestige and power. Apart from their "crowns" they are said to occupy "fraudulent seats, in which they have undeservedly been installed" (§III.2, AR 104, RJ 15). Alfred Ivry has suggested that al-Kindī has in mind the Mu'tazila, who were the dominant school of speculative Muslim theology during the middle of the ninth century, when *On First Philosophy* was written. Ivry must be right that the targets of al-Kindī's ire are theologians of some description, since he grants them a reputation for "speculation" and also says that they trade in religion. But it is painting with too broad a brush to identify these opponents with the Mu'tazila generally. For one thing, the whole notion of a Mu'tazilite "school" is somewhat anachronistic in this context. The middle of the ninth century saw a number of competing figures within *kalām*, and it was only later that the differences between these figures seemed minor enough to group them under a single Mu'tazilite heading. It seems unlikely that al-Kindī is thinking of such a broad and varied phenomenon in this passage, and more likely that he has in mind a specific group of theologians. Who these might be is a matter for guesswork, not certainty. But I suspect that, far from being "Mu'tazilite" thinkers, they are in fact more likely to be traditionalists like Ibn Ḥanbal and his supporters.[3] In any case, what seems to be distinctive about the opponents is not so much that they are influential theologians, but that they are detractors of the philosophical inheritance of the Greeks. This is why al-Kindī attacks them just after praising the Greeks for their pursuit of truth. He goes on to say that the opponents deny the necessity to acquire the "knowledge of things in their true natures," that is, philosophy. Their position is incoherent, al-Kindī argues, because anyone who denies the need to do philosophy would owe us a philosophical argument for why philosophy is unnecessary. But by offering this argument they would of course engage in philosophy, and thus refute themselves (§III.4, AR 105, RJ 15; this argument goes back to Aristotle's *Protrepticus*).

Al-Kindī concludes his attack with what is probably the most rhetorically charged passage in any of his extant works. It is worth quoting in full:

> *On First Philosophy* §III.5 (AR 105, RJ 15–17): We beseech Him who can see into our hearts—who knows our efforts towards establishing a proof of His divinity, making manifest His oneness, driving away those who stubbornly resist Him and do not believe in Him by using proofs that refute their unbelief and tear aside the veils of their shamefulness and declare openly the deficiencies of their destructive creed—to protect us and whoever follows our path with the fortification of His unceasing might, to dress us in the armor of His preserving shelter and grant us the aid of the edge of His piercing sword, and support through the might of His victorious strength, so that He may thereby let us reach the end of our intention in aiding the truth and supporting what is right, and so that He may thereby let us reach the degree of those whose intention is pleasing to Him, those whose action He approves, and those to whom He gives triumph and victory over His opponents who do not believe in His grace, and who contravene the path of truth that is pleasing to Him.

What is particularly striking about the rhetoric here is its religious context. Al-Kindī is not saying that the philosophical pursuit of truth is to be detached from religious belief. Rather, al-Kindī argues that the rejection of his own project amounts to "unbelief [*kufr*]." This is a startling accusation. Al-Kindī bases it on the fact that the opponents reject the attempt to use philosophy in supporting the main tenets of Islam: God's oneness and divinity. Insofar as philosophy can contribute to knowledge of these truths, to reject philosophy is in effect to reject Islam itself.

This tells us a great deal about the project of *On First Philosophy* and al-Kindī's project in general. As was already suggested by the characterization of metaphysics as theology at the outset of the work, *On First Philosophy* is an attempt to use philosophy to prove the central truths of Islamic theological dogma. And it is not only the uncontroversial claims that God exists, and that God is one, that are at issue here. As we will see, the extant remains of *On First Philosophy* culminate in an argument for a broadly negative understanding of divine attributes, which is a position associated with none other than the Mu'tazila. This suggests that al-Kindī's invective here is not directed against Mu'tazilite theological positions or indeed the practice of speculative theology. After all, al-Kindī is in the process of trying to persuade the reader to endorse the *philosophical* speculative theology of *On First Philosophy*. His aims and even his ultimate doctrines are like those of the Mu'tazila; it is only the Greek materials on which he draws that distinguishes his project from theirs.[4] His quarrel, then, is with any theologian (or, presumably, anyone at all) who wishes to deny the utility of Greek philosophical texts for supporting positions within Muslim theology.

The Sources of *Falsafa*

Up until now I have spoken rather loosely of the "Greek tradition" and "philosophical texts" that inspired al-Kindī, whose use he was so keen to defend. Before we can go further and discuss how he saw the Greek tradition he was promoting, we need to be more specific about which texts he was able to read, and in what form. Of course the Greek philosophical corpus would have appeared much different to al-Kindī from how it does to us. Probably the biggest difference is that he may not have known a single Platonic dialogue in complete form. He seems to have had access at least to summary accounts of some dialogues, such as the *Timaeus* and *Phaedo*, but in general his knowledge of Aristotle was much greater than his knowledge of Plato. And even his knowledge of Aristotle was very incomplete.

A second difference, so obvious that one is in danger of overlooking it, is that al-Kindī was reading these texts in Arabic translation. Although later reports credit al-Kindī with having "translated" various Greek works, this probably means that he had the works in question translated by others in his circle.[5] It is now generally agreed that he read no Greek, and was dependent on his translators to provide him with Arabic versions of Greek texts (and, perhaps, oral reports about works that had not yet been translated). Now, when we look at some of the translations produced in his circle, it becomes obvious that what al-Kindī was reading was not normally a pellucid rendition of the original Greek. His circle produced two kinds of translations: one kind could be faulted for being so literal as to be difficult to comprehend, while the other could be faulted for being more a loose paraphrase than a translation. The star example for the latter category is the Arabic Plotinus, which is not only loose in its handling of the Greek but sometimes adds long original sections with no basis at all in Plotinus' *Enneads*. The Arabic version of the *De Anima* is similarly distant from its Greek exemplar. These translations could also be selective. For example, the Arabic Plotinus consists only of versions of parts of the second half of the *Enneads*. This is quite possibly because the earlier parts of the Plotinian corpus did not seem worth the expense and effort of rendering them into Arabic.

Nor was the Arabic of either sort of translation necessarily a pleasure to read.[6] Al-Kindī is said to have "corrected" numerous texts, which probably means that he fixed the Arabic of his translator colleagues, who were not native speakers of Arabic, to something somewhat less barbarous.[7] Ideally, then, if one wants to know what al-Kindī thought was in a Greek author, one should always read the Arabic translation he used and bear in mind how difficult a task he faced in divining the original intent of that Greek author. Thus I will cite from the Arabic versions of the texts he was reading, when they are available, and sometimes indicate how these diverged from the Greek. On the bright side, it should be mentioned that the Kindī circle seems usually to have translated directly from Greek, whereas the circle of Ḥunayn b. Isḥāq, for example, often used a Syriac intermediary translation. But it is not always possible to know whether a given text known to al-Kindī was based directly on Greek or on a Syriac model.

With these caveats out of the way, let us quickly survey the main texts used by al-Kindī. The greatest influence on him in metaphysics and logic is from a handful of Aristotelian and Neoplatonic works. Some works from the *Organon* are very important for al-Kindī, especially Porphyry's *Isagoge* and Aristotle's *Categories*. This is unsurprising because there was a well-established tradition of reading these works already in the Syriac tradition, starting centuries before al-Kindī's birth. Aristotle's *Metaphysics* is tremendously influential on al-Kindī's *On First Philosophy*, as can be seen merely by glancing through Ivry's commentary on this work. Fortunately, we have the Kindī circle version of the *Metaphysics*—ascribed to an otherwise unknown Usṭāth—preserved in Averroes' *Long Commentary on the Metaphysics*.[8] From the Neoplatonists, there were Arabic versions of Plotinus' *Enneads* and Proclus' *Elements of Theology*. Like the Arabic Plotinus the Arabic Proclus differs considerably from its source; for example Proclus' complex metaphysical system of hypostases is simplified into something more like the Plotinian world of cosmos, soul, intellect and God.

As for influences on al-Kindī's physics, we know that Ibn Nā'ima al-Ḥimṣī, translator of the Plotinus materials, also did an Arabic version of some of the *Physics* (as well as the *Sophistical Refutations*). Al-Kindī seems to have known the *Meteorology* and *On the Heavens* as well. His cosmology is also deeply indebted to treatises by the Aristotelian commentator Alexander of Aphrodisias (see chapter 8). Most famously, though, al-Kindī drew on the work of John Philoponus in his arguments that the physical world is not eternal (see chapter 4). With regard to psychology and ethics, at some point al-Kindī would have been able to read the Arabic paraphrase of the *De Anima*. But, as mentioned above, at least some of his psychological works seem curiously untouched by the doctrines of the *De Anima*. He did know at least parts of the *Parva Naturalia*, it would seem—this is shown by his treatise *On Sleep and Dream* (see chapter 5). His sources in ethics, though, were much thinner than in metaphysics and psychology; in particular there is no evidence that he made use of an Arabic *Ethics* in any of his extant works. As we will see (chapter 6), al-Kindī's ethical thought is as a result broadly Platonist, inspired by the figure of Socrates and encouraging a kind of intellectualizing asceticism. Al-Kindī's *On Dispelling Sadness*, his most elaborate ethical work, also borrows an image from Epictetus' *Enchirideon*. But there is no reason to think he read this entire work in Arabic.

In science and mathematics, Euclid's *Elements* seems to have been a great influence on al-Kindī, as was his *Optics* in the recension of Theon of Alexandria. Nicomachus of Gerasa's *Introduction to Arithmetic* was an important source for both mathematics and a Pythagoreanizing version of Platonism which can be detected in various Kindian treatises. Al-Kindī "corrected" a translation of this work by Ibn al-Bahrīz, adding glosses of his own.[9] As we will see shortly, these mathematical works exerted a powerful influence on his philosophical methodology. Al-Kindī was also well-acquainted with the works of Ptolemy, a major influence on al-Kindī's astronomical theory. The *Almagest* is said to have been translated for al-Kindī and he knew the *Tetrabiblios* as well.[10] He also knew medical treatises, such as Galen's works on compound drugs, to which he refers in *On Degrees* (see chapter 7). It may well be that al-Kindī's access to scientific texts like these outstripped his access to philosophical works.

And that, sadly, is almost all we can be sure of. There remain many uncertainties about what other works al-Kindī could have known. One of the biggest questions is how much, if anything, al-Kindī was able to read from the translations of his eminent contemporary Ḥunayn b. Isḥāq (Ḥunayn died in 873, so about at the same time as al-Kindī). If he had access to Ḥunayn's productions then the list of Greek works al-Kindī could have read would expand greatly. He may also have known texts produced by other early translators. For example Yaḥyā b. al-Biṭrīq (fl. ca. 815) translated the *Timaeus* and zoological works by Aristotle.[11] Since al-Kindī quotes from his translations of *On the Heavens* and the *Meteorology* he may well have known these as well.[12] It is a matter of controversy whether al-Kindī knew certain other works—e.g. the *Divine Names* of the Pseudo-Dionysius, the *Optics* of Ptolemy, and the *Commentary on the De Anima* of Philoponus, to name just a few.

Space does not permit me to explore the range of questions that arise here. But it is worth making the general point that, just as we today have many texts al-Kindī did not, so he knew Greek works that are lost to us. For instance, it is clear that he knew summaries and epitomes of Greek works or overviews of Greek authors, which probably came down to him from the Alexandrian philosophical schools. Such summaries may have provided him with his only access to the Platonic dialogues. One work which probably depends on an earlier summary is al-Kindī's overview of the Aristotelian corpus, titled *On the Quantity of Aristotle's Books*. When al-Kindī wrote this treatise, he had first-hand knowledge of some of Aristotle's works (like the *Categories*), and he gives us well-informed accounts of these. But his remarks on other works are so cursory as to suggest that he knows nothing about them apart from their titles ("*On the Length and Brevity of Life*," al-Kindī helpfully informs us, "is about the length and brevity of life," §XI.4). *On the Quantity of Aristotle's Books* most likely depends on a summary of the topics of each item in the Aristotelian corpus. This summary was presumably itself translated from Greek, but we do not know when, or what the source text was.

A final consideration to be raised about al-Kindī's sources is the question of how he used them. It has sometimes been wondered whether al-Kindī added much to his sources, or whether his own treatises are just pastiches of Greek material in translation. Sometimes an entire work by al-Kindī has even been assumed to be little more than a paraphrase of some (lost) Greek work.[13] Certainly some Kindian works do seem to fit this description. For instance *On the Sayings of Socrates* may be culled entirely from a Greek source or from several sources, with nothing of al-Kindī's own added. But when we do know al-Kindī's sources it is clear that he selects, manipulates, and combines them in surprising and philosophically interesting ways, as well as adding arguments of his own. A good example is *On First Philosophy* itself, as we will see in chapters 3 and 4. In reading al-Kindī we would do well to abandon the notion that philosophical innovation is precluded by close dependence on prior sources.

Indeed, it is often in interpreting his sources or trying to reconcile sources that al-Kindī's creativity emerges.[14] We have already seen that al-Kindī was determined to persuade his contemporaries of the value and power of Greek thought. This meant, of course, that it would have been exceedingly inconvenient for him to admit that Greek thought itself was riven by disagreement. Rather he needed to present it as a single, harmonious body of true doctrines. Thus we frequently find him stressing the agreement of several philosophers on a core set of positions: for example his *Discourse on the Soul* has Plato, Pythagoras, and Aristotle presenting a united front in claiming that the soul is immaterial and immortal. Another treatment of the soul, the *Short Statement on the Soul*, asserts the internal consistency of the views of Plato and Aristotle, as well as the harmony of these two philosophers with one another (see chapter 5 for both works). To be sure, al-Kindī does sometimes disagree with Greek thinkers. For example, he must have known that Aristotle held the world to be eternal. But in his proofs that the world is not eternal, he never admits as much, allowing the disagreement to remain tacit. The only explicitly critical discussions of Greek thinkers to be found in al-Kindī appear in the scientific works that I take to be from his later career (see chapter 1).

The Structure of *Falsafa*

What, then, did this body of agreed truths consist in? For al-Kindī, following Greek precedent, philosophy can be broadly divided into practical and theoretical disciplines.[15] Thus *On First Philosophy* begins with the assertion that "the objective of the philosopher is to achieve the truth with his knowledge, and to act truthfully with his action." This division is reflected in other works.[16] However, as we have seen in our survey of his sources, al-Kindī had much less access to works on practical philosophy than he did to works on theoretical philosophy. His own writings reflect this, as do his treatments of the structure and methodology of philosophy. For him the question of philosophy's structure is primarily the question of how the *theoretical* side of philosophy is structured. The central difficulty to be confronted here turns out to be al-Kindī's attitude towards mathematics—which he considers to be a philosophical science—and how it relates to the rest of philosophy. For, as we will see, al-Kindī presents two conflicting versions of the place that mathematics occupies within the philosophical curriculum. On both versions, though, mathematical methodology is crucial for philosophy as a whole.

Let us begin with *On the Quantity of Aristotle's Books* (hereafter *Quantity*), the extant Kindian work devoted most explicitly to these concerns. In it he gives the following division of philosophy, which he will use to classify Aristotle's writings:

> *Quantity* §II.1 (AR 264–5): After propaedeutic science there are four types of books: the first of the four is the logical books; the second is the physical books; the third is those that deal with what may in itself dispense with the physical in order to persist, having no need of bodies, even though it exists together with bodies and is connected to them in some way; and the fourth deals with what has no need of bodies and is completely unconnected to them.

As just suggested, the division of the four types of books seems restricted to the theoretical sciences. Indeed the final division of objects into material, immaterial but connected to the material, and utterly immaterial, comes ultimately from a division of theoretical science found in Aristotle himself (*Metaphysics* E.1, 1026a13–19). When we turn to the rest of *Quantity* we find that the practical sciences of ethics and politics sit rather uneasily in the analysis of Aristotle's corpus. Al-Kindī lists the works of

Aristotle twice, once to list and order them and once to identify the "purposes [*aghrāḍ*]" of each. (In between, we get a surprising digression on the nature of Muḥammad's prophecy, which I will discuss below.) In both lists, the ethical treatises come at the end and are presented almost as an afterthought. This may be in part because al-Kindī has not read any of Aristotle's ethical works; he seems even to be hesitant about how many there are and what they are called.[17]

Leaving practical philosophy aside, then, we have logic and then three sciences identified in terms of their objects. It is the logical works (especially the *Categories*) that receive the most attention in both of al-Kindī's lists, which is probably because these are works he knows first-hand and has studied carefully. Unfortunately he says nothing about how logic relates to the other sciences. This may be because, as we will see shortly, al-Kindī is much more interested in how the propadeutic sciences prepare the way for philosophy, than he is in how logic does so. But we can piece together an answer to the question. Philosophy, like any discipline, expresses its findings in language. And, as his discussions of the *Organon* make clear, for al-Kindī Aristotle's various logical works are devoted to various kinds of speech. The *Categories* deals with "terms [*maqūlāt*]," i.e. subjects and predicates (§III.1, AR 366): the 10 categories are the 10 types of terms. *On Interpretation* deals with propositions or "judgments": what types of propositions there are and how they are composed (§IX.5, AR 380). The *Prior Analytics* is about syllogisms generally, and the *Posterior Analytics*, *Topics* and *Sophistics* about different types of syllogism (§IX.10, AR 381). The *Rhetoric* is then about the discourse of persuasive argument, and the *Poetics* is of course about poetic discourse. Thus the *Organon* precedes the rest of theoretical science by determining which modes of discourse will be appropriate to it.

It is then the remaining three sciences that actually deal with the objects of theoretical philosophy. As we saw, these sciences are differentiated in terms of the different kinds of objects they study. One science studies physical objects, i.e. bodies; a second studies things that may be in bodies but can persist without bodies; and the third studies things with no connection to bodies. The first category comprises the physical sciences, obviously enough. Aristotle's corpus is generous in its investigation of these sciences, including not only the *Physics* but (by al-Kindī's count) seven more books, including *On the Heavens* and the *Meteorology*. In *Quantity*, al-Kindī says that the second category is psychology, because the soul, according to al-Kindī, can survive without the body but also has a connection of some kind to the body. On this topic al-Kindī mentions the *De Anima* and also the *Parva Naturalia*. Although al-Kindī elsewhere again identifies psychology as the intermediate science,[18] he is not consistent on the point, as we will see below.

Finally there is the science that deals with what has no connection to bodies. According to al-Kindī Aristotle devoted only his *Metaphysics* to this science. We might find this characterization of the *Metaphysics* odd. After all, don't the middle books of the *Metaphysics* deal primarily with substances that are composites of matter and form? It is not until book *Lambda* that we get to objects that are explicitly said to be immaterial, namely God and the movers of the heavenly spheres. Even after that, we have the mathematical books, which according to Aristotle himself deal with objects of the second class (immaterial things that may be connected to body). But al-Kindī's explanation of the "purpose" of the *Metaphysics* is more than odd, it is astonishing:

> *Quantity* §XI.5 (AR 384): His purpose in his book called *Metaphysics* is an explanation of things that subsist without matter and, though they may exist together with what does have matter, are neither connected with nor united to matter; and the oneness [*tawḥīd*] of God, the great and exalted, and an explanation of His beautiful names, and that He is the complete agent cause of the universe, the God of the universe and its governor through His perfect providence and complete wisdom.

It now becomes easier to see why al-Kindī could say that his own *On First Philosophy* could be both a treatise on metaphysics and an investigation into the nature of God: for al-Kindī these are the same thing. To put it another way, for al-Kindī metaphysics is theology (indeed, *Muslim* theology, given the references here to *tawḥīd* and God's "beautiful names"). Or, to put it still another way, for him the study of being reduces to the study of the First Cause of being. In chapter 3 we will see how al-Kindī works this out in detail.

For now let us step back and consider theoretical science as a whole. The three-fold division gives al-Kindī an orderly way of thinking about these sciences, and thus a way of ordering Aristotle's corpus. But it also raises a question: how are the three sciences interrelated, and how do we progress from one to the next? The question is pressing because the three sciences seem to be defined in opposition to each other. Each science has a discrete realm of objects, and there is no attempt to show how, for example, the insights yielded in physics could be helpful for metaphysics or vice-versa. In chapter 5 we will see that there is a good reason for this. Al-Kindī's epistemology presents serious obstacles to the idea that the study of physical objects as such could be relevant to the study of psychology or metaphysics. But *Quantity* suggests a more mundane reason for al-Kindī's presentation of the three kinds of theoretical science as autonomous from each other: he does not know enough Aristotle. For Aristotle, the various sciences could be interrelated using his theory of demonstrative syllogisms, as put forth in the *Posterior Analytics*. One science (for example mathematics) provides premises that are put to use in another (for example optics). This notion of the subordination of sciences seems almost wholly unknown to al-Kindī, which must be in part because his knowledge of the *Posterior Analytics* is at best indirect and sketchy.[19] Thus whenever he raises the question of the ordering of the sciences, he ranks them in terms of the eminence of their objects or just insists that they do have a proper order, without explaining how the earlier sciences actually contribute to our understanding of the later sciences, or how the later sciences could retrospectively justify the principles of the earlier sciences.[20]

All of this raises a further set of questions. What method does al-Kindī think we should be using in philosophy, and how does al-Kindī think philosophy is structured, if he does not draw on the philosophical method and structure described in the *Posterior Analytics*? To answer this question, we need to return to the topic of the propaedeutic sciences. These are, al-Kindī tells us, the mathematical sciences, namely arithmetic, geometry, harmonics and astronomy. They study whatever is numbered, namely the varieties of quantity and quality: discrete quantities (arithmetic), quantities relative to one another (harmonics), unmoving qualities (geometry), and moving qualities (astronomy) (§VII.2, AR 377). In stark contrast to his handling of logic, al-Kindī tells us at length and emphatically why the mathematical sciences must be studied before we proceed to the others. Our path to knowledge begins with our grasp of sensible objects, and this is always by way of their quantities and qualities (§V.6, AR 372). So we begin from the sciences that study quantity and quality, and these are the mathematical sciences. Without these it is impossible to attain any other kind of philosophical knowledge, since knowledge of secondary substance (i.e. universals) depends on knowledge of primary substances (i.e. sensible particulars).[21] Al-Kindī explored this point in another work that is now lost, mentioned in the *Fihrist*, titled *That Philosophy Can Only Be Acquired through the Science of Mathematics*.

The structure of philosophy, then, seems clear enough: mathematics sets us on the road towards theoretical science, and logic teaches us how to express the truths we will discover in that science. The core of theoretical science itself consists in three apparently autonomous inquiries, into bodies, souls, and the divine respectively; presumably all three inquiries are a matter of grasping universals or "secondary substances." But there is a problem. Al-Kindī is not consistent in saying that it is psychology that is the intermediate theoretical science. He sometimes claims that this science is mathematics. When he does so he is following the aforementioned passage (*Metaphysics* E.1, 1026a13–19) in which Aristotle gives the three-fold division of the sciences. Aristotle identified the intermediate science as mathematics, not psychology (cf. *Physics* II.2 for the status of mathematicals).

There are three texts that show al-Kindī following this alternate scheme, with mathematics between physics and metaphysics. The first is a report of his views by the later author Ibn Nubāta;[22] the second is in a work on music, *On Stringed Instruments*;[23] and the third is the concluding remark in a mathematical work having to do with the finiteness of the created world.[24] This scheme may also be assumed in *On First Philosophy* itself, which says that "figure [*shakl*]... has no matter but may be perceived together with matter" (§IV.7, AR 108, RJ 21). Furthermore, *On First Philosophy* has the following to say about the use of mathematics regarding the physical world:

> *On First Philosophy* §IV.13–14 (AR 110–1, RJ 23–5): For this reason many who have contemplated things that are above nature have been confused, because in their inquiry they used the images of these things in their souls, inasmuch as their habits were the result of sensation, like children.... [Conversely they were confused] about natural things when they used mathematical investigation. For this is appropriate only for what is immaterial, because matter is subject to being acted upon, and is moved. Nature is the first cause of everything that moves and is at rest, and therefore everything natural possesses matter. Thus it is not possible to use mathematical investigation in the perception of natural things, since it is proper to the immaterial. If this is the case, and such an investigation is for things that are not natural, whoever uses it in an inquiry into natural things has turned away from and missed the truth.

This passage seems to be in direct conflict with the teaching of *Quantity* that the mathematical sciences are the sciences that study sensible particulars ("primary substances" in the language of the *Categories*, which is taken over in *Quantity*). For it seems that these particulars must be identified with the "natural things" mentioned here in *On First Philosophy*. Far from saying that mathematics is the science through which we grasp such particulars, al-Kindī now tells us that using mathematics to study sensible particulars can only lead to confusion.

We can partially resolve this tension by insisting on al-Kindī's behalf that the "qualities and quantities" are not *themselves* sensible particulars. Rather they are abstract entities, like numbers, ratios, or shapes. Even in *Quantity* itself (§V.6, AR 372), we find al-Kindī saying that "sensation does not make contact with its object directly, but contacts it through the intermediary of quantity and quality." This suggests that qualities and quantities are something distinct from, and inhering in, the particulars. They are themselves incorporeal but have a "connection" to bodies. If this is right, then *Quantity* too sees the mathematical qualities and quantities in themselves as "intermediary" objects, on a par with the soul. Kindian works like *On Degrees* could provide concrete examples, such as the ratio of 3 parts hot to 1 part moist in a given pharmacological compound. The compound is a sensible particular, but the ratio of 3 to 1 is not. In light of this, perhaps al-Kindī had good reasons to consider both mathematics and psychology to be intermediate sciences.

There are still two lingering tensions, though. First, there is no getting around the inconsistency in the division of theoretical philosophy: is it physics-*mathematics*-metaphysics or physics-*psychology*-metaphysics? Here al-Kindī seems simply to have repeated different versions of the curriculum handed down from antiquity. It is unsurprising that he does not present mathematics as the middle science in *Quantity*. Aristotle may have identified it as such, but Aristotle's corpus contains no separate works devoted to mathematics. So the curriculum with psychology as intermediate, and mathematics as propaedeutic, is far more useful in this context. A second, deeper problem is the methodological tension between *Quantity* and *On First Philosophy*. Whether or not qualities and quantities are themselves sensible particulars, *Quantity* states explicitly that the mathematical sciences are primarily (perhaps only) used to study sensible particulars. *On First Philosophy* by contrast seems to counsel against this with equal explicitness. This raises issues about al-Kindī's broader epistemology and scientific method, which we will not be able to pursue until chapters 5 and 7.

For now let us note that when al-Kindī speaks of using a "mathematical investigation [*al-faḥṣ al-riyāḍī*]" in *On First Philosophy*, he does not then proceed to engage in anything obviously mathematical. Rather, he continues on to a discussion of the eternity of the world. This is not, however, a *non sequitur* on al-Kindī's part. As we will see (chapter 4), al-Kindī's treatment of the eternity of the world in *On First Philosophy* is indeed "mathematical" in the sense that it uses a mathematical methodology.[25] The methodology in question is the axiomatic proof. Al-Kindī first lays out several principles which are undefended and apparently in no need of defense: he says that they are known "immediately" or "without an intermediary" (*bi-lā tawaṣṣut*, §VI.1, AR 114, RJ 29). The argument then deploys these premises to reach the desired result. This form of proof is known to al-Kindī above all from the works of Euclid, not only the *Elements* but also the *Optics*. Al-Kindī imitates Euclid's method in his own *On Perspectives*, which is inspired by the *Optics*. And it is to this that al-Kindī refers in *Quantity* when he extols geometry for its "great method of demonstration [*al-'aẓīma 'l-burhān*]" (§VII.3, AR 377).

It is worth noting that in another passage from *Quantity*, one of the few claims al-Kindī associates with the *Posterior Analytics* is that "the principles of demonstration do not need to be demonstrated, since they are obvious and clear to the intellect or to sense" (§X.1, AR 381). Aristotle does indeed argue in *Post. An.* I.3 that all demonstration terminates in indemonstrable first principles. This scrap of information may have encouraged al-Kindī to assume that in the *Posterior Analytics* Aristotle set out an axiomatic method just like the one used in Euclid. In any case al-Kindī certainly would have had other models for the use of Euclidean geometric proof in subjects like metaphysics. One source would have been Proclus' *Elements of Theology*, which was rendered into Arabic in al-Kindī's circle (some of the resulting texts were drawn together to form the *Book on the Pure Good*, later the *Liber de Causis*). In the *Elements of Theology* Proclus uses an axiomatic method deliberately styled on that used by Euclid in his own *Elements*.[26] As we will see, al-Kindī's aforementioned arguments against the eternity of the world draw heavily on John Philoponus, and Philoponus also used an axiomatic argument in one of his own discussions of this topic.

Mathematics, then, gave al-Kindī one paradigm for philosophical method: the axiomatic proof. A second style of argument is even more prominent in al-Kindī: the *reductio ad absurdum*. Such an argument has the form, Either A or B, but if B, either C or D, but neither C nor D, so not-B; therefore A. (Obviously it can be more elaborate, for instance by introducing more than two possibilities at any stage; however most of the arguments of this sort in al-Kindī start with a dichotomy.) A good example is the argument at the beginning of the third section of *On First Philosophy* (§IX, AR 123–4, RJ 41–3), which can be schematized as follows:

Either (1) something can make its own essence, or (2) nothing can make its own essence.
If (1) something can make its own essence, then either:
(1a) it is a being, and its essence is not a being;
(1b) it is a non-being, and its essence a being;
(1c) it is a non-being and its essence a non-being;
or (1d) it is a being and its essence a being.
But (1a–d) are, for various reasons, all impossible.
Therefore (2) nothing can make its own essence.

This sort of argument appears throughout al-Kindī's corpus, with such frequency that one is tempted to speak of *reductio ad absurdum ad nauseam*.

As a method of philosophical argument, the dichotomous argument has the advantage that it claims to explore *all* the possibilities—in the example just given, (1a–d) are logically exhaustive. So such an argument rules out any unexplored avenues. But the method also has disadvantages. First, the whole argument is only as strong as the sub-arguments used to rule out the options on the false side of the dichotomy. So in this example, we must accept al-Kindī's arguments against each of (1a–d); in al-Kindī these sub-arguments are sometimes also by dichotomous *reductio*. Second, and more important, such an argument, if successful, does establish the truth of the only possibility to remain standing; in our example this is (2). But it gives us no insight as to why this possibility is the true one. It is not a "demonstrative" proof in Aristotle's sense, because it does not give the *reason why* the conclusion is true, it only tells us *that* the conclusion is true. To take another example, there is a classic dichotomous argument in *That there are Incorporeal Substances*, to the effect that a species cannot be a body (§§7–10). We get an exhaustive refutation of the suggestion that species are bodies, but no clue at all as to why we might find it attractive to think of species as incorporeal substances, even though this is the conclusion of the argument. Rather it is something we are meant to accept because the other options are all foreclosed. Al-Kindī's lack of access to the *Posterior Analytics* again seems relevant. Had he read this work he might have put less stock in these *reductio* arguments.[27]

The Integration of *Falsafa*

Al-Kindī thus had a coherent vision of the contents, structure and methods of philosophy as handed down from the Greeks. Using methods of proof borrowed from mathematics, the most rigorous of the sciences, philosophy would investigate all kinds of objects in a set of complementary disciplines, culminating in metaphysics, which would yield an understanding of God himself. The different Greek philosophers would be seen to agree, in most cases, on the findings of metaphysics and the other sciences. Presenting Greek thought as fulfilling these requirements was of course an ambitious undertaking, but in a sense this conveys only half of al-Kindī's ambition. The other half was the integration of this received philosophical wisdom into the intellectual currents of al-Kindī's own culture.[28]

Such an integration required overcoming numerous challenges. There was first of all the problem of even identifying the important figures in the Greek tradition and saying what their doctrines had been. A work produced near the time of al-Kindī's circle, the *Opinions of the Philosophers* ascribed to "Ammonius," shows both how interested al-Kindī's contemporaries were in this project, and how wildly inaccurate their information was.[29] The *Opinions* puts Neoplatonic metaphysical doctrines into the mouths of everyone from Thales to the late ancients. This text is closely related to the burgeoning tradition of gnomological literature: lists of pithy sayings and anecdotes about Greek wise men.[30] Such literature also contributed to the "historical" project of supplying doctrines and personalities to go with the famous names of Greek tradition. Al-Kindī himself is the author of one of the first such gnomological treatises, a list of sayings ascribed to Socrates (see chapter 6).

Another, still more daunting task was the integration of philosophy into the Arabic language itself. Even assuming that he did not know Greek, through his close involvement with the work of numerous translators al-Kindī would have been keenly aware of the difficulty of rendering Greek philosophy into Arabic. The obstacles confronting translators were many. They ranged from the problem of finding Arabic grammatical constructions that could render Greek grammatical constructions, to understanding the references to Greek history and literature that litter the works of Aristotle and other Greek philosophers. Above all, there was a need for an Arabic technical vocabulary that could convey the technical vocabulary of Greek texts. With a few exceptions, al-Kindī could not rely on the work of previous authors writing in Arabic. He and his translators needed to establish an entirely new vocabulary that could not only stand in for Greek vocabulary—both in translations and in original treatises like the ones al-Kindī was writing—but also make some sense to Greek-less readers of Arabic. Thus we sometimes see al-Kindī giving us a Greek term in transliteration, telling us the equivalent Arabic term, and explaining the intended meaning so that there can be no confusion. His handling of the titles of Aristotle's *Organon* in *Quantity* is one example. Another is the following passage:

> *On Sleep and Dream* §III.1 (AR 295): If this is as we have said, then it is already evident what dreams are, as long as the faculties of the soul are known. For among them is a faculty called "imaginative [*muṣawwira*]," i.e. the faculty which makes us perceive the forms [*ṣuwar*] of individual things, without matter—i.e. when those things bearing the forms are absent from our senses. This is what the ancient Greek philosophers called *phantasia*.

In passages like these al-Kindī is trying to establish a new philosophical vocabulary in Arabic. His success was mixed. The word *muṣawwira* is in fact used by later authors, including Avicenna, to refer to an aspect of the imaginative faculty. But some of the most striking terminology, including several neologisms, to originate in al-Kindī's circle quickly fell into disuse.[31]

Another work that displays al-Kindī's project of producing new Arabic terminology does seem to have been influential.[32] This is *On Definitions*, which consists of a list of about 100 Arabic terms with definitions. Sometimes the same term is given several definitions, and the entries "philosophy" and "the human virtues" each receive a lengthier discussion. A few entries show clearly that this work was produced through engagement with Greek texts. For example it mentions etymologies for the Greek terms that stand behind the Arabic words being defined (including "philosophy" at §70A, AR 172; see also §88, AR 176, "rancor").[33] An entry on "imagination" (§21, AR 167) shows how fluid technical terminology could be in al-Kindī's time. As we just saw, in *On Sleep and Dream* al-Kindī uses the phrase *quwwa muṣawwira* for the imaginative faculty. But the entry on "imagination" in *On Definitions* does not use this term at all, instead giving *tawahhum* as the term to be defined and using *takhayyul* as a synonym within the definition itself. On the other hand, just as in *On Sleep and Dream*, we are given the transliteration *fanṭāsiyyā* to show the underlying Greek.

Assessing the role that *On Definitions* played in al-Kindī's wider project is made difficult by its complex textual transmission. It is preserved in three very different versions in different manuscripts (definitions from it also appear in the *Muqābasāt* of al-Tawḥīdī). One manuscript contains only a handful of the definitions found in the version of the Istanbul manuscript, and seems to have had some non-Kindian material added to these. Another adds more than 30 entries beyond what is present in the Istanbul version. Worse still, doubts have been raised about the authenticity of the treatise. I have dealt with the questions of transmission and authenticity elsewhere.[34] Here let me say only what is relevant for present purposes, which is that *On Definitions* seems to have been compiled from various texts known to al-Kindī's circle. It may have been compiled by al-Kindī alone, or (more likely, in my view) by him together with his translators and/or his students. Alternatively it may even have been a resource produced by these associates without al-Kindī's direct involvement. But the important point is that the definitions were culled, by someone in al-Kindī's circle, from Greek texts. Yet the terms being defined are Arabic; it is only rarely that the underlying Greek word is even mentioned. *On Definitions* thus embodies the project of creating an Arabic version of the Greek philosophical vocabulary. It also shows that native Arabic speakers might need a lexicon to understand this new Arabic terminology.

The question of terminology provides a concrete example of the process I have described above, in which Greek philosophy was integrated into an Arabic-speaking culture. This holds true for Greek ideas as well as for Greek language. In al-Kindī's hands the Greek heritage becomes not only "Arabized" but also "Islamicized," woven into the project of defending and explicating the truths handed down to the Prophet. I will spend much of this book describing how al-Kindī does this with regard to divine predication, the creation of the world, the immortality of the soul, divine providence, and so on. But for now let us take some even clearer cases where *falsafa* is pressed into the service of interfaith disputation and Koranic exegesis. These cases arise in three texts that will be discussed in greater depth later in this book; for now I want only to indicate their importance for understanding how al-Kindī saw the relationship between philosophy and Islam.

We saw already that al-Kindī wrote numerous "controversial" works, in which he attacked both doctrines of other faiths and doctrines held by theologians within Islam. Most of these are lost, but we do still have a very brief treatise of his written against the Christian doctrine of the Trinity, and this provides us with our first example. The polemic is preserved for us by Yaḥyā b. 'Adī, who quotes it in order to refute it and thus unintentionally preserves al-Kindī's words for posterity. Al-Kindī is explicit that his purpose here is to use ideas from the Greek tradition, despite the theological context. He says at the outset that he will show the "falsehood of the Christians' doctrine of the Trinity on the basis of logic and philosophy" (§1, RJ 123). And indeed, the text moves through the five "voices" of Porphyry's *Isagoge*, showing that the three divine Persons cannot be accommodated under any of these logical concepts (at the end he also mentions and makes use of Aristotle's *Topics*). Al-Kindī explains his use of Greek logical works as follows:

> *Against the Christians* §9 (RJ 125–7): Actually the falsehood of [the doctrine of the Trinity] is clear in many ways, but we wished to refute it using the *Isagoge* because it is the book that youths and beginning students train with. Thus this [refutation] can be grasped by the understanding even of someone of mean speculation and paltry learning. Also because this book we have used in our rebuke of [the Christians] can be found in just about every one of their homes. So perhaps this will increase their suspicions and help to awake them from their slumber.

This is a rather revealing passage. It adds to our evidence that at least the early parts of the *Organon* (which included Porphyry's *Isagoge* as an introduction to Aristotelian logic) were being studied widely in al-Kindī's day. But it also tells us something about al-Kindī's attitude towards the Christians, who, after all, included most of the translators with whom he collaborated. He is no doubt exaggerating when he says that in his day, pretty much every Christian home boasts a copy of the *Isagoge*. But the remark shows his respect for the learning of the Christians, who had anticipated his own interest in philosophical works, and who were now providing him with Arabic translations of those works.

Furthermore, the whole treatise shows that for al-Kindī, philosophy can be used to show the superiority of Muslim doctrine to the doctrines of other religions. No doubt he also used philosophical weaponry in his attacks on other sects, like the Manicheans, which are lost but mentioned in the *Fihrist*. Here one might be tempted to assume—especially given al-Kindī's own emphasis on the Christians' knowledge of Greek logic—that he appealed to philosophy only as a "neutral" discourse, so as to argue from common ground when he disputed with members of other faiths. But he was no less confident of the value of philosophical argument when speaking to his coreligionists about the truths of Muḥammad's revelation. Nothing shows this more clearly than two works in which he uses philosophy to explicate the Koran itself.

The first of these is *On the Prostration of the Outermost Sphere*, the entirety of which is devoted to glossing a verse from the Koran (55:5[6]): "and the stars and the trees prostrate themselves." He says he is responding to a request from Aḥmad, the caliph's son, to explain this verse. But one suspects that al-Kindī may have suggested the topic himself, since it gives him such a perfect chance to explain his cosmology and theory of divine providence, according to which God's will is achieved through the motions of the heavens (see chapter 8). In any case al-Kindī does not simply move straight into his philosophical account, but rather first makes some pointed comments about the dangers of misinterpreting passages from the Koran. He points out that all languages, and especially Arabic, have ambiguous terms, and that one must be careful not to insist on the most obvious, literal interpretation of any word that may arise (§I.2, AR 245, RJ 177–9). Surely, though al-Kindī does not say so, part of what he has in mind here is the fact that the Koran speaks of God in anthropomorphic terms, talking for instance of His "face" or of His sitting on a throne. This point about ambiguous terms also arises regarding figurative readings of such passages, which al-Kindī would no doubt himself adopt given his views on God's nature. Similarly, when the stars are said to "prostrate" themselves, this should not be taken literally, since the stars obviously cannot physically prostrate themselves. Rather "prostration" here simply means "obedience" (§II.1, AR 246, RJ 179). Al-Kindī even quotes a non-Koranic passage from Arabic poetry to illustrate the point (§II.2, AR 246, RJ 179).

Only then does he go on to a philosophical treatment of why it makes sense to think of the stars as "obeying" God.

Here, then, we see al-Kindī engaging in two disciplines that are later thought of as "Arabic" or "religious" sciences, in contrast to the foreign Greek sciences. Most obviously, he is showing his ability in Koranic exegesis or *tafsīr*. In addition, he is drawing on Arabic grammar to help him disambiguate the passage at hand. He alludes to the "inflection and derivations" that one must be aware of in reading an Arabic text (§I.2, AR 245, RJ 177) and makes a technical grammatical point in his remarks on the classical Arabic poem he cites (§II.2, AR 246, RJ 179).[35] Of course one of al-Kindī's aims here is simply to demonstrate his own proficiency, and to scold those who read the Koran without his degree of subtlety. But implicitly, he also demonstrates that *falsafa* can be used alongside, and even in the service of, the disciplines and projects of his own culture.

A third and final example, which again shows how al-Kindī uses philosophy within the context of *tafsīr*, gives us our best evidence as to his belief in the harmony, even the identity, of the truths of philosophy and the truths of Islam. The passage in question is the aforementioned "digression" on prophecy in *On the Quantity of Aristotle's Books*. Al-Kindī has just been insisting that we cannot achieve philosophical knowledge without training in the propaedeutic sciences. This leads him to a contrast between the knowledge available to a prophet through revelation, and the knowledge attained in philosophy. The human sciences (*al-'ulūm al-insāniyya*), he says, "are of a lower rank [*martaba*] than divine knowledge [*al-'ilm al-ilāhī*]," because the latter can be acquired "without study, effort, or human methods, and without time" (§VI.1, AR 372). The prophets simply "know through the will of Him, the great and exalted, and by their souls' being purified and illuminated with the truth" (§VI.2, AR 373). Indeed, their instant and effortless access to the truth is a proof that their knowledge does indeed come from God (§VI.3, AR 373).

Of course, al-Kindī is here favorably contrasting prophetic knowledge to "human" or philosophical knowledge. But he does not say that prophets have access to any more or different knowledge from that attained in philosophy. Rather prophets have access to precisely the same truths, but instantly and without effort or study.[36] He underlines this in what follows by giving a specific example, namely a passage from the Koran (36:79–82). In this passage, Muḥammad has been challenged by the unbelievers to explain how God could raise the bodies of the dead at Judgment Day ("who can revivify the bones when they have decayed?"). The answer was revealed to him:

> Say that He will revivify them who brought them forth the first time, the one who knows every created thing; He who made fire for you from the green tree, so that you might kindle flame from it. Or is He who created the heavens and the earth unable to create their like again? Surely, He is the Creator, the knowing. When He wills something, He says to it, "be," and it is.

Al-Kindī admires this answer as "more clear and brief" than any that philosophy could give (§VI.4, AR 373),[37] but this does not stop him from giving an extensive philosophical account of the meaning of the revealed answer. This account provides us with one of al-Kindī's most interesting discussions of creation (see chapter 3). Though his treatment of the question is philosophical, we find him again quoting classical Arabic poetry to illustrate a point about interpreting the Koranic passage (§VI.9, AR 376). As in *Prostration*, the literary allusion is given in support of a figurative reading of the passage at hand.[38]

This lengthy digression on prophecy tells us a great deal about how al-Kindī thinks philosophy can be used in a Muslim society. Revelation sets out its truths in a more precise, brief, and compelling way than any human could hope to achieve. But revelation does not add truths which are unavailable to human reason (as would be held by, say, Thomas Aquinas).[39] Nor does it fall short of philosophy by failing to provide rigorous demonstration, and by being merely rhetorical or symbolic, intended for the masses who cannot hope to master philosophy (as al-Fārābī and Averroes would have it). This means that philosophy can simply be integrated directly into the task of expounding the Koran: when the meaning of the Koran is unclear or disputed, philosophy is given pride of place as an interpretive tool. But its use does not rule out the deployment of more traditional techniques in the burgeoning *tafsīr* tradition. Particularly telling is that in both of these texts al-Kindī draws parallels from classical Arabic poetry and makes points about Arabic grammar. This is why I have spoken of his project as the integration of philosophy into Islamic and Arabic culture. Philosophy is not put forward as an alternative that is either superior or inferior to ongoing intellectual endeavors of al-Kindī's contemporaries. Rather it is offered as a new, powerful tool for achieving exactly the same aims, in concert with the indigenous disciplines that were developing in al-Kindī's day. Logic, and philosophy generally, can for instance be used to attack false theological doctrines such as the Trinity, and to explicate the Koran. More generally, they can be used to defend and expound true theological doctrines, such as the Muslim belief in absolute, rigorous monotheism, or in creation *ex nihilo*. In the chapters 3 and 4 we will see how al-Kindī undertook this task.

3

METAPHYSICS

Oneness and Being

Al-Kindī's most famous work is *On First Philosophy*, and deservedly so. Not only is it one of his longest surviving treatises, but it also contains his fullest discussions of the two philosophical doctrines for which he is best known, the denial of the world's eternity and the ineffability of God. Al-Kindī himself saw the treatise as an important achievement, as is clear from his remarks at the beginning of the later *Proximate Agent Cause*, thanking his sponsors in the caliphal family for their support while he was writing *On First Philosophy*. He also refers back to it in other treatises. Unfortunately, *On First Philosophy* has not come down to us complete. We have only the first "part [*juz'*]" which consists of four "sections [*funūn*]." We know there was more, because what is extant ends with the statement "this is the end of the first part," and because other authors have relayed two fragments from the rest to us.[1] In the text as we have it, the first section consists of an introduction and the defense of philosophy I discussed in chapter 2. The second section includes some methodological remarks, followed by al-Kindī's famous argument against the eternity of the world. The third and fourth sections are a meditation on the concept of oneness, drawing on Aristotelian logical texts and Neoplatonic works, and culminating in the proof that God, whom al-Kindī calls "the true One," transcends all description. In chapters 4 and 5, I will discuss these themes of God's nature and the world's eternity, focusing on *On First Philosophy* but also drawing on other relevant Kindian treatises.

God as the True One

The third section of *On First Philosophy* can be divided into three main subsections. The first was mentioned in chapter 2 as an example of al-Kindī's *reductio* style of argument. The argument makes extensive use of the Arabic word *dhāt*, which can as a technical term mean "essence," but can also mean simply "self."[2] Thus the question posed—*hal yumkinu [al-shay'] anna yakūnu 'illa kawn dhātihī*—could be translated "can something be the cause of itself?" or "can something be the cause of its own essence?" Al-Kindī seems to exploit this ambiguity in what follows, so I will simply leave the term untranslated.

Al-Kindī proceeds by setting out a distinction between a thing (*al-shay'*) and its *dhāt*, and explains that what he is interested in here is the generation (*kawn*) of the *dhāt*. Can the thing itself be the cause for this generation? There are two possibilities: either the thing exists or it does not. If it does not exist, it cannot be a cause for anything. But if it does exist, it cannot be the cause of its *dhāt*, because it is identical with its *dhāt* (AR 124, RJ 41). This latter claim is bound to take us by surprise, because it seems to undercut the distinction that began the argument, between a thing and its *dhāt*. But perhaps al-Kindī is now telling us that the distinction between a thing and its *dhāt* is merely conceptual or apparent. Even though we can think or speak of them as if they were two items, in fact they are one and the same.[3]

Suppose then that the thing is identical with its *dhāt*: can it be the cause of its *dhāt* in that case? No, since if X is identical to Y, then X cannot be the cause for Y. This is because, if X and Y are identical, what "holds true [*ya'riḍu*]" of one must hold true of the other (§IX.3, AR 123–4, RJ 41).[4] Obviously if X caused Y, but not vice-versa,[5] this requirement would not be satisfied; in particular it would hold true of X that it is a cause of Y, but this would not hold true of Y itself. Thus al-Kindī takes himself to have shown that nothing can be the cause of its own *dhāt*. That is, nothing can bring its own essence into being, or, put more simply, nothing can cause itself. There is some question as to why al-Kindī bothers with this argument at all, since it is not clear how its conclusion helps him towards his ultimate aim of understanding God's oneness. But although he never explicitly refers back to this argument, I believe it does have an important role to play in what follows.

The second subsection goes through a classification of different types of "utterance [*lafẓ*]." Al-Kindī later calls these items *maqūlāt*; literally "things that are said." This is frequently translated as "predicates" or "predicables," but I believe that this is too narrow a translation. Really al-Kindī has in mind anything that can be put into words. Thus I will use "terms," which seems suitably broad.[6] Terms are classified following Porphyry's *Isagoge*: genus, species, difference, individual, proper accident, and common accident. The purpose of this middle subsection is then to investigate how "one" is said within each of these types of utterance or term. What we discover is that in every case, when we speak of something's being "one," it turns out that this oneness is qualified by some sort of multiplicity. For example, though we would be right to insist that *animal* is one genus, we must also admit that this single genus can be divided into multiple species. Differences, accidents, and species are similarly all applicable to multiple individuals. We might suppose that at least a single individual is unrestrictedly "one," but this would be wrong. An individual has parts that are united to one another either by nature (like a man's body parts) or by art (like the parts of a house). In order to understand this kind of unity, al-Kindī adds a new set of terms having to do with part and whole.[7] Since any individual is a whole made up of parts, even individuals are not unrestrictedly one.[8] Al-Kindī repeatedly expresses his findings in this second subsection by stating that in the case of each term, the unity in question is "accidental" or not "in the true nature" of the unified thing.

This is a central point in al-Kindī's analysis, so it is worth pausing to consider further what he means before we go on to the third subsection. From his arguments, it is clear that when he says that something is only "accidentally" one he means that it is qualified just as much by multiplicity as it is by unity. Why put the point in this way? In the same section of *On First Philosophy* (§X.2, AR 125, RJ 43), al-Kindī defines an "essential" feature of something as follows: "by 'the essential' I mean that which makes subsist the essence of the thing: through its existence is the subsistence and stability of the thing's being, and through its absence is the destruction and corruption of the thing." An obvious example, which he gives elsewhere, is that it is essential to me that I be alive, since if I stop being alive I will stop existing completely, at least as the sort of thing that I am. The same is true of features like *rational*, since if I stop being rational I stop being human (assuming for the sake of argument that *human* is defined as rational animal).

Now, a striking aspect of these predicates is that in each case they must be true of me not only for as long as I exist, but also in such a way as to exclude their opposites. That is, I cannot be both alive and dead, nor can I be both rational and irrational (i.e. both capable of reasoning and incapable of reasoning). With accidental features, the reverse is the case. At different times, I may be both sitting and standing. At one and the same time, I can be both short and tall in comparison to different people. Thus it is natural to think of accidental features (like *sitting*, *standing*, *shortness,* and *tallness*) as being precisely those features that are "compresent" with their opposites in the very same, subsisting subject—either at the same time or at different times in the subject's career. Al-Kindī here expresses a classically Platonic principle using the Aristotelian language of essential and accidental predication. The Platonic principle is that S is P in the true or paradigmatic sense only if it is P and in no sense not-P. Plato himself applies the principle in arguing for the Forms, for instance in the *Phaedo*, when he introduces the Form of the Equal as that which is in no sense unequal. Al-Kindī will instead go on to apply the principle to God. For God, we will discover, is the "true One," who unlike His creatures is "essentially one." In other words, He is the only being completely unaffected by multiplicity.

This takes us to the third subsection, which argues precisely from the compresence of oneness and multiplicity in all (created) things to the claim that there must be a cause of oneness in these things, a cause which is itself utterly one and in no way multiple. Jean Jolivet has shown that this subsection depends on the *Platonic Theology* of Proclus,[9] though it remains unclear how this work, or a report of its contents, might have been known to al-Kindī (we know only of an Arabic version of Proclus' *Elements of Theology*). It is worth attending to the transition from the second to the third subsection. After his proof that each type of "term" involves both unity and multiplicity, al-Kindī says:

> *On First Philosophy* §XIII.14 (AR 132, RJ 53): And since we have shown that oneness is in all these things by accident, they belong to something else by essence and not by accident. Thus the oneness that is in something by accident is a oneness that is acquired by it, from what has oneness in it by essence: here is necessarily a true One whose unity is not an effect.

Since it is God who is the "true One" in question, this is nothing short of a proof for God's existence. Al-Kindī seems to realize immediately that it is too quick, or at least that it requires further explanation. So he marks the beginning of a new stretch of argument with the comment, "but let us show this more fully than we have so far." The lengthy proof that follows establishes that it is impossible for multiplicity to exist without unity, and vice-versa. The arguments for this are extremely abstract, and have their ultimate basis in Plato's *Parmenides*, by way of Proclus.

The two theses in question are handled rather differently. I will call the two theses (M) and (U). (M) is the claim that there is only multiplicity, with no unity. (U) is the reverse: the claim that there is only unity, with no multiplicity. A typical argument against (M) is this: if there is only multiplicity, then all things will be multiple. But they will therefore agree, or be similar to each other, insofar as they share the common feature *multiplicity*. This means that they partake in a kind of unity, namely their sharing in one and the same feature (viz. multiplicity). This is a contradiction, so there must be unity as well as multiplicity. A typical argument against (U) is this: if there is only unity, then nothing will have distinct parts, because distinct parts of the same thing must be multiple. But things *do* have distinct parts. So there must be multiplicity as well as unity. Now, what is striking is that the argument against (U) has what we might call an empirical or factual premise, namely the premise "but things *do* have distinct parts." By contrast the argument against (M) does not depend on any fact about the way the world really is. It relies on pure conceptual analysis, showing that we cannot posit multiplicity without thereby positing unity as well. All but one of the arguments against (M) are free of factual premises.[10] More important, it turns out that every single argument against (U)—and there are eight of them—has a factual premise. The arguments always run like this: Suppose there is only unity. On this supposition, it turns out that some feature of the world (for instance contrariety, motion, agreement, continuity) will not exist. Then, the factual premise: this feature does exist. Therefore the supposition is false, so there is multiplicity as well as unity.[11]

The reason this is important is that al-Kindī will go on to show that there is indeed a case where we have unity without multiplicity, namely the case of God Himself, the true One. So it had better not be conceptually impossible that unity exist in the absence of multiplicity, or God will be conceptually impossible.[12] Rather, what al-Kindī wants is to show that *in the created world*, that is, in every case other than the case of God, unity and multiplicity always co-exist. Thus when he states his conclusion, he is careful to qualify it: "it remains then that unity is associated with multiplicity, that is, is associated with it *in all sensible things*, and all that is concomitant to the sensible things" (§XVI.2, AR 141, RJ 63–5, my emphasis).[13] For it was facts about the sensible world, rather than an argument to conceptual impossibility, that allowed us to refute (U). Still, even if the arguments against (U) leave open the possibility of a pure unity free of multiplicity, why should we accept that such a pure unity exists?

The reason is that, according to al-Kindī (and Proclus, whom he is still following here), there must be an external cause for the very co-existence of unity and multiplicity in all sensible things. For there are only three possible hypotheses: either (a) things just happen to be both one and many by chance, and there is no cause for this at all; or, (b) the set of things that are one and many include within themselves the cause for this association of unity and multiplicity; or, (c) there is a cause for this association, but this cause is outside the set of things that are one and many. It cannot be (a) by chance that they are both one and many, because then it would be *possible* that they be either only many or only one, and this we have already refuted.[14] Further, (b) the cause for the association of unity and multiplicity cannot be internal to the set of things that display this association. For then, they would be their own cause. Al-Kindī dismisses this quickly, citing the threat of an infinite regress; his argument is sketchy and incomplete. We can flesh it out for him, though, by invoking the results of the first subsection. We discovered there that nothing can be the cause of its own generation. Now we are considering those things that must be both one and many. To cause such a thing to exist is to produce an association of unity and multiplicity. Thus no such thing can cause itself to be both one and many, because if it did it would be the cause of its own generation. Also, there cannot be a chain of things, in which each is caused to be one and many by the prior element in the chain. That is what al-Kindī explicitly rules out here, when he rejects the infinite regress. The only other option would be to say that there is reciprocal causation, i.e. that some things in the set cause others to be one and many, and these others return the favor. But this might also thought to fall afoul of the arguments of the first subsection: if X causes Y, and Y causes X, then X in effect causes itself.

That leaves only the final possibility, that (c) there is an external cause for the association of unity and multiplicity in the sensible world. And this, of course, is God, the true One. He cannot be both one and many, because we introduced Him to serve as the *external* cause for the things that are both one and many. Nor can He be only many, for as we saw, multiplicity without unity is conceptually impossible. So we are left with a cause external to the set of things that are one and many, which is itself one but not many. This convoluted set of arguments, then, has yielded the core of al-Kindī's theology, which consists of three claims. First, there is a unique cause for all things. Second, this cause is the cause of their unity. Third, this cause is itself one, and in no respect multiple.

Thus al-Kindī is led, in the fourth and final extant section of *On First Philosophy*, to his famous demonstration that God's unity precludes there being any "description" of Him. We should not be surprised at this conclusion, since we have already seen that any "term," that is, anything we can say, implies both unity and multiplicity. The fourth section begins to expand on this theme by introducing a mathematical analogy. The relationship between God and creation is like the relation between 1 and the numbers. Notice that I say "between 1 and the numbers," not "between 1 and the *other* numbers." For, whereas we nowadays think of 1 as simply the first number (or, at least, integer), al-Kindi denies this. One is not a number at all,[15] but rather the principle from which numbers are generated and composed. You get 2 by adding 1 to itself, you get 3 by adding 1 to 2, and so on. Al-Kindī spends quite a while showing this, but says little to explain why it is important in the present context. To some extent, though, the purpose of the analogy is clear. Just as God is utterly one while His creatures are subject to multiplicity, so the mathematical 1 is simple, while the numbers are all composed. And as just mentioned, 1 is the principle and source of the numbers, since these are composed from "units," that is, by adding 1 to itself repeatedly. The mathematical 1 is external to the numbers and is their cause, just as God is external to created things and is their cause. The mathematical analogy captures both God's distinctness from creation, and His causal relationship to creation.[16]

I think there is a more subtle point lurking here as well. Al-Kindī's discussion of number begins with a reference to relations of "more" and "less" between different quantities. Every quantity, al-Kindī argues, is "more" or "less" only relative to some other quantity. For instance, 10 sacks of flour are more than 9 sacks and less than 11 sacks. Even if we imagined something greater than any other actually existing quantity, it would still be small compared to some potentially existing quantity, such as a multiple of itself. For example, if the diameter of the physical cosmos is the longest actual line, there is nothing incoherent in imagining a line twice or three times that length.[17] So there is, as al-Kindī puts it, no "absolutely large" or "absolutely small." Since quantity is measured by number, the discussion of number as contrasted to the mathematical one thus returns us to the theme of the compresence of opposites. Unlike the numbers, 1 does not enter into relations of great and small, more and less (it is not, as one might think, the "intrinsically less," i.e. the smallest number). Rather it is the principle of things that enter into these relations, relations which involve the compresence of more and less. By the same token we cannot really *compare* 1 to the numbers. Rather, when we compare, we compare things that are numbered, i.e. quantities. For these are the things that enter into relations of more and less. This prepares us for the thought that God, the true One, cannot be "compared" to His creatures. As the Koran says, "nothing is like to Him [*laysa ka-mithlihī shay'*]" (42:11). Al-Kindī puts the point differently, by saying that there is no genus which God shares with anything else. Since comparisons always happen within a genus (e.g. bodies are compared to bodies, lines to lines, times to times), God is literally "incomparable": "the One in truth admits of no relation with anything in a shared genus, and it has no genus that admits of being in a relation to anything in a shared genus" (§XIX.1, AR 153, RJ 83).

Notice that phrase "the One in truth." This reflects a terminological shift from the third to the fourth section of *On First Philosophy*. Whereas previously al-Kindī spoke only of things that were "accidentally one" as opposed to "essentially one," now he contrasts things that are "one metaphorically [*bi-'l-majāz*]" to God, who is "One in truth [*al-wāḥid bi-'l-ḥaqīqa*]" or the "true One [*al-wāḥid al-ḥaqq*]."[18] The meaning, however, is the same: what is "metaphorically" one is what is both one and many. The "true One" is only one, not at all multiple. In the rest of *On First Philosophy*, al-Kindī will therefore try to specify the sense of "oneness" that applies to God. However, he does this largely by enumerating the senses of "one" that do *not* apply to God. For this reason, al-Kindī's treatment of how we speak of God—what one might call "theological discourse"—is usually thought of as being thoroughly negative. If this is right then in the end all al-Kindī has to say about God is that we can say nothing: He is utterly ineffable, inaccessible to language or thought. I think it would be more accurate to say that al-Kindī, in these final passages, is surveying the senses in which "one" might be understood, and narrowing down to the correct sense by a process of elimination.

Along the way he considers and dismisses numerous proposals for how to conceive of divine oneness. For instance, he argues that neither soul nor intellect is "the true One," because thinking involves a motion from thought to thought, and intellect grasps a multiplicity of universals (we will return to this passage in chapter 5). Thus he follows Plotinus' rejection of Aristotle's understanding of God as a pure intellect, on the basis that intellect falls short of absolute simplicity.[19] Nor, to take a contrasting possibility, does God have the unity appropriate to material things, namely the unity that comes with having continuous matter. Rather God is immaterial, since all matter is divisible and thus involves multiplicity. On the other hand, the senses in which we say things are "indivisible" are equally inappropriate to God—whether something is "indivisible" because it would be destroyed, were it divided (like a man, who ceases to exist if he's cut in half), or for the more prosaic reason that it is just practically speaking impossible to divide the thing in question (like a diamond, which is too hard to cut, or something smaller than any available cutting tool).

In general, al-Kindī continues, we can distinguish between two broad classes of unity, neither of which is applicable to God. Confusingly, he uses the terms "essential" and "accidental" unity for these two classes. Here "accidentally one" does not mean "both one and many," nor does "essentially one" mean "excluding all multiplicity," as it did in section 3 (and will again at the close of this section, when he gets back to God). Rather, in this context, the "accidentally one" is what is "one" for wholly extrinsic reasons, for example if it just happens to have the same name as something else and thus be "one in name" (like the animal "dog" and the "dog" star). And in this context something is "essentially one" if it is one "in substance," in other words if it has a kind of unity that it must have in order to keep existing. But this, of course, just returns us to the study of terms in section 3. For having a unity of substance means either being a single individual, or being one in form (i.e. one in species) or one in genus. These senses of unity can obviously be excluded from God on the strength of previously given arguments.

Al-Kindī has, then, finally reached his intended conclusion:

On First Philosophy §XX.2 (AR 160, RJ 95): Thus the true One possesses no matter, form, quantity, quality, or relation. And is not described by

> any of the other terms: it has no genus, no specific difference, no individual, no proper accident, and no common accident. It does not move, and is not described through anything that is denied to be one in truth. It is therefore only pure unity, I mean nothing other than unity. And every one other than it is multiple.

This looks like unqualified negative theology, since it denies that God can be "described [*mawṣūf*]" in any way. We might be further encouraged to take it that way if we attend to al-Kindī's historical context. For he seems to be reacting to at least two different traditions in his treatment of divine attributes (*ṣifāt*, from the same root as *mawṣūf*). On the one hand, there are the Arabic translations of works by Plotinus and Proclus.[20] On the other, there is contemporary *kalām*, which devoted considerable attention to the topic of theological language and especially the status of divine attributes. Thinkers grouped under the "Muʿtazilite" heading also give a generally negative treatment of divine attributes, so numerous readers of al-Kindī, including myself,[21] have seen a link between al-Kindī's discussion of theological discourse and *kalām* speculation.

Yet the same historical links might make us wary of taking his conclusions here to be purely negative. Both *kalām* figures and the Arabic Neoplatonic texts find a variety of ways to explain how some such discourse can be retained. *On First Philosophy* follows them not only in its broadly negative theology, but also by preserving a doctrine of positive divine attribution that can withstand the requirements of simplicity and transcendence. I have already said that, in section 4, al-Kindī seems to be trying to specify the sense in which God is one by a process of elimination. This observation rests on the obvious fact that, whatever his claims about negative theology, al-Kindī is nonetheless insistent that we can call God "one." The problem is not to see whether this statement is permissible, but to see in what sense it is true.

Now, someone who wanted to insist that al-Kindī's theology is thoroughly negative might suggest that when al-Kindī calls God "one" he means nothing more than "God is indescribable," given that all description implies multiplicity. But this does not seem to do justice to al-Kindī's treatment of God's oneness. For he not only denies multiplicity of God but also emphasizes that God is the *cause of unity* in everything else. This would seem to be another Platonic inheritance. Just as a Platonic Form can explain F-ness in sensible, particular objects by being F and in no way not-F, so God is a suitable cause for unity in sensible things precisely because

He is one and stands outside the set of things that are both one and many. In light of this, it hardly seems that we can understand God's oneness in a purely negative way, as a mere denial of attributes. For it is in virtue of His oneness that God exercises causality over His creation. Section 4 of *On First Philosophy* does not go back on the claims of section 3 to have proven the existence of a principle that is perfectly one and the cause of unity. Rather it cautions us against misunderstanding this claim, by associating inappropriate, inferior kinds of oneness with God.

This becomes particularly clear at the close of section 4:

> *On First Philosophy* §XX.5–6 (AR 161–2, RJ 97): Since every one of the sensible things, and what attaches to sensible things, has both unity and multiplicity in it together, and any unity in it is an effect from a cause, and is accidental in it and not by nature, and multiplicity is necessarily a collection of unities, therefore it is necessary that if there is no unity, there is no multiplicity at all. So the bringing-to-be of every multiplicity occurs through unity, and without unity the multiple would have no being at all. All bringing-to-be is a being-acted-upon that makes exist that which did not exist. So the emanation of unity from the true, first One is the bringing-to-be of every sensible thing, and everything that attaches to the sensible. It makes every one of them exist when it brings-to-be through its being. The cause of the bringing-to-be is then from the true One; which is not given unity by any giver. Rather, it is essentially one. . . . So it is the originator of all things that are brought-to-be, and since there is no being that is not caused by unity, and its being-made-one is its being-brought-to-be, it is thus through unity that all things subsist. If unity were taken away, they would depart and disappear, as soon as it was taken away, in no time. Thus, the true One is the first Originator, that which supports all that is originated, and anything that is freed from His support and His power must depart and disappear.

This passage says explicitly what has been implicit throughout sections 3 and 4: as the source of unity in sensible things, God is in fact their Creator. Since the "being [*huwiyya*]" of multiple things requires their being unified, God makes things be, or exist, by making them be one. However, being and unity are not completely identical in created things. Indeed al-Kindī specifies that it is only in the "intrinsically one," that is, in God Himself, that unity and being are the same (§XX.4, AR 161, RJ 97). Similarly, in the passage just quoted, we have the intriguing claim that the true One "brings things to be through its being [*bi-huwiyyatihī*]." This again affirms the identity of being and oneness in God, and says that God creates through this being or oneness. By contrast, in created things, unity is distinct from being. But even in created things, unity is a necessary condition for being, so that if its unity is withdrawn from something, that thing ceases to be. This only stands to reason, if we bear in mind that any description of anything imputes some sort of unity to it. Think in particular of the kinds of "essential unity" applied to created things in section 4: for me to have a body, or to be an individual, a human, or an animal, is for me to be "one" in a certain way. None of these things can be true of me if unity is withdrawn, so without unity I will literally cease to exist.

Clearly, despite the Platonic lineaments of his theology, al-Kindī does not want us to understand God to be something like the Form of oneness. God is doing something much more active than being a paradigm for other things to participate in. This is suggested not only by al-Kindī's calling God a "Creator" or "Originator" (*mubdi'*) but also by his reference here to "emanation [*fayḍ*]," which seems to bring us close to something more Neoplatonic than Platonic. Of course this is also supposed to underwrite the Islamic doctrine of God as Creator. In the final paragraph of *On First Philosophy* that survives to us, al-Kindī identifies his "true One" with "the Giver and Originator, the Powerful, the Supporter . . . who is great and exalted above the attributes of the heretics" (§XX.7, AR 162, RJ 97–9). So God is not just a principle of oneness; He is an agent.

God as the True Agent

Despite its incompleteness, the extant version of *On First Philosophy* thus manages to end on a rather emphatic note. But this final passage on God as a Creator raises as many questions as it answers. What is the exact relationship between God and each individual thing He creates? Does that reference to "emanation" suggest that, like the Neoplatonists, al-Kindī thought that God acts on some of His creatures only indirectly? If being and oneness are not identical in creatures, then why does al-Kindī seem to think God's "bringing something to be" is tantamount to a bestowal of unity? And what about the fact that creatures are many as well as being one? After all, God is not "the true Many"— indeed, He is not many at all. So it doesn't look as though He bestows multiplicity on His effects. Where, then, does multiplicity come from? Quite possibly the lost parts of *On First*

Philosophy would have supplied the answers to at least some of these questions. To judge by the little we know of the missing sections, they would seem to have dealt (at least in part) with the dispersion of God's providential activity through the created universe. Al-Kindī himself suggests this in *Proximate Agent Cause*, when he refers back to *On First Philosophy* and says that he there showed that God "makes some things reasons and causes for other things" (§I.3, AR 215). Evidence outside of the Kindian corpus also supports this conjecture. An intriguing passage found in Ibn 'Abd Rabbih al-Andalusī purports to quote *On First Philosophy* (under the title *On Oneness*) on the topic of God's choice to create the best of all possible worlds.[22]

Still, without more evidence than this our best hope is to supplement the account of *On First Philosophy* by turning to other Kindian works. The most promising text is *On the True Agent*, or, to give it its full title, *On the True, First, Complete Agent and the Deficient Agent That Is Metaphorically [an Agent]*. In light of its brevity and lack of prologue, it may well be not an independent treatise, but a fragment from a lost larger work—perhaps even from the lost sections of *On First Philosophy*. At any rate, *On the True Agent* sets out to explain just what the title says. God is a "true agent [*al-fā'il al-ḥaqq*]" whereas His effects are only agents "metaphorically [*bi-'l-majāz*]." For God "is the agent who acts without being acted upon by any agent," whereas created things both act and are acted upon—they are both agents and patients. The terminology of having some feature "metaphorically" as opposed to "truly" means precisely what it meant in the fourth section of *On First Philosophy*. For any feature F, being "metaphorically" F means suffering from the compresence of F and not-F. The only difference is that here the roles of F and not-F are played by agency and passivity, rather than unity and multiplicity.[23]

What then does it mean to say that God is only an agent, whereas His effects are both agents and patients? It could mean that God acts directly on each thing, and that then these things additionally act upon each other. But that is not what al-Kindī has in mind. Rather, he says:

> *On the True Agent* §3–4 (AR 183, RJ 169–71): What is below [God], i.e. all the things that He creates, are called agents only metaphorically, not in truth, because, that is, they are all in truth acted upon. The first of them is from its Creator, may He be exalted, and [thereafter] they are from one another. For the first of them is acted upon, another is acted upon due to its being acted upon, yet another is acted upon due to this

> [second effect's] being acted upon, and so on until the last of the effects is reached. The first effect among them is called an agent metaphorically, owing to the effect [that comes] from it, since it is the proximate cause of its effect. Likewise for the second [effect], since it is the proximate cause of the third [effect] in its being acted upon, until the last of the effects is reached. But the Creator, may He be exalted, is the first cause for all of the effects either through an intermediary or without an intermediary, in truth, because He is an agent who is not acted upon at all. But He is the proximate cause for the first effect, and a cause through an intermediary for His effects that are after the first effect.

Here al-Kindī sets out a fairly abstract, but nonetheless clear account according to which God's action is, with one exception, mediated. His initial act has only a single direct effect, referred to here as "the first of the effects." This first effect is then the "proximate" cause of the second effect, and so on until we reach "the last of the effects." My guess is that this last effect, which presumably exercises no agency at all, is matter, since it needs to be something purely passive.

We seem therefore to be in the presence of a classically Neoplatonic theory of divine action, which also appears later in al-Fārābī and Avicenna: God has a direct causal relationship only with the first thing He creates, and this thing passes on His action to everything else. Such a position has the well-known advantage of solving (or at least ameliorating) one of the difficulties just mentioned, about where multiplicity comes from. It does not come from God, the true One, but is only brought about indirectly, through God's effects. Although al-Kindī does not speak here, as he had in *On First Philosophy*, of "emanation," his language is nonetheless influenced by his Neoplatonic translations. He speaks of the true agent as that which makes an "impression [*athar*]" in its effect without receiving an impression, and of the metaphorical agent as that which both makes and receives such an impression (§2, AR 183, RJ 169). This train of thought and terminology also appear in the Arabic Plotinus.[24]

On the other hand, we should not overlook the Aristotelian lineaments of al-Kindī's discussion here. In *Physics* VIII.5, Aristotle considers cases in which one thing moves another through an intermediary, for example if someone pushes a stone with a stick: the hand moves the stick, and the stick moves the stone. He argues that such a chain of movers cannot regress indefinitely, so there must be a first cause of motion. And he specifies that the earlier a cause is in the chain of movers, the more that cause should be considered a mover (257a10–12). Thus what Aristotle here calls the "first" mover is more a mover than any other. Aristotle stresses that this mover is not moved by any other mover, just as al-Kindī stresses that his true Agent is not acted upon by any other agent. This is part of Aristotle's argument for the existence of an immaterial first unmoved mover, who is God. So al-Kindī may well have both Aristotle and the Neoplatonists in mind when he describes God as directly causing only a "first effect," which passes on His causality to other things.

Unfortunately al-Kindī gives us no hint here about what the "first effect" in this chain is supposed to be. If Aristotle is uppermost in his mind then it must be the heavens. This would fit with *Proximate Agent Cause*, where al-Kindī portrays divine action as being mediated by the action of the heavens. Immaterial principles do not figure in that account at all. *On the True Agent* overlaps terminologically with *Proximate Agent Cause* (most strikingly, the contrast between "remote" and "proximate" causes appears in both), just as it does with *On First Philosophy*. And the introductory remarks of *Proximate Agent Cause* show that it was written after *On First Philosophy*, indeed shortly thereafter. So it would be natural to take all three texts as closely related and as having been written at around the same time. If we read the doctrine of *Proximate Agent Cause* into *On the True Agent*, then we should understand al-Kindī to mean that the heavens are the direct effect of God, and the intermediary causes for things in the sublunary world.[25]

On the other hand, in *On First Philosophy* al-Kindī suggests tentatively that "one might think" that intellect is the "first multiple" (§XIX.6, AR 155, RJ 87). This suggests that we could see what he elsewhere calls "the intellectual world" as being a further intermediary between God and the heavens, which in turn are causes for the sublunary world. If that is his position, then al-Kindī is following the Arabic Proclus and Plotinus materials. The *Liber de Causis* says explicitly that intellect is God's first effect and the intermediary between God and everything else.[26] This interpretation has its advantages. In particular, it would make room in al-Kindī's metaphysics for soul and intellect as immaterial causes, which would help us integrate his psychological works into the picture presented in his metaphysical and cosmological writings. Though it is hard to be certain of al-Kindī's considered opinion, the evidence of *Proximate Agent Cause* suggests that it is the Aristotelian picture of divine action mediated through the heavens that is described in *On the True Agent*. By contrast he never explicitly asserts a hierarchy like that of the Neoplatonic writings, with God followed by intellect, soul, and the physical world.[27]

In the remainder of *On the True Agent* (§5, AR 183–4, RJ 171) al-Kindī makes a distinction between two sorts of agents. One sort performs an "act [*fi'l*]" in the strict sense, whose effect lasts only as long as the agent is acting. A person who is walking, says al-Kindī, is an agent in this sense, because the result of his acting, namely the fact that he is walking, will cease as soon as he stops acting. Let us call this a "sustaining" agent. The other sort of agent produces an independent, lasting effect, which is properly not called an "act" but a "product [*'amal*]"—for example a carpenter who builds a table. Let us call such agents "productive." Now, al-Kindī explicitly says that this distinction applies to the "metaphorical" agents that are God's effects. But it is hard to avoid the suspicion that God Himself is meant to be a sustaining, and not a productive, agent: that God's act maintains the created world in existence at all times. That al-Kindī means to imply this is suggested by the fact that the term "act" in the strict sense is reserved for sustaining causes. Presumably if God is a "true and complete agent [*fā'il*]," He too will perform an "act [*fi'l*]" in this narrower sense. Comments made elsewhere by al-Kindī seem to support this, for instance when he specifies that the heavens will persist only as long as God maintains them in existence.[28]

Unfortunately, *On the True Agent* leaves off there, without even saying explicitly why the distinction between the two kinds of agents, sustaining and productive, was introduced. However, there is one remark made at the beginning of *On the True Agent*, which I have passed over until now:

> *On the True Agent* §1 (AR 183, RJ 169): We say that the true, first act is the bringing-to-be of beings from non-being [*ta'yīs al-aysāt 'an laysa*]. It is clear that this act is proper to God, the exalted, who is the end of every cause [*ghāya kull 'illa*]. For the bringing-to-be of beings from non-being belongs to no other. And this act is a proper characteristic [called] by the name "origination [*ibdā'*]."

Unfortunately it is not easy to reconcile this remark with the two features of divine action explained in the rest of the treatise—that God's act is passed on by intermediary causes, and that God is (apparently) a sustaining cause for the world. Regarding the first point, are we meant to understand that this special kind of causation, honored with the word *ibdā'*, meaning "creation" or "origination," is enacted only once, in order to create God's first effect? Or does God directly create each thing in the created world? If the latter is the case then in what sense is divine causation mediated? Regarding the second point, one can imagine someone saying that God brings a creature into being continually, so that "creation" could be an enduring, sustaining relationship between God and His effects. But it is hard to see why al-Kindī, of all people, would want to say that, because he is famous for insisting that nothing created can be eternal. If creation is an enduring relationship between Creator and creature, why does it matter how long this relationship lasts? Surely, one is tempted to say, even an eternal thing could be "created" in the sense just described, so long as it depends on God for its being at every moment of its existence. The rest of this chapter will be concerned with confronting these two problems. This will mean turning our attention away from the provocative but all too brief *On the True Agent*, and surveying several other texts in which al-Kindī discusses creation.

Creation and Being

Al-Kindī is consistent in defining creation as God's bringing being from non-being. He formulates this using terminology that he seems to have introduced himself, drawing a contrast between *aysa*, "being," and *laysa*, "non-being."[29] We just saw an example in *On the True Agent*. Here are two more:

> *On Definitions* §6 (AR 165): Origination [*ibdāʿ*]: manifestation of something from non-being [*iẓhār shayʾ ʿan laysa*].[30]
>
> *Proximate Agent Cause* §I.3 (AR 215): God is the true One, who is in no way multiple, the first cause who has no cause, the agent who has no agent, the completer who has no completer, and what brings all things to be from non-being [*al-muʾayyis al-ḳull ʿan laysa*].

These neologisms are not the only words used for "being" and "non-being" by al-Kindī and his circle. The term that has attracted the most scholarly interest is *anniyya*.[31] A synonym for this, used especially in the Arabic Plotinus but also by al-Kindī, is *huwiyya*. This is potentially confusing, since *huwiyya* is used by later authors, such as Avicenna, to mean "essence." But in al-Kindī it always means "being," and is synonymous with *aysa* and *anniyya*.[32] Finally there is *wujūd*, "existence," which remains an important term in later authors. For non-being, al-Kindī uses *lā shay'*, literally "no thing," and *'adam*, which also appears in ninth-century *kalām* in related contexts.

The same terminology appears in al-Kindī's most elaborate treatment of creation. This comes in the digression on prophecy at the center of *Quantity*—a digression we already explored in chapter 2, to see what it had to tell us about the relation between religious truth and philosophical inquiry. We have not yet looked at the meat of the passage, though, which is an analysis of God's creative act. Remember that al-Kindī is explicating a Koranic verse which tells us that God must be able to resurrect the bodies of the dead, given that He also "strikes fire from the trees." Here is what al-Kindī has to say about these verses:

> *Quantity* §VI.7–8 (AR 374–5): He made fire from what is not fire, or heat from what is not heat. Thus something is necessarily generated from its contrary. For if what comes to be did not come to be from the substance of its contrary, there being no intermediary between the two contraries—by "contrary" I mean "it" and "what is not it" [*huwa wa lā huwa*]—it would have to come to be from itself [*min dhātihī*]. But then its essence [*dhāt*] is always fixed, eternal and without beginning. For, if fire does not come to be from not-fire, then it must come from fire, so that fire will come from fire, and [this] fire from [another] fire, and inevitably there will endlessly and eternally be fire from fire and fire from fire. Therefore fire would always exist, and there would never be a state where it is not. Thus there would never be fire after there was no fire. But fires *do* exist after not being, and are destroyed after existing. So the only remaining possibility is that fire is generated from not-fire, and that everything that comes to be is generated from something other than itself. So everything that is generated is generated by something which is not it. Then, in order to explain the generation of a thing from its contrary, he [sc. the Prophet] said: "or is He who created the heavens and the earth unable to create their like again?" And then he said what necessarily follows from this, "Surely, He is the Creator, the knowing." Because in their hearts the unbelievers denied the creation of the heavens, since they had formed an opinion about the period of time needed for their creation based on an analogy with the acts of mankind—for, in the case of human acts, the greater the work produced, the longer is the period [of time] required, so that for [humans]

> the greatest of sensible things [i.e. the heavens] would take the longest amount of time to produce—[God] said that He, great be His praise, needs no period [of time] to originate. And this is clear, because He made "it" from "what is not it." He whose power is such that He can produce bodies from not-bodies, and bring being [*aysa*] out of non-being [*laysa*], since He is able to perform a deed with no material substrate, has no need to produce in time. For, since mankind cannot act without a material substrate, He who does not need to act upon a material substrate has no need to act in time. "When He wills something, His command is to say to it: 'Be!' and it is." That is, He only wills, and together with His will there comes to be that which He wills.

Remarkably, this passage weaves into its exegesis of the Koran ideas from a Christian Greek commentator, John Philoponus. Philoponus will be very important in chapter 4, because he is the main influence on al-Kindī's arguments against the eternity of the world. Still it is surprising to discover that here, in a passage devoted to explicating the Koran, al-Kindī is drawing on ideas from Philoponus' *Against Aristotle on the Eternity of the World*.[33]

The most obvious parallel to Philoponus in this passage is al-Kindī's rejection of an eternal regress in the production of fire (see *Against Aristotle*, Fr. 120). The fact that Philoponus used the example of fire was serendipitous, given that the same example of causing fire appears in the Koranic passage al-Kindī is discussing. But more important are three other theses taken over from Philoponus, all found in fragments from book VI of *Against Aristotle*. First, God creates without a material substrate (Fr. 115); I will return to this point shortly. Second, God creates without any time elapsing during His creative act (Fr.115, 129). Rather "mere willing suffices for Him to give substance to things" (Fr.115), and these things come about instantaneously upon His willing them. (Compare this with the end of the quotation above from al-Kindī.) Third, God's creating something consists in bringing something into being "out of non-being [*mê on*]" (Fr.116, 119). Conversely, if God annihilates something He "turns it back into complete non-being from which it came to be as well" (Fr.131).

Although Philoponus and al-Kindī disagree with Aristotle, the disagreement is not as stark as it might appear. For Aristotle too speaks of "coming-to-be from non-being into being" (*hê* [*genesis*] *ek tou mê ontos haplôs eis ousian*), which is "coming-to-be in the absolute sense [*genesis haplôs*]" (*Physics* V.1, 225a15–16). Aristotle likewise describes corruption (*phthora*) in the absolute sense as a change from being into non-being

(225a18). Also Aristotelian is the idea, emphasized particularly by al-Kindī, that all coming-to-be is from a "contrary [*naqīḍ*]." Aristotle says that every change is from an *enantion* (e.g. white to black) or *antiphasis* (e.g. white to non-white). Aristotle sets out this principle in *Physics* V.1, where he also seems to identify being and non-being as "contraries" in the requisite sense when the change in question is generation or corruption. Aristotle even allows that in some changes, indeed precisely these changes that count as generation and corruption, the change is instantaneous (see *Physics* VI.5, 236a5–7). When a man is generated, there is an instant at which the man begins to be. The process is not gradual, extended over a period of time. Thus, when the generation or corruption of a substance is in question, Aristotle is very close to Philoponus and al-Kindī: such a substance comes to be from non-being, and does so at an instant. The difference between them is that Aristotle rejects the idea of something's coming to be from nothing at all. He allows that man can come to be from something that was not-man—namely appropriate matter not yet organized as a man—but denies that man can come to be from utter privation.

According to Philoponus and al-Kindī, though, God can create without a pre-existing substrate. Philoponus says that just as "man is generated from not-man and house out of not-house" (compare al-Kindī's talk of producing fire from not-fire, and bodies from not-bodies), the world itself is generated out of "not-world" (Fr.69). And while Aristotle would say that, on such a hypothesis, the world would require a pre-existing substrate, Philoponus believes that in the special case of divine creation, no such substrate is required. Philoponus is particularly insistent upon the point, because in the course of his arguments for the world's eternity, Aristotle had claimed that every motion or change requires a prior substrate, the thing potentially moved or changed (*Physics* VIII.1). For Philoponus, though, God's ability to create both matter and form simultaneously shows His superiority to nature (Fr.119, 131) Thus, when God creates something, we have what might be called a "supernatural change," by which I mean a transition from complete and utter privation, or absolute non-being, to the thing that is created.[34] Natural change, by contrast, consists in the modification of something already present. In the case of substantial change, a substrate gains a substantial form (e.g. blood becomes a man), or the substance is destroyed and a substrate is left behind (e.g. a man dies and leaves a corpse). In the case of accidental change, meanwhile, an already constituted substance loses one property for another (e.g. a man goes from not-white to white). Again, there is something that persists through the change.

This contrast between divine creation and the natural processes of generation and corruption sheds some light on the first question posed at the end of the previous section: in what sense is God's agency mediated? We have seen that al-Kindī composed a work arguing that the heavens, and not God, are "the proximate cause *of generation and corruption*." What might it mean to say that God is the cause of being, but the heavens the cause of generation and corruption? Al-Kindī tells us, "by 'falling under corruption' I mean transformation from one essence [*'ayn*] to another" (*Outermost* VIII.1). Or, in a more detailed passage already cited above:

> *On First Philosophy* §X.2 (AR 125, RJ 43): By "the essential" I mean that which constitutes the essence of the thing: through its existence is the subsistence and stability of the thing's being, and through its absence is the destruction and corruption of the thing. For example life is essential to the living thing. The essential is called "substantial" because through it is the subsistence of the substance of the thing.

For instance, what is gained in a man's generation, and lost in a man's death, are those features that are essential to the man, such as rationality and life. The heavens bring about the generation and corruption of all sublunary substances. They account for the essential properties belonging to these substances, by manipulating the four elements that make up those substances. In other words, they always work with pre-existing matter, whereas God creates *ex nihilo*. So the heavens bestow or remove essential properties, but they do not bestow or remove *being*. That is the prerogative of God alone.[35]

This takes us to the difficult problem of what it means to distinguish between a cause of "being" and a cause of attributes or properties. In *On First Philosophy* we do find, even in passages not devoted to discussions of divine causality, a distinction made between "being" on the one hand and predicates or attributes on the other. For instance, in his discussion of the four types of inquiry from Aristotle's *Posterior Analytics* II.1,[36] al-Kindī says that the question "whether?" (*hal*, Gk. *ei esti*) is "an inquiry into being alone [*anniyya faqaṭ*]" (§I.4, AR 101, RJ 11). He then adds, "but every [individual] being [*anniyya*] has a genus, so 'what?' is an inquiry into the genus." It seems unwise to read much into this passage. But we find a similar contrast later, in a passage that seems to have clear ontological implications:

> *On First Philosophy* §V.2 (AR 113, RJ 27): Corruption is only a change of the predicate [*al-maḥmūl*], not of the primary bearer of predication [*al-ḥāmil al-awwal*]. As for the first bearer of predication, which is being [*aysa*], this does not change, because for something corrupted, its corruption has nothing to do with the "making be" of its having being.

This passage is very compressed, but it rewards close scrutiny. The last phrase contrasts corruption with "the 'making be' of [something's] having being [*ta'yīs al-aysiyya*]." This seems to support the idea that, for al-Kindī, the process of generation and corruption is distinct from the process of granting and removing being. More difficult is the rest of the passage, which treats being [*aysa*] as though it were a synonym for matter.[37] For it is, says al-Kindī, that which underlies all predication and subsists even through corruption.[38]

That this is not quite what al-Kindī has in mind is suggested by a similar passage from the *Liber de Causis*, the paraphrase of Proclus produced in his circle. The first proposition of the *De Causis* reads in part as follows:

> *De Causis* §1: Every primary cause has in it a greater emanation on its effect than the secondary, universal cause. When the secondary, universal cause has removed its power from the thing, the primary universal cause does not remove its power from it. For the primary, universal cause acts on the effect of the secondary cause before the second universal cause (which follows [the primary cause]) acts on it. When the secondary cause (which is followed by the effect) acts, its act cannot function without the first cause (which is above it). So even if the secondary cause separates from the effect (which follows it), the primary cause (which is above [the secondary cause]) does not separate from [the effect], because it is the cause for its cause. Therefore the primary cause is more a cause for the thing than its proximate [*qarība*] cause, which it comes after.
>
> We can represent this with [the example of] being [*anniyya*], life, and man. For something must first be being, then living, then man. Life is the proximate cause of the man, and being is its remote cause. So being is more a cause for the man than life, because it is the cause for life, which is the cause of the man. Likewise, if you say that reason is a

> cause for man, being is more a cause for the man than reason, because it is the cause for his cause. The proof of this is that when you remove the rational power from the man, he does not remain man, but he remains living, ensouled [*mutanaffasan*], and sensing. When you remove life from him, he does not remain living, but he remains a being, because being was not removed from him, but life. For the cause is not removed through the removal of its effect. Thus, the man remains a being. When the individual is not a man, it is a living thing, and when not a living being, it is only a being [*anniyya faqaṭ*].

In the thought experiment in the second paragraph, the author imagines removing a series of features from "man"—it becomes clear in the last sentence that he has in mind an individual man, and not the type or species *man*. Suppose that we remove the man's reason. This yields something non-rational, yet still alive and sensing: the thought here seems to be that when we take a *rational animal* (i.e. a man), and remove *rational*, we are left only with *animal*. Similarly we may remove the features that belong to something insofar as it is an animal or living thing (*ḥayawān*), by removing *life* (*al-ḥayy*). This leaves us with *anniyya faqaṭ*: "only a being" or "being alone."

Now consider the context of the thought experiment. The *De Causis* is arguing that the higher a cause is, the more fundamental and inseparable is its effect. This is what the example is supposed to bring out. The cause that gives rationality, for instance, must be inferior to the cause that gives being, because being is prior to rationality. Nor is this a randomly chosen example: since being belongs to everything there is, and can only be separated from anything by annihilating it, the cause of being will be the very highest cause. So the cause of being will be the first cause, God. (This will be made explicit a bit later, in *De Causis* §4.) Notice that *De Causis* §1 uses the same terminology as does al-Kindī by contrasting "remote" and "proximate" causes, the latter being intermediaries whose causal efficacy depends on the causes prior to them. Thus we have, here in the *De Causis*, the same idea of God exercising His causal act via intermediary causes that stand closer to the ultimate effects.

But could this really be al-Kindī's own considered view? In *On First Philosophy*, al-Kindī portrays God first and foremost as the cause of *unity*. And in the same work, it is made abundantly clear that in created things unity always manifests itself in the form of some determining feature (something picked out by a "term" or "expression"). Features like *rational* and *human* are instances of unity, as we saw. So the doctrine of *On First Philosophy* would seem to indicate that what God does when he creates is precisely to bestow these determining features on His creatures. On this view, God would make a man rational, human, or tall, insofar as each of these is a type of unity. We should remember, though, that a feature like rationality, humanity, or tallness is always an example of multiplicity just as much as it is an example of unity. Here it may be useful to return to our comparison between God and Platonic Forms. The Form of Equal is supposed to explain why a 3-inch stick is equal to another 3-inch stick, but not to explain why it is unequal to a 4-inch stick. In the same way God should be the cause *only* for the unity of His creatures, and not for anything that smacks of multiplicity. Thus if God creates, say, an elephant, He should be responsible for the fact that this is *one* elephant, but not for the fact that it is one *elephant*. For nothing can be an elephant without having multiplicity, for instance by having many parts.

Al-Kindī seems to be making something like this point at the end of *On First Philosophy* when he writes:

> *On First Philosophy* §XX.4 (AR 161, RJ 95–7): Every one of the effects of unity only goes from its unity to what is other than its being [*min waḥdatihī ilā ghayr huwiyyatihī*], I mean that it is not made multiple insofar as it exists [*min haythu yūjadu*]. [The effect] is many, not intrinsically one [*wāḥid mursal*]; by "intrinsically one" I mean not multiple at all, and not having its unity be anything other than its being.

This passage too is very compressed, but the first sentence says clearly that God does not make something multiple just by making it exist. It is only in the case of God, who is "intrinsically one," that unity and being are identical.[39] In everything else, that is, in everything that God creates, unity is other than being. And God should not be a cause for unity in this sense, unity that is compresent with multiplicity. Rather, He only makes something be, and this sheer "being" does not imply multiplicity. Other factors must explain the thing's falling short of complete unity.

So to return again to the first question posed at the end of the previous section, it would seem that God does indeed have an immediate relationship with every created thing. For He gives each thing its being. But on the other hand, He gives only being. Other, intermediary, causes must be invoked to explain the features of each thing that make it the sort of thing that it is. It must be admitted that working out the details of this account is a difficult task. The doctrine as it applies to sublunary things is fairly clear: God causes their existence, the heavens do the rest. But what about the heavens themselves? What explains their size, speed of rotation, and all the other features that make the heavens so heavenly? As we will see al-Kindī is insistent that the heavens did come into being, so we know that God has bestowed, and will remove, existence from them. But al-Kindī also argues that the heavens do not undergo the sort of generation and corruption that is present in the sublunary world. This suggests that the heavens are directly created and destroyed by God, along with all their essential properties. This would make sense of al-Kindī's calling God the "remote" cause of generation and corruption, since He directly causes the heavens, which are the "proximate" cause. But it would mean that in the case of the heavens God does more than create being: he creates heavenly spheres, and bequeaths to them all their properties. In short, He creates not the being of the heavens, but the heavens.

Actually, despite the passages we have examined there is room for doubt as to whether al-Kindī really distinguishes consistently between the being of a thing and that thing itself. After all, in the passage from *Quantity* with which we began, God is described not only as bringing being from non-being, but also as creating fire from not-fire, and bodies from not-bodies. Or, as he says more generally, God makes "it" from "not-it" [*huwa min lā huwa*]. This suggests that when he says that God creates "being," he might mean simply the thing that comes to exist as a result of the creative act. Here we run up against an ambiguity in the metaphysical terminology used in al-Kindī's circle. The words *aysa*, *huwiyya* and *anniyya* can refer to "being" in two different senses. They can mean "being" in the abstract sense, as in the passage cited above explaining the import of the question "whether?" as an inquiry into "being alone [*anniyya faqaṭ*]." In this first sense it is natural to distinguish between a thing and its being. But in a second sense, the same terms can mean *a* being, in other words, the thing that exists. This is particularly clear from the fact that all of these terms can appear as plural nouns, for instance in the passage from *On the True Agent* cited above: creation is bringing "beings [*aysāt*]" to be from non-being.[40] Here *aysāt* clearly means the various things that God creates.[41] In this sense, then, words like *aysa* and *anniyya* seem to mean something like "substance" (bear in mind that Aristotle's word for "substance," *ousia*, is related to *einai* and *on*, "to be" and "being").

In light of this it is perhaps not surprising that al-Kindī gestures towards two conflicting theories of creation. Sometimes he is close to anticipating Avicenna's distinction between essence and existence, insofar as he contrasts being with a thing's attributes, and views God as providing only being (in the first, more abstract sense).[42] But sometimes he seems to have the more straightforward idea that God directly creates the thing itself. In such passages, when God is said to create *aysa* or *anniyya*, this means He is creating "a being," a substance or fully constituted entity. So it is not clear that we should credit al-Kindī with a well worked-out, consistent theory of creation. But his inclination towards seeing God as the cause of being in the abstract sense is philosophically interesting, and as we have seen it suggests how he could have explicated the theory of mediated divine agency in *On the True Agent*.

The Creator as Mover

What of our second question, the question of why the world must be temporally bounded, if creation consists in an enduring relation between the world and God as its sustaining cause? Here our long passage on creation from *Quantity* can be of some help. It showed that, however distinctive creation might be, it nonetheless has in common with all other causation that it brings about some X from its contrary, not-X. In the case of creation, being is brought from non-being. Now, this immediately raises a difficulty for anyone who thinks that God is an *eternal* sustaining cause: in what sense does such a cause bring the world to be from non-being? For the world is permanently in a state of being. I would not want to suggest that this is an insurmountable difficulty, but it is a difficulty that seems to have helped convince al-Kindī, following Philoponus, that the world cannot be eternal. We can see why if we return to the contrast made in *On the True Agent* between sustaining and productive causes. Al-Kindī's example of a sustaining agent there was a walker, whose act causes his walking. Such an agent does not go from not-walking to walking at each moment during his walk. Rather, there is a time prior to his walking at which he is not-walking, and his beginning to be a sustaining cause is what brings about a change from not-walking to walking. God's creative act can be understood the same way. It exercises sustaining causality, but the exercise of this causality is temporally bounded. Only then will God bring about a *change* when He creates.

In this regard we should take note of a passage from section 2 of *On First Philosophy*, which comes in the midst of the argument against the eternity of the world. Here al-Kindī says that the world's "being-brought-into-being from non-being [*tahawwiyahū aysan 'an laysa*]" would count as a motion (§VI.12, AR 118, RJ 33–5), since it would be a generation (*ḳawn*) and generation is a type of motion. One should note that "motion [*ḥaraḳa*]" here does not only mean locomotion, i.e. change of place. Al-Kindī specifies that locomotion is only a subspecies of motion and that in general motion is just "the change [*tabaddul*] of something" (§VI.9, AR 117, RJ 33).[43] Here then we see the same thought process that we found in the Koranic exegesis from *Quantity*: creation is bringing something to be from non-being. But the fact that bringing-to-be is explicitly called a "change" or "motion" is a significant addition to the theory. It is a particularly surprising addition in light of Aristotle's own statement that *genesis* is not *ḳinêsis*, given that it is impossible for non-being to move (*Physics* V.1, 225a25–6).

Yet this is not a slip of al-Kindī's pen. At the culmination of *On First Philosophy*, he combines many of the themes we have seen him associate with creation into a single passage, and one of these themes is motion:

> *On First Philosophy* §XX.6 (AR 162, RJ 97): What is brought to be has not always existed, and what has not always existed is originated; that is, its being-brought-to-be is from a cause. That which is brought-to-be is originated, and since the cause of its being-brought-to-be is the true, first One, the cause of origination is the true, first One. But the cause from which motion is originated, I mean, the mover, is the agent.

Obviously this passage is deeply un-Aristotelian in a number of respects. It countenances absolute coming-to-be, it rejects the eternity of the world, and it favors the Neoplatonic idea of God as the One over Aristotle's conception of God as thought thinking itself (remember that al-Kindī has only a few pages earlier rejected the claim that the true One is intellect). But of course the idea that God is a cause of motion is perfectly Aristotelian. In both the *Physics* and *Metaphysics* Aristotle establishes the existence of God precisely on the basis that there must be some "first mover," an unmoving cause of all motion. By classing creation as a type of motion, al-Kindī is thus able to retain what must have seemed to him to be the central tenet of Aristotle's theology: because God is a Creator, He must also be a mover. And elsewhere, it should be added, he makes it clear that God is unmoved, providing another point of agreement with Aristotle.[44]

As this passage also shows, the fact that God is a mover is supposed to underwrite the now familiar claim that God is an agent, that is, an efficient cause. Most modern-day readers would count this as another departure from Aristotelian orthodoxy on al-Kindī's part. For it is commonly held nowadays that in the *Metaphysics*, if not in the *Physics*, Aristotle holds that God is a final and not an efficient cause. But it is doubtful that al-Kindī would have seen things in this way. Certainly the later Greek commentatorial tradition would not have forced this interpretation on him; far from it. In fact Ammonius, the head of the school at Alexandria and the teacher of Philoponus, authored a treatise which argued specifically that Aristotle's God should be understood to be an efficient as well as a final cause. There is, as far as I know, no evidence that al-Kindī knew this treatise, but he was nevertheless in agreement with Ammonius in thinking that God is an efficient cause, and it seems almost certain that like Ammonius he thought Aristotle agreed with him on the point.[45] The view that God is an *efficient* cause of being, and that Aristotle knew it, becomes a commonplace in Arabic philosophy, and al-Kindī should be credited with anticipating this important feature of the later tradition.

In complete contrast is al-Kindī's refusal to accept Aristotle's doctrine that the world is eternal. Here al-Kindī surely knows that he is in disagreement with Aristotle. And unlike his view that God is an efficient cause, which would command wide agreement in later Arabic thought, al-Kindī's stance on the eternity of the world would be almost universally rejected by later *falāsifa*. The passages I have examined from *Quantity* and *On First Philosophy* suggest that al-Kindī took this stance in part because he thought of creation as a genuine change or motion. Since change is always a passage from one contrary to another, the world must be preceded by non-being. This is why an eternally sustaining cause could not, for al-Kindī, be a genuine Creator. It is curious that viewing creation as a motion or change from one contrary to another lies behind al-Kindī's most Aristotelian theological claim (God is an unmoved mover) and also his least Aristotelian theological claim (the world is not eternal). However this is not al-Kindī's only reason for rejecting the eternity of the world. His motives for doing so, and the arguments he presents against an eternal world, will serve as the topic of chapter 4.

4

ETERNITY

Infinite Creator and Finite World

In the century that followed al-Kindī's, al-Fārābī began his work proving the agreement of Plato and Aristotle by remarking, "I see a great many people in our time absorbing themselves in and disputing the question whether the world is created [*ḥudūth*] or eternal."[1] Not much had changed since late ancient times. Greek Platonists and Aristotelians had also disputed whether the world is eternal, and whether or not Plato agreed with Aristotle on this issue. Aristotle left no doubt that he believed the world to be eternal, arguing for this at length in the *Physics* and *On the Heavens*. But in the *Timaeus* Plato seemed to say that a divine Demiurge created the physical cosmos with a beginning in time. As we will see, though, most Platonists interpreted him as agreeing with Aristotle that the world is eternal. In the Arabic-speaking world al-Fārābī and Avicenna also uphold the world's eternity. Thus al-Ghazālī takes this as a central example of overweening philosophical pretension, singling it out for sustained criticism in his *Incoherence of the Philosophers*: for al-Ghazālī to be a *faylasūf* is in part to believe in the eternity of the world.

Philoponus and al-Kindī are the dissenters from this tradition of orthodoxy. Philoponus' motives for denying the world's eternity are fairly clear. He was a Christian, and sought to defend the revealed truth that the world is created with a beginning in time. He was also a Platonist who, unlike most late Platonists, was happy to disagree with Aristotle. And he read the *Timaeus* as meaning just what it says, namely (conveniently enough) that the world is created with a beginning in time. At first glance, al-Kindī's stance is far more surprising. Of course, he writes before any orthodoxy could be established amongst Muslim Aristotelians, but he surely knows that he is departing from Greek orthodoxy and from Aristotle himself by taking this position. He may simply be deeply impressed by Philoponus' arguments, which inspire his own. And he may be convinced that the Koran unambigously says the world was created with a temporal beginning, and so feel obliged to defend this view. Still, there is no obvious need for al-Kindī to bother with the issue at all. As a propagandist for the virtues of Greek thought, why highlight this divergence between Aristotle and Islam? Yet far from suppressing the difficulty, al-Kindī positively lavishes attention on the problem of the world's eternity. The claim that the world has finite duration is not only the thesis for which al-Kindī is most famous, but also the thesis that engages his interest more than any other, at least in the works that have come down to us. Also surprising is that his most elaborate treatment of the issue surfaces in *On First Philosophy*. The rejection of eternity dominates section 2 of the surviving text, and is the first major thesis al-Kindī tries to establish in the text as a whole. This has occasioned less perplexity among commentators than it should. Why should a treatise on *metaphysics* focus on the duration of the *physical* cosmos?

This chapter, then, involves numerous tasks. Most obviously, the details of al-Kindī's arguments against the world's eternity must be examined. Before looking at these arguments, though, I will need to set out their Greek background, which means discussing not just Philoponus but the complex tradition to which Philoponus was himself responding. Finally, I will explain why al-Kindī was so determined to prove that the world is not eternal, and why he gives it such a prominent place in *On First Philosophy*.

The Greek Background

Aristotle is the first Greek philosopher to give extensive arguments for or against the eternity of the world. As already mentioned, these arguments appear in his *Physics*, especially VIII.1, and in book I of his *On the Heavens*. The *Physics* arguments are based on the impossibility of a first motion or a first moment of time. It is significant that when Aristotle first formulates the issue at hand, in the opening lines of VIII.1 (250b11–15), he asks whether *motion* "ever came to be, having first not been [*poteron de gegone pote kinêsis ouk ousa proteron*]" and whether *motion* will cease. He does not, that is, see the problem as one about the eternity of the world's very existence, but rather its motion.[2] In fact Aristotle is mostly concerned to rule out a hypothesis according to which the world is first eternally at rest, and then begins to move (251a23–4). Even on this rejected hypothesis, the world would still be eternal; it is only its motion that would have a temporal beginning. Aristotle also wants to reject the claim that time itself has a beginning, but this should not be confused with the claim that the world as a whole comes to be *ex nihilo*. For time, according to Aristotle, is what numbers motion; if there is no motion there will be no time either (251b12–13). Even here, then, it is the possibility of a first motion that is at issue.

Aristotle excludes this possibility by arguing that whatever moves first must have had a prior potentiality for motion. A still prior motion would be required to actualize this potential, so our supposedly first motion would not be first after all. Thus it is incoherent to posit a first motion (251b5–10). Now, if there can be no first motion, then likewise there can be no first moment of time, as we have already seen. But Aristotle has an additional reason to rule out a beginning of time. He understands the moment or instant of time, which he calls "the now [*to nun*]," as a division between past and future. Such a "now" is not an extended part of time, but rather an indivisible limit between two stretches of time. By this reckoning there can be no first moment: there would be no past from which such a moment would divide the future. Similar arguments regarding motion and time show that they cannot end: motion and time are eternal both *ex parte ante* (into the past) and *ex parte post* (into the future).

It is worth underlining again that these arguments are not aimed directly against a position like that of Philoponus or al-Kindī, according to which the world, and motion and time along with it, come to be *ex nihilo*. Aristotle simply assumes in his argument that any motion will require something prior that is potentially moved. Granted, he has argued for this elsewhere, as we saw in chapter 3. But still it is clear that absolute coming-to-be is not Aristotle's worry in VIII.1, for he is happy to assume the need for a pre-existing substrate of motion as a premise in his main argument. Similarly, as Philoponus will point out, no one who thought that time had a beginning would accept Aristotle's definition of the "now," because it immediately excludes the possibility of a first moment. All of this suggests that Aristotle has not envisioned an opponent for whom the entire world is radically contingent, in the sense that it may not have existed at all. Rather he wants to rule out, for instance, that the world goes through periods of complete rest followed by periods of motion (he associates this with Empedocles, 252a7), or as already mentioned, that the world was eternally at rest and then moved.

Although motion is eternal, it is not the case that all things are always in motion. In *Physics* VIII.3 Aristotle divides things into three kinds: things that move only sometimes, things that always move, and things that never move. This division sets the agenda for the rest of book VIII. That there are things that both rest and move is plain to the senses; these are the things of our familiar surroundings in the sublunary world.[3] But the eternity of motion, thinks Aristotle, cannot be explained only with reference to such intermittent movers. There must be some moving things that move always, with continuous (*suneches*) motion (VIII.6, 259a15–16). Only circular motion can be regular and eternal as required; so it is the heavenly spheres, with their unceasing rotations around the earth, that make up the second class of things that always move (VIII.8–9). Finally there must be things that never move, because it is impossible for every motion to be caused by something that is itself moved, or by self-motion (VIII.5). The only remaining alternative is a mover that is itself unmoved. Book VIII concludes with a densely argued chapter that will be exploited by Philoponus. In order to show that an unmoved mover of eternal motion must be immaterial, Aristotle argues that no finite thing (such as a body) can cause motion through infinite time. For to do so it would need to have infinite power (*dunamis*), which, Aristotle argues, is impossible (VIII.10, 266b5–6).

While these are Aristotle's best-known ideas regarding the eternity of motion and the cause of motion—ideas that will be further elaborated in *Metaphysics,* book Λ—a more technical set of arguments to be found in *On the Heavens* would prove equally important for late ancient discussions of eternity. Let us return to the idea that eternal, regular motion must be circular. Why is this? Aristotle argues that nothing made up of the four elements could move eternally and regularly. For the elements all have natural motions that are rectilinear: fire and air go straight up by nature, and earth and water go straight down. Of course one may impose nonrectilinear motion on the elements or compounds of the elements, but this will always be "unnatural" forced motion, and motion that is eternal and regular cannot be unnatural. Thus the heavens must be made of something else, the so-called "fifth element" or aether (*On the Heavens* I.2).

Conversely, given that aether is naturally suited to circular motion, it must be admitted to be ungenerable and incorruptible (*On the Heavens* I.3, 270a12–22). For circular motion, unlike rectilinear motion, has no contrary (*On the Heavens* I.4). The reason for this is that two motions are contrary when the starting-point of one motion is the finishing-point of the other; a trip from London to Boston is contrary to a trip from Boston to London. But in circular motion the starting-point and finishing-point are the same. And, as I discussed in chapter 3, "generation and corruption occur in opposites" (*On the Heavens* I.3, 270a22). Since aether, the material that makes up the heavens, moves with a motion that has no contrary, the heavens can be neither generated nor corrupted. This provides Aristotle with yet another reason for thinking that the heavens, and thus the cosmos as a whole, are eternal.

On the face of it, and according to Aristotle himself (*Physics* VIII.1, 251b17–18, *On the Heavens* I.10, 280a30), this elaborate theory differs starkly from the views of Plato in the *Timaeus*. On some issues the two philosophers are clearly in agreement: the *Timaeus* makes it clear that the cosmos is eternal *ex parte post*, in a passage (41a–b) in which the Demiurge promises not to unmake the cosmos owing to its goodness and beauty. The *Timaeus* also emphasizes the importance of the heavens' regular circular motion, albeit for rather different reasons, and links time to heavenly motion. However, there are at least two points of apparent disagreement. For one thing, the Demiurge does not seem to be very like the unmoved mover of the *Physics* and *Metaphysics*. He providentially ordains what would be best for the cosmos, and enlists the help of "younger" gods to bring about his providential aims. He also seems to take an explicitly active role in the composition of the cosmos, which is what led to the question of whether Plato disagreed with Aristotle in seeing God as an efficient cause. As we saw in chapter 3, late ancient commentators managed to bring Aristotle into line with Plato on the latter point. And in chapter 8 we will see that they managed a similar feat with respect to divine providence.

But the most important seeming disagreement for our present concerns is over whether the world is eternal *ex parte ante*. Plato has his main speaker Timaeus say the following at 28b:

> Regarding the heaven as a whole [*ho pas ouranos*]—let us call it the "cosmos," or whatever other name is most appropriate—we must put the same question one must ask about anything at the outset: whether it has always been, having no beginning of generation, or whether it has come to be, from some starting-point [*poteron ên aei, geneseôs archên echôn oudemian, ê gegonen, ap' archês tinos arxamenos*]. It has come to be [*gegonen*]. For it is visible, tangible, and has a body.

Even in Plato, few passages provoked as much commentary in later ancient writings as this one.[4] Prior to the advent of Neoplatonism in the work of Plotinus, some Platonists like Atticus and Plutarch were happy to understand this statement in the "literal" sense that the world has a temporal beginning.[5] But even during this period others devised alternative interpretations that turned on the words "generated [*gegonen*]" and "beginning [*archê*]." We know a fair amount about the history of these interpretations, thanks in part to the highly informative *Commentary on the Timaeus* of Proclus. Proclus himself, like all Neoplatonists apart from Philoponus, follows a "non-literal" interpretation in his commentary. He also compiled 18 arguments *On the Eternity of the World* in order to refute the "literal" interpretation.[6] Some of these arguments are drawn from Aristotle. But most derive from debates over Plato's true meaning in the *Timaeus*, debates which had already been raging for generations.

Proclus offers an ingenious reading of *Timaeus* 28b which exploits the ambiguity of the two key terms *archê* and *gegonen*. *Archê* can mean "beginning" but it can also mean "principle." Proclus thinks that Plato is affirming that the cosmos has an *archê* in the sense of a causal principle, rather than a temporal beginning, in other words that the cosmos depends for its existence on the Demiurge. Giving a suitable interpretation to the other term, *gegonen*, is more difficult. The early Platonist Taurus compiled a list of possible interpretations,[7] one of which was that something is "generated" if it has an extrinsic cause. But the special sense in which the physical cosmos is generated cannot just be that it has such a cause. For in Neoplatonism transcendent, immaterial things too may have superior, extrinsic causes; for example the universal intellect is caused by the One, and the soul by the intellect. Proclus does not want the physical cosmos to be "generated" in the same sense as these immaterial things.[8] He solves this problem by turning to the context of *Timaeus* 28b. Just prior to the passage, at 27d–28a, Plato has distinguished between "being [*to on*]" and "becoming [*to gignomenon*]." The world of becoming is that of physical things that undergo change, while the world of being is the intelligible realm of simple, unchanging things. Proclus argues that when Plato says the cosmos is "generated" he means that it belongs to the realm of becoming. As such it is unable to subsist eternally under its own power, and yet it is eternal, for it is constantly renewed in being by its transcendent cause. Thus the Demiurge of the *Timaeus*, on Proclus' reading, is an eternal *sustaining* cause of the sort I described in chapter 3.

These interpretive moves make it possible for Proclus to maintain the eternity of the physical cosmos as a genuinely Platonic theory. However, he is happy to claim common cause with Aristotle as well. In the *Timaeus* commentary he writes:

> Just as body, by its proper nature [*kata tên heautou phusin*], has limited power [*dunamin*], so by its proper nature, it is perishable. Not in the sense that it is adapted [*epitêdeion*] for destruction, but as not having a nature such that it preserves itself [*all' hôs heauto sôzein ou pephukos*]. Nor as being potentially perishable, yet actually preserving itself. Rather, as incapable of giving itself indestructibility. Whence then does [the body of the cosmos] have eternity [*to aidion*], and whence does it receive infinite power? From the maker cause [*apo tês poiêtikês . . . aitias*], one must say. So that it is moved by that, and comes to be [*ginetai*] from that, and is always coming to be. For everything that comes to be from an unmoved cause partakes of the nature that always endures, as the divine Aristotle too says. Thus, according to this argument, the cosmos has eternity from an unmoved, prior, demiurgic cause. But since, according to its own nature, it is generated [*genêton*], it is always coming into being [*aei ginetai*] due to its father.[9]

Here Proclus avails himself of the principle established in *Physics* VIII.10, that no finite body can have an infinite power, to show that the world cannot be eternal without an external cause. This is rather different from Aristotle's use of the principle, since for Aristotle it established not the need for a first mover but the immaterial nature of that mover. Another difference is that as I have noted above, Aristotle does not engage with, or perhaps even consider, the notion of the world's being brought into *being* by a transcendent cause. His concern is whether there is a beginning of motion, not a beginning of existence. By contrast Proclus believes that the physical cosmos, though eternal, is continually being brought into being by the Demiurge. Proclus' position thus has some overlap with Aristotle's, because he agrees with Aristotle that the world is eternal, and some overlap with a position like the one Philoponus and al-Kindī will adopt, because he agrees with them that there must be an extrinsic cause to explain the world's continuing to exist (and not just be moved) for any length of time at all.

The contrast between a Platonist view like that of Proclus and the Aristotelian outlook will become clearer if we turn back to the earlier Aristotelian commentator Alexander of Aphrodisias. Alexander devoted a brief essay, now collected as one of his *Quaestiones*, to showing "that it is not possible for the world to be incorruptible through the will of God, if it is corruptible by its own nature."[10] This is directed against Platonist interpretations of the aforementioned passage in the *Timaeus* where the Demiurge says he will preserve the cosmos forever due to its beauty and goodness. Although Alexander is of course happy to agree that the world is eternal *ex parte post*, he rejects the idea that eternity could be granted to the world without the world's having a natural disposition towards eternity. In general, he claims, it is impossible for anything to take on a property for which it has no natural disposition; examples might be that fire cannot become cold, nor a human immortal. But the Platonists, according to Alexander, say that "according to its own nature [*kata tên hautou phusin*]," the world is disposed towards corruption and not eternity. Alexander argues that even God could not make such a thing eternal, since, as he says, "what is impossible in this way, since it is impossible for all, is impossible even for the gods" (32.3–4). In short, if the world is corruptible by nature, then it has no intrinsic possibility for eternal existence, so the gods cannot make it exist eternally.

Would Proclus be vulnerable to this criticism? In some passages Proclus seems to agree with Alexander that the world is by nature indestructible. For example, in *On the Eternity of the World* he makes use of the Aristotelian argument that since the heavens have natural circular motion, they have no contrary and are thus by nature indestructible. Regarding the Demiurge's promise not to unbind the cosmos, he says in his sixth argument that the world is therefore indestructible, since only the Demiurge can destroy it, and the Demiurge would not do so. On the other hand we may doubt whether, given the account of the *Timaeus* commentary, the world could have an intrinsic natural disposition towards eternal existence. For it belongs to the realm of becoming, and it is only the extrinsic power of the Demiurge that renews it in existence from moment to moment. One reason it is counted as "generated" is that it is composite, and

Proclus himself elsewhere makes use of the Platonic principle that what is composite is corruptible.[11] He also argues, in a passage quoted above, that the cosmos cannot have an infinite power of its own for existence, since it is a finite body.

Proclus wrote another work in which he defended the *Timaeus* from Aristotelian criticisms; this work is lost but some passages are preserved by Philoponus. These passages again invoke the impossibility of there being an infinite power in a finite cosmos. But this time the purpose is an *ad hominem* attack on Aristotle: since the world is finite, Aristotle's own principles commit him to rejecting the eternity of the world. Philoponus pounces on these arguments and indulges in some *ad hominem* arguments of his own. In light of Proclus' criticism, Proclus himself must admit that the cosmos "does not have everlasting being in its own right [*eph' heautô to aei einai ouk echôn*] but is something that comes to be and perishes . . . if one were to separate from it the cause of its continuous becoming and of its everlasting movement, it will on account of not itself possessing infinite power experience a cessation of movement and therefore also of existence, since every finite power perishes."[12] A bit later, though, he makes the more measured claim that Proclus wants the world to be eternal both in its own right *and* through the will of God (*ek tês oikeias phuseôs . . . kai ek tês tou theou boulêseôs*).[13]

If this last remark is accurate then Philoponus' position is diametrically opposed to Proclus'. For Philoponus, the cosmos is of such a nature as not to be eternal, and it is also beyond God's power to make the world eternal *ex parte ante*. The only concession he will make is that God can, and will, override the world's nature to give it eternal existence *ex parte post*. These positions emerge from several works in which Philoponus discusses the eternity of the world. The first of these is his *Commentary on the Physics*, which briefly rehearses some of the arguments that will appear in his later polemical works. These polemical works include *Against Aristotle*, which I have already had occasion to discuss, and a point-by-point refutation of Proclus' set of 18 arguments, *Against Proclus on the Eternity of the World*. This massive work, which fortunately is almost entirely extant, seems to have been written later than *Against Aristotle*, to which it refers. Ironically, just as Philoponus' enemy Simplicius preserves almost all the extant fragments of *Against Aristotle*, so Philoponus preserves Proclus' arguments by quoting them in order to refute them. (The first argument by Proclus is extant only in Arabic, because the very beginning of Philoponus' treatise is lost.) Philoponus wants to show not only that Proclus' arguments fail to prove that the world is eternal, but also that Atticus and Plutarch were right to say that Plato himself rejected the world's eternity *ex parte ante*. There was also a work, now lost but again quoted by Simplicius, devoted specifically to the issue of infinite power. Of these polemical works it seems that the latter treatise and at least parts of *Against Aristotle* were translated into Arabic, while parts of *Against Proclus* appear in texts ascribed to Alexander of Aphrodisias.[14]

We have already seen that, in *Against Aristotle*, Philoponus rejected the arguments of *Physics* VIII.1: there is no reason to think that there cannot be a first motion or first moment of time, since God can bring a moving world into being *ex nihilo*, and time along with it. But most of *Against Aristotle* (at least, of the parts of it that are extant) is directed against the aether theory of *On the Heavens*. In books I–V Philoponus demolishes the Aristotelian theory that contrasts the rectilinearly moving elements, which are subject to generation and corruption, with the eternal, circularly moving heavens. For one thing, says Philoponus, according to Aristotle himself there is a sphere of fire rotating around the earth, just below the sphere of the moon. So Aristotle is committed to thinking that fire has natural circular motion after all. Furthermore, Philoponus claims the authority of Plato in arguing that the heavens are made of the same stuffs as the sublunary world—a thesis which particularly outrages Simplicius. And in any case, it is not right to say that circular motion has no contrary and that what moves circularly is therefore incorruptible. For circular motion at least has a *privation*, namely no motion at all, and it is privations that are required in order for corruption to occur. Finally, in the separate treatise on infinite power, Philoponus seems to have followed the arguments he himself quotes from Proclus in *Against Proclus*, by turning *Physics* VIII.10 against its author. The world is a finite body, and Aristotle himself shows that no body can have infinite power (*dunamis*). If we construe eternal existence as requiring such an infinite power, then the cosmos cannot be eternal, at least not in its own right.

The upshot is that for Philoponus, the heavens and thus the cosmos as a whole are by nature generable and perishable. Of course if he followed the view of necessity maintained by Alexander in his *Quaestio*, this would be the end of the discussion. For, according to Alexander, what has no natural propensity for eternal existence cannot be eternal. Philoponus disagrees with this, however. He himself holds that God "overrides" the cosmos' natural tendency to perish and grants it indefinite existence.[15] He is driven to this both by his Platonism and by his Christianity. As we have seen the *Timaeus* makes it crystal clear that the Demiurge will maintain the cosmos in existence forever, and for Christians God's creation will never be destroyed, even though it may take on a different form following the Last Judgment.[16] Driven especially by the need to show Plato's position to be coherent, Philoponus argues at the end of *Against Proclus* VI that it is possible for the world "to receive an acquired and [continually] restored immortality from a power that is higher than that which belongs to its own nature."[17]

But this puts Philoponus in a difficult position with regard to eternity *ex parte ante*. As we saw, Philoponus' arguments against Aristotle are fought on the ground of what is in the nature of the physical cosmos: as a body, it cannot have infinite power, and as constituted from the four elements, it must be generable and destructible. But why not say that God has willed that there should be a world that is naturally generable and corruptible, which is nonetheless eternal both *ex parte ante* and *ex parte post*? This is a particularly pressing question if we think that this is precisely what God would or must do, unless it is impossible even for Him. Several of Proclus' arguments in *On the Eternity of the World* urge this point on us. For example, the first argument says that since the creator of the cosmos is maximally generous, he must give the greatest possible gift to his creation, i.e. eternal rather than limited existence. The fourth argument similarly says that the creator must be immune to change, so he cannot go from potentially creating the world to actually creating it.[18]

Of course Philoponus has specific counter-arguments against these claims. But in order to demonstrate that the world *cannot* be eternal *ex parte ante*, it is not enough to show that the nature of the world is such that it has no disposition for eternity *ex parte ante*. For Philoponus admits that the world has no disposition for eternity *ex parte post*, yet he thinks it receives this nonetheless. Philoponus needs an argument that shows not just the limitations on the world's nature, but the limitations on what God can create. He gives just such an argument in *Against Aristotle* VI (Fr. 132), repeated in *Against Proclus* I. He exploits Aristotle's claim, from *Physics* III.8, that there can be no such thing as an actual infinity: hypothesizing such an infinity leads to contradictions. But, says Philoponus, were the world to be eternal *ex parte ante* then we would be committed to an actual infinity, for example the number of years that have already elapsed. Worse still, we would have an actual infinity that is still increasing. For example, the number of years that had elapsed when Socrates was alive has increased since then, so we would have one actual infinity that is bigger than another, which is (according to both Philoponus and Aristotle) impossible. I will call this the "counting argument."

The counting argument helps Philoponus in two ways. First, it shows why there should be an asymmetry between the past and future eternity of the world. Since future eternity just means an indefinitely increasing finite number of years will elapse, it commits us only to what Aristotle calls a "potential infinity," which all agree is possible. (A potential infinity occurs when one can keep adding indefinitely without limit, for example by counting upwards through the integers; see *Physics* III.6, 207a7–8.) But past eternity would commit us, claims Philoponus, to an actual infinity of years that have already elapsed,[19] and all agree an actual infinity is impossible. Second, the counting argument shows why not even God can make a world that is eternal *ex parte ante*: if He did it would be impossible to reach any given time within that world, since the infinite cannot be traversed. This is not an appeal to the nature of the world as a body, or as constructed from elements. Rather it is an appeal to the idea that not even God can make an actual infinity or cause it to be traversed. Philoponus himself does not single out the counting argument in the way I have. In fact, in *Against Proclus* I.3, even as he is putting forward the counting argument he says that it is only "because of the very nature of what has come to be [*di' autên tên tou ginomenou phusin*]" that God cannot make an eternal world.[20] But the contrast I have drawn, between what one might call "natural" and "absolute" possibility—that is, what is possible for the world given its intrinsic nature, and what is possible for God even if we assume that He can override the nature of what He creates—will turn out to be central to al-Kindī's adaptation of Philoponus' arguments in *On First Philosophy*.

The Arguments in Context

Al-Kindī devoted no fewer than four treatises[21] directly to the question of the world's eternity; three of these are reworked versions of one another. Of those three the shortest is *On the Quiddity of What Cannot Be Finite, and What Is Said to Have Infinity* (hereafter *Quiddity*). An expanded version of the same material, with slightly more complex argumentation and a conclusion about God, is called *On the Oneness of God and the Finiteness of the Body of the World* (hereafter *Oneness*). The same arguments, with yet more small additions, appear in section 2 of *On First Philosophy*. I believe the three texts were written in this order, and that *Quiddity* and *Oneness* represent, if you will, preparatory sketches for *On First Philosophy*. This is shown by the gradual accumulation of detail in the arguments. For example, as we will see the arguments begin by setting out several axioms, and *Oneness* gives a different set from that used in *Quiddity*; the axioms from *Oneness* are then retained in *On First Philosophy*. However all three texts overlap verbatim, to a large extent, so the changes seem to have been in the form of adding material rather than rephrasing or rewriting earlier versions.[22]

The fourth text, *Explaining the Finiteness of the Body of the World* (hereafter *Finiteness*) written at the request of one Aḥmad b. Muḥammad al-Khurāsānī, does not have exact parallels with these other three. Instead it offers mathematical demonstrations of several principles, rather than assuming these principles as undefended axioms (the principles have some overlap with the axioms in *Oneness* and *On First Philosophy*). Then al-Kindī uses these principles to show that the world is finite in magnitude. Although he does not explicitly draw the conclusion that the world is therefore eternal, the finite magnitude of the world is central to al-Kindī's argument in the three previously mentioned works. It seems likely that *Finiteness* was written to elucidate the argumentation that had been put forward in *On First Philosophy* and its predecessors.[23] We may even speculate that the recipient, al-Khurāsānī, was unconvinced by the earlier version of the arguments and asked for a justification of al-Kindī's axioms.

A fifth work that should also be considered here deals with the composition of the heavens, a theme that was central to Greek discussions on the eternity of the world, as we have seen. Recall that Aristotle argued in the first book of *On the Heavens* that the heavens must be composed of indestructible matter, since they move circularly. Al-Kindī agrees with this account in a short treatise entitled *That the Nature of the Celestial Sphere Is Different from the Natures of the Four Elements*. He advises us that "the greatest indications of the natures of movable things are their motions, whose differences from one another distinguish the natures of the movable things" (§2, AR^2 40). The nature of the four elements, or "simple bodies," is distinguished by their rectilinear motions up or down: the hot (or "light") elements, fire and air, move up, and the cold (or "heavy") elements, water and earth, move down. Since the heavens move circularly, they must be neither hot or cold (§11, AR^2 45).

Al-Kindī faithfully follows this Aristotelian demonstration to its conclusion: since the heavens are not made of the elements, they are not composed of conflicting materials. Therefore the heavens are to be contrasted with that which "passes out of existence, changes, flows, and corrupts at every moment in time," i.e. sublunary things compounded out of the elements (§13, AR^2 46). Thus al-Kindī sides against Philoponus and with Aristotle and Simplicius over the issue of the composition of the heavens, insisting that they have an incorruptible nature.[24] This gives rise to the suspicion that, at least when he writes this short work, al-Kindī has not read books I–V of Philoponus' *Against Aristotle*.[25] If he has, then he is giving Philoponus' viewpoint surprisingly short shrift. But even so, how can al-Kindī reconcile his rejection of the world's eternity with this embrace of the Aristotelian theory of aether? The answer is found in a rather blithe aside towards the end of the treatise. The heavens, he says, are "fixed in their state for the time of their duration which their Creator, the great and exalted, allotted to them—so that they will pass out of existence just as they began, since He wished this" (§13, AR^2 46). In other words, the incorruptible nature of the heavens is irrelevant to the eternity question, because God has given them only a finite existence. Aristotle's theory is reduced to the more modest claim that during this finite existence, they are not subject to corruption in the way that sublunary things are.

In other treatises, al-Kindī likewise accepts Aristotle's cosmology but adds the same qualification of finite duration. In *On the Prostration of the Outermost Sphere* al-Kindī denies that the celestial realm falls under corruption, and immediately adds the caveat "during the interval [of time] appointed for it both as a whole and each of its individuals" (§VIII.2, AR 257, RJ 195, cf. §II.5, AR 247, RJ 181). And in *Proximate Agent Cause* he summarizes Aristotle's position on aether together with the obligatory qualification:

> *Proximate Agent Cause* §IV.1 (AR 219–20): The outermost body of the world, I mean what is between the level of the moon up to the limit of the body of the celestial sphere, is neither hot nor cold, neither moist nor dry, [and] no generation or corruption befalls it *for the period of time appointed for it by God*, great be His praise, and generation and corruption are only in what is below the sphere of the moon.

Whereas Philoponus thought the aether theory so crucial that he devoted five books of *Against Aristotle* to attacking it, al-Kindī seems to dismiss with a shrug the relevance of the theory for the eternity of the world. Ironically, though, al-Kindī's position is not so unlike that of Philoponus. Philoponus was determined to show that the heavens and entire cosmos are by nature corruptible, even though God overrides this nature so as to make them eternal *ex parte post*. Al-Kindī instead is happy to accept that the heavens are by nature *in*corruptible, but he thinks that God overrides this nature to give them a temporal beginning and end. This suggests that, for al-Kindī, the question of the nature of the physical world is even less decisive in the eternity debate than it had been for Proclus or Philoponus. For him determining what is naturally necessary to the cosmos is not even a preliminary issue. The eternity debate revolves entirely around the question of whether or not God would create a finite or infinite world.

So far this is a weighty conclusion supported by slender evidence, but it is a conclusion confirmed by section 2 of *On First Philosophy*. A curious feature of section 2 is that the eternity arguments are preceded by a lengthy discussion of philosophical methodology and epistemology. Indeed, this constitutes al-Kindī's most detailed discussion of philosophical method. No one, to my knowledge, has offered any explanation as to what these methodological considerations have to do with the eternity arguments they introduce. Yet I believe that the epistemological introduction is in fact crucial to understanding the intended status of the arguments, as well as how they fit into the rest of *On First Philosophy*. In this introduction, al-Kindī distinguishes between two kinds of "perception [*wujūd*, literally 'finding']," sensory and intellectual. Sensation grasps particulars, which are unstable due to their continuous change. As a result sensation too is unstable and we can retain an "image" of a particular object only by using imagination and memory (we will return to this in chapter 5). Intellection grasps universals, and because the intellect does not use images or concern itself with changing particulars, its perception "is perfectly certain, through the confirmation of the intellectual principles that are necessarily intelligible" (§IV.5, AR 107, RJ 21).

Al-Kindī helpfully gives us two examples of the sort of thing he means by intellectual perception. The first is that the same thing cannot be one thing and its opposite without changing (this is roughly the law of non-contradiction). The second is more complicated: al-Kindī claims that the intellect knows with certainty that outside the universe there is "neither void nor plenum." This "is not something grasped by sense . . . [but] something that the intellect perceives necessarily." It does so by means of the following argument:

> *On First Philosophy* §IV.9–10 (AR 109–10, RJ 21–3): The meaning of "void" is a place with nothing placed in it. But place and what is placed are in a relation in which neither one is prior. If there is place, there is necessarily something placed, and if there is something placed, there is necessarily place. Therefore it is impossible that there be a place with nothing placed [in it], but this is what we mean by "void"; therefore no existence belongs to absolute void. Then, we say that if the plenum is a body, either the body of the universe is infinite in size, or it is finite in size. But it is impossible that there be anything infinite in actuality, as we will show shortly. Thus it is impossible that the body of the universe be infinite in size. So there is no plenum beyond the body of the universe, because if there were, then this plenum would be a body, and if there were a plenum beyond this plenum, and a plenum beyond every plenum, then the plenum would be infinite. Then there would necessarily be a body infinite in size, which would necessitate something infinite in actuality. But the infinite in actuality cannot exist. Therefore the body of the universe has no plenum beyond it, and no void beyond it, as has been shown.

This does not look much like a necessary law of reason, such as we met in the first example. Rather al-Kindī is here supporting a thesis defended in Aristotle's *Physics*: the impossibility of void and the denial that there is anything (even empty space) outside the limits of our finite physical universe. Still, as Ivry notes in his comment on this passage, "al-Kindī is thinking of the void in some absolutely logical sense, which allows him to establish an immediate self-contradiction in terms."[26] Al-Kindī is not, in other words, giving an empirical argument against the possibility of void, but insisting that void is conceptually impossible. He therefore concludes the argument by remarking, "this is absolutely necessary [*wājib iḍṭirāran*] and there is no form for it in the soul; it is only perceived intellectually [*ʿaqlī*] and necessarily." Note that in the argument against void, al-Kindī also refers ahead to the arguments against the world's eternity, and their demonstration that there can be no actual infinity. Since this appears here as a premise in what is supposed to be a purely "intellectual" argument, it stands to reason that the argument against actual infinity will also be such an intellectual argument.

The methodological section continues with a caution that we must use the correct method for any given subject of inquiry. In particular, one must not use "images" drawn from sensation when one is studying "things that are above nature [*al-ashyā' allatī fawqa 'l-ṭabī'a*]." He compares those who attempt this to children, who cannot break free of the habit of using sensation. Conversely, in a passage already quoted in chapter 2 (§IV.14, AR 111, RJ 23–5), al-Kindī adds that we must not use mathematical investigations when studying "natural things [*al-ashyā' al-ṭabī'iyya*]." For this sort of investigation is proper to the immaterial. I do not believe that al-Kindī is here saying that it is illicit to employ mathematical concepts with regard to sensible things. Indeed, as we will see in chapter 7 the use of mathematics is the most striking feature of his work in the physical sciences. He speaks rather of mathematical *investigation* (*faḥṣ*). What he rules out here is thus the geometrical, axiomatic style of demonstration that he learned from the works of Euclid (see chapter 2).[27] This is of some significance for our understanding of the eternity arguments, which, as already mentioned, use such a geometrical procedure: axioms are assumed and used in a *reductio ad absurdum*. Here it is also worth recalling that in *Finiteness* al-Kindī gives explicitly mathematical proofs of a similar set of axioms and concludes from these that the world is a finite magnitude, as he will also argue in the eternity arguments.

If this is right then the relation between the two halves of section 2 is clear. The first half makes a distinction between sensory and intellectual perception, gives some examples of the latter, and urges us to observe the correct method with respect to each subject of inquiry. This paves the way for the second half by explaining what sort of inquiry will be involved in the discussion of the eternity of the world. Though al-Kindī provides almost nothing in the way of a transition between the two halves, there are signs that he is consciously giving "intellectual" arguments regarding eternity. The most obvious is that when he introduces the aforementioned axioms, he says that they are "first, certain premises known without an intermediary" (§VI.1, AR 114, RJ 29). Compare this to his description of how we know that nothing can be one thing and its opposite: "this is perceived by the soul without sensation, and by necessity, with no need for an intermediary" (we have already seen too that "certainty" is a feature of intellectual arguments).

My interpretation has the virtue of bringing together the apparently unrelated elements of section 2, but it also has two broader implications.

The first has to do with the unity of *On First Philosophy* as a whole. At the beginning of this chapter I raised the question of why al-Kindī would involve himself in a discussion of the eternity problem in a work devoted to metaphysics. We now have part of the answer: in the methodological section he describes intellectual demonstrations as the ones that are to be used for what is "above natural things," namely for things that do not move. These are the things that may be grasped directly by the intellect, without the use of sensation. It is easy to see why God, the subject of sections 3 and 4, would be a fitting object of such an inquiry. But the fact that al-Kindī uses a "mathematical" procedure and "intellectual" demonstration with regard to the eternity of the world shows that he believes that this, too, is an issue to be addressed by the methods of "first philosophy," that is, metaphysics. For it is an issue decided by the use of intellect alone, without recourse to sensation. How can this be, since the world whose finiteness is being proven obviously does move, and is a physical object? I believe the answer is that al-Kindī considers himself to be dealing not so much with the actual physical cosmos as with abstract concepts like infinity and magnitude. In other words, he is showing how the intellect can grasp immediately, through pure reflection, that an actual infinity is impossible, and that the eternal by definition cannot have limit. Asserting the temporal finiteness of our actual world is merely an application of these abstract truths.[28]

This leads us to the second significant implication. If what I have just said is right, then the arguments show the *absolute* impossibility of there being a universe that is infinite in any magnitude, including time. Not even an infinite power could create an infinite magnitude, because the assumption of such a magnitude is self-contradictory. (Compare this to al-Kindī's discussion of void. He claims that the notion of void is simply incoherent, which entails that not even God could create a void.) Thus these arguments need to accomplish the same thing as Philoponus' counting argument, which, perhaps not coincidentally, is the only argument al-Kindī borrows directly from Philoponus. Al-Kindī thus completes a process in which ancient thinkers steadily moved away from Aristotle's approach to the eternity question. The orthodox Neoplatonists and Philoponus had already asked whether the very being of the universe begins, rather than whether motion begins. But once we admit the existence of a cause that creates being, rather than simply moving the movable, we have accepted a cause that does not act in the way that natural causes do. This throws into serious doubt a position like Alexander's, where natures are the last word on what is possible. Philoponus makes the obvious move of not only of denying that God must act as natural agents do (He can exercise causality without a pre-existing substrate), but also insisting that God can override the nature of what He creates. Al-Kindī goes further still, by removing the question of the intrinsic nature of the universe from the eternity debate altogether. He ignores the incorruptible nature of the heavens, because this nature is subordinated to higher "metaphysical" considerations. All that matters is what God, the cause of being, can and does will to create. And pure reflection tells us that even if He creates a world made partially of incorruptible material, that world cannot be infinite.

The Eternity Arguments

Now, finally, let us turn to the arguments themselves, which are four in number. Argument (1) is actually more a declaration of al-Kindī's intent than a proper argument. It explores the concept of eternity itself, reaching conclusions that foreshadow the later sections of *On First Philosophy*. I will set this passage aside for now and return to it later. Argument (2), which proves the impossibility of an infinite magnitude, is the longest. Al-Kindī includes it in all his works on the eternity of the world, fine-tuning it in each new version. Argument (3) is subsidiary to argument (2); it begins with the new topic of composition, but reverts to invoking the impossibility of an infinite magnitude. In his pioneering work on al-Kindī's debt to Philoponus, H.A. Davidson saw argument (3) as a failed attempt to develop a separate line of reasoning from argument (2). My view of the argument is somewhat more optimistic, but on any reading it would seem that (2) and (3) are closely linked. Argument (4) is what I have called the counting argument, i.e. the argument that an infinite time cannot elapse. It appears in *Quiddity*, *Oneness* and *On First Philosophy*, and is the argument with the strongest parallel in Philoponus. Arguments (1) and (3) appear only in *On First Philosophy*.

Let us begin with arguments (2) and (3). Argument (2) is lengthy, so it is useful to subdivide it into four parts. First (2a), there are the aforementioned axioms or premises, on which al-Kindī depends in what follows. For example, if two finite bodies are combined, the result is finite. We will see al-Kindī using this premise shortly. I have already tried to explain the importance of al-Kindī's using an axiomatic style of argument here. It seems worth adding that when Philoponus gives the counting argument in *Against Aristotle*, he too seems to have used this style of argument. Simplicius tells us that prior to the counting argument Philoponus assumes three "axioms [*axiômata*]," one of which is that an actual infinity is impossible.[29] This may have encouraged al-Kindī to employ a Euclidean argument form in the present context, though as we have seen he was fond of this style of argument anyway, and no doubt needed little encouragement.

With his axioms in hand, al-Kindī goes on to prove (2b) that there can be no such thing as an actual infinity. He does so by means of the following thought experiment (§VI.2–5, AR 115–6, RJ 29–31). Suppose that there is an actually infinite magnitude,[30] and that we subtract a finite portion of this magnitude. Imagine, if you like, an infinitely tall stack of books, from which we remove, say, the collected works of Shakespeare. Now we have a dilemma: are the remaining books a finite or infinite stack of books? If the resulting stack is finite, then when we add Shakespeare back to the pile we should get a finite stack of books, since we have added one finite amount (Shakespeare's works) to another (the finite resulting stack). But this can't be right, because all we have done is subtract and replace a part of the infinite magnitude. So it would seem that, when we take out Shakespeare, the resulting stack must be infinite. But this is impossible as well. For suppose we compare the two infinite stacks, the one with Shakespeare, and the one without Shakespeare. Are they the same size? How could they be, since one contains more than the other? Even worse, if they are the same size then when I put Shakespeare back into the stack, it won't get any bigger. And how can I add books to a stack without making the stack bigger? Yet neither can they be of different sizes, since they are both infinite.[31] Therefore the stack without Shakespeare can be neither finite nor infinite; and the same argument will work for any magnitude. So our original assumption of an infinite magnitude is, by *reductio*, impossible.

From a modern point of view this argument is of course wrongheaded. This is because we now have a different notion of infinity, which allows that a finite magnitude can be subtracted from an infinite magnitude leaving an equally infinite result. Consider, for example, the integers, which are an infinite set. If we subtract, say, the integer 1 from this set, we are left with an infinite set. The complete set of all the positive integers is not "greater" than the incomplete set of all positive integers apart from 1.[32]

However, from an ancient point of view al-Kindī's argument would have been persuasive, and even today it has a good deal of intuitive appeal.

This takes us to the next stage of the argument (2c). Time, says al-Kindī, is predicated of a magnitude, namely body. For time is the number of motion, and the only thing that moves is body. So if we assume that no body can be infinite, as proven in the first part of the argument (2a),[33] and that nothing predicated of a finite thing can itself be infinite, then we will see that time cannot be infinite. Of course the sticking point here will be the second assumption. Is it really so obvious that nothing infinite can be predicated of something finite? Ironically, al-Kindī may have been emboldened to make this assumption on the authority of Aristotle himself. In *Physics* VI Aristotle discusses the divisibility of magnitude, time and motion, and insists that time will be divided in just the same sense as motion and magnitude (VI.1, 231b18–20). For example, if a hare is running across a field, then the time it takes the hare to cross the field, the width of the field, and the hare's motion itself, can all be co-divided indefinitely. (If the distance is halved, so will be the required time, and so on. This will later help Aristotle against Zeno's paradoxes of motion.) Then, in VI.2 (233a17–21), Aristotle expands on this to remark that "if either [time or magnitude] is infinite [*apeiron*], so is the other, and in the same way. For instance if time is infinite in both directions, then so will be the extent [*mêkos*] in both directions, and if time is divisible, so is the extent, and if time is [infinite] in both respects, then so is the magnitude."[34] So perhaps al-Kindī is here following Philoponus' strategy of using Aristotle against himself.

Al-Kindī definitely uses this strategy in what follows. He has just claimed that time will be finite so long as body, and the motion of body, are finite. But what if someone admitted that motion is finite, but still thought the world is eternal because it undergoes an infinite period of rest before moving? As we saw, Aristotle already showed how to deal with this hypothesis in *Physics* VIII. Thus in the final part of this extended argument (2d),[35] we have the strange spectacle of al-Kindī using Aristotle's arguments in favor of the eternity of motion as part of his own argument against the eternity of the world. Both of them need to rule out the possibility of a universe that is at rest for an infinite time before it moves. However, as Ivry has remarked, "al-Kindī is here eliminating the last possible chance for an eternal universe, while Aristotle is pointing the way to just such a conclusion."[36]

This establishes the intended conclusion of argument (2), namely that time, motion, and body are inseparable from one another, and none can be actually infinite in magnitude. This is also the conclusion of argument (3), which introduces the new point that the physical cosmos is composed of parts. As we saw, Philoponus appeals to the world's composition in arguing that it cannot have infinite power. Al-Kindī and Philoponus even use the same examples: the world is composed from matter and form, and is extended in three dimensions.[37] However al-Kindī, after giving these examples, does not go on to exploit *Physics* VIII.10 as had Philoponus. Rather, he simply drops back into the same argumentation that he gave previously: "composition is a change of the state that is not itself composition. Thus composition is motion, and if there is no motion there is no composition. Body is composed, so if there is no motion, there is no body. Thus body and motion are not prior to one another" (§VII.1, AR 120, RJ 37). This leads to a reiteration of the proof of the finiteness of time already presented in argument (2). Davidson believes that al-Kindī is here unable to reproduce Philoponus' argument, and in his confusion argues circularly: if the universe is composed, i.e. created, it must undergo the motion of being put together . . . so it must have been put together at some first moment, i.e. created.[38] A more generous reading would be to say that argument (3) supplies a new reason for accepting a key premise of argument (2), that the world can never have existed without motion. For if the world is composed, and anything composed comes to be as the result of a motion—namely the motion that puts together the elements of the composition—then the world can never have existed without there having been motion. If this is right, then argument (3) is not intended as an independent proof of the eternity of the world.

The upshot of (2) and (3), then, is as follows:

> *On First Philosophy* §VI.15 (AR 120, RJ 35): It has then been made clear that time cannot be infinite, since there cannot be a quantity, or anything that has quantity, that is infinite in actuality. Thus all time has a limit in actuality, and body is not prior to time. So it is impossible that the body of the universe be infinite, because of its being [*li-anniyyatihī*]; the being of the body of the universe is necessarily finite, and the body of the universe cannot have existed always.

Aristotle would no doubt find this passage rather frustrating. Al-Kindī is very clear that he has only intended to show that no magnitude, including time, can be *actually* infinite. But as we have seen above, Aristotle's view was precisely that the eternity of the world involves only a *potential* infinity. It would seem then that al-Kindī has devoted a great deal of effort to proving something that is in fact common ground between himself and Aristotle, namely that the world cannot be actually infinite. What he ought to be doing is arguing that eternity does in fact require actual, and not just potential, infinity. Instead, so far he seems only to have assumed it, as when he says, following the second part of argument (2), that "time is a quantity, so it is impossible that there be an actually infinite time; therefore time has a finite beginning" (§VI.6, AR 116, RJ 31). For Aristotle, this would not follow at all. He would say that time could be potentially infinite *ex parte ante*, and still lack a finite beginning.

Argument (4) finally gives us some reason to disagree with Aristotle. It is a version of Philoponus' counting argument, which (as al-Kindī presents it, at least) may be understood as relying on the impossibility of completing an infinite number of tasks. If we think of reaching a given moment as a task, we will see that in a world that is eternal *ex parte ante*, an infinity of such tasks would need to be completed before the present moment, or any moment, is reached.[39] How good is this argument? The obvious retort would be that it is perfectly possible to complete an infinite number of tasks so long as one has an infinite time in which to do it. But Aristotle himself, as Philoponus emphasizes, rejects the possibility of traversing the infinite. So the obvious retort may be one Aristotle could not give. A better response from an Aristotelian point of view would be the following. Al-Kindī seems to imagine beginning at some particular moment that is infinitely far in the past, and then trying to get to the present moment by waiting around for long enough. (He thus speaks of getting "from infinity to a determinate, known time.") That does indeed sound impossible. But in fact, there is only a finite duration between any *particular* moment in the past and the present moment. This is all that is required for saying that the eternal past constitutes a potential infinity: however large a finite duration you care to name, the world has already existed longer than that. So there is no question of an infinite period of time having elapsed between any given past moment and the present.

In *On First Philosophy* al-Kindī also attempts something that neither his own earlier versions nor Philoponus had done: it applies the counting argument to future as well as past time. Here al-Kindī yet again draws on the *Physics*, this time by using the Aristotelian definition of the instant as a boundary or limit between two times, past and future. His definition implies that any temporal duration is bounded by a limit at both ends. For example a single day is bounded by the limit between Friday and Saturday and the limit between Saturday and Sunday. But this means that as the future unfolds, and we add more and more temporal durations (be these seconds, minutes, days, or what have you), we will never have "infinite" time. For infinity is that which has no bound or limit. (Indeed, the Arabic term used throughout for the infinite is simply *mā lā nihāya la-hū*, "that which has no limit"; the Greek term *apeiron* has a similar etymology, often meaning "unlimited.") So the future must necessarily remain finite.

Here Aristotle's frustration would no doubt return. What al-Kindī is saying is that no matter how many years pass, the future will never reach "infinity." And he is right: for the same reason, you can keep counting up through the integers indefinitely without getting to an infinite number.[40] But Aristotle would agree to this. What is un-Aristotelian is al-Kindī's claim that this shows that future time is not "eternal." For Aristotle, an "eternal" future just is a future whose duration will increase indefinitely while always remaining finite. It might be tempting to think that al-Kindī is confused here, or that he is misunderstanding Aristotle's position.[41] But I do not think that is the case. Rather, he explicitly accepts (§VI.7, AR 116, RJ 31) that the world may be potentially infinite in either size or duration. There is no conceptual impossibility that results from assuming a potential infinity. His only quarrel with Aristotle then is the one embodied by the first part of argument (4); al-Kindī is convinced by Philoponus' claim that eternity *ex parte ante* would constitute an *actual* infinity. And as we know from arguments (2) and (3), an actual infinity is impossible. He is then aware of the asymmetry, exploited by Philoponus, between eternity *ex parte ante* and "eternity" *ex parte post*: the former yields an actual infinity, the latter only a potential infinity.

Though al-Kindī thus disagrees with Aristotle about past time, he is otherwise strikingly faithful to Aristotle. This helps to explain why he was willing to go against his most respected authority on this issue: the scope of disagreement was actually not all that large. Indeed, where Aristotle and Philoponus are in conflict, al-Kindī usually takes the side of Aristotle. For instance al-Kindī retains Aristotle's definition of time, which Philoponus said was question-begging, and he retains the doctrine of the incorruptibility of the heavens, which Philoponus rejected. Moreover, like Philoponus he accepts "eternity" for future time in just the way Aristotle did, understanding it as merely potential infinity. To be sure, al-Kindī says in passages quoted above that the heavens would in fact cease to exist if God willed it. But he might nonetheless believe that future time will keep increasing indefinitely. Like Philoponus, he may believe that the present cosmos will be replaced by some other form of created world after the Last Judgment. But for his present purposes this does not matter: all he wants to do is show that the world is in no sense *actually* infinite. For al-Kindī genuine eternity must involve actual infinity—what he calls "infinite being" in his conclusion to argument (2).

Created or Eternal

This leaves us with the question of why al-Kindī is concerned only with eternity in the strong sense of an actual infinity. We can get some insight into this question by returning to argument (1), which I set aside in the last section. It begins as follows:

> *On First Philosophy* §V.1 (AR 113, RJ 27): We say that the eternal is that for which non-being is absolutely impossible. With regard to existence [*kawniyyan*] the being of the eternal has no "before." The eternal does not subsist because of anything else. The eternal has no cause: the eternal has no subject, nothing predicated of it, no agent, and no explanation (that is, something for the sake of which it would exist), because there are no causes other than the ones just mentioned.

This looks more like a series of assertions than an argument, and the same goes for what follows. To summarize: since the eternal has nothing predicated of it, it can have no genus. And it cannot corrupt, since this would be a change in predicate (I quoted this passage in chapter 3). For similar reasons it cannot change. Finally, the eternal is perfect, because what is deficient is what has a potential for changing to become more perfect, but as we just saw the eternal cannot change. It is rather "stable [in its] state, through which it is excellent" (§V.3, AR 114, RJ 29).

We are some distance here from Aristotle's deliberations about eternal motion. Needless to say, al-Kindī is here already anticipating the arguments of sections 3 and 4 of *On First Philosophy*, and "the eternal" which is perfect and has no predicate is God. The present passage offers a much more rudimentary line of argument, though. It rests on the claim that the eternal is what has no cause. Perhaps we could understand this as follows. Remember the passage on creation in *Quantity*, which argues that what exercises causality must make something go from one contrary to another. Since the eternal is never in a state of non-being, it can never have been brought into being, and therefore it has no cause. Al-Kindī also says, in the first sentence of argument (1), that "the eternal is that for which non-being is absolutely impossible [*al-azalī huwa alladhī lam yajib* [*mā*] *laysa huwa muṭlaqan*]." God, in other words, exists necessarily. A link between necessity and eternity is also made in *On Definitions*, which defines "the necessary" as "that which is always actually in what it describes" (§33A, AR 168).

This suggests one reason for al-Kindī's reserving genuine eternity for God: if the eternal is the necessary, then claiming that God alone is eternal means claiming that He alone is necessary, while everything else is contingent. However, unlike later Arabic philosophers like al-Fārābī and Avicenna, al-Kindī's theology does not focus on the idea of God's necessity. The overall thrust of argument (1) has to do not with God's modal status, but rather His transcendence. Because God is uncaused, He has no genus, in other words no predicates. Al-Kindī also associates eternity with transcendence in *Oneness*, which on closer inspection proves to be something of an *On First Philosophy* in miniature. As already mentioned, it is mostly taken up by versions of arguments (2) and (4). But it concludes with a brief section on the uniqueness of God:

> *Oneness* §16 (AR 207, RJ 147): [God] is not multiple, but one, without multiplicity—may He be praised—and He is much higher than the attributes of the heretics. He is not like His creation, because there is multiplicity in all of the creation, but none in Him at all, because He is a Maker and [created things] are made, and because He is eternal and they are not eternal, since the states of what changes change, and what changes is not eternal.

In this treatise, we find al-Kindī already linking the concepts of divine oneness (here meaning both monotheism and divine simplicity), immutability, and ineffability with the concept of eternity.

This is confirmed in another work, mentioned several times already, in which al-Kindī uses material from Porphyry's *Isagoge* to refute the Christian doctrine of the Trinity. The treatise begins with a general argument against the Trinity:

> *Against the Trinity* §1 (RJ 123): [The Christians] assert that [each of] the three Persons is a single, eternal [*lam yazal*] substance. By "Persons" [the Christians] mean "individuals [*ashkhāṣ*]," and by "single substance" they mean that each one of [the Persons] exists with its own proper characteristic. Therefore the concept of substance is found in each one of the Persons, and they agree in this; but each one of them [also] has an everlasting proper characteristic through which it is differentiated from its companions [sc. the other two Persons]. So it is necessary, given this, that each one of them is composed from substance, which is common to [all of] them, and proper characteristic, which is proper to it [alone]. But everything composed is caused, and everything caused is not eternal [*azalī*]. Therefore the Father is not eternal, nor is the Son eternal, nor is the Holy Spirit eternal. Therefore the eternal is not the eternal, and this is a repugnant contradiction.

The crucial premises in this argument are given in the antepenultimate sentence: "everything composed is caused, and everything caused is not eternal." Here, just as he does in argument (1), al-Kindī asserts without explanation that the eternal is uncaused. But he does more than this: he claims that anything uncaused is simple. This is because anything that has a cause is "put together" or composed by that cause. An example might be that to make a physical object, matter must be combined with form (compare with argument [3], discussed above). Eternity, uncausedness and utter simplicity turn out to be mutually entailing.

Al-Kindī returns to this point throughout *Against the Christians*. Going through each of the five "voices" of Porphyry's *Isagoge*—genus, species, individual, difference, and common accident—al-Kindī shows that a Person of the Trinity can be none of these. For each of these voices involves some composition or multiplicity. Al-Kindī's arguments are very like those of section 3 of *On First Philosophy*. For instance a genus cannot be simple because it is made up of a multiplicity of species, which are in turn made up of multiple individuals (§2, RJ 123). Each stage in the argument reasserts that God cannot be subject to these multiplying concepts because He is eternal. So again, eternity is equated with absolute simplicity, which means of course that nothing other than God can be called truly eternal.

Above, I argued for the unity of *On First Philosophy* on methodological grounds, on the basis that the eternity arguments are purely "intellectual" and thus have a proper place in a work on metaphysics. Now we can see that *On First Philosophy* is unified at the doctrinal level as well. The eternity arguments are meant to establish the uniqueness and transcendence of God indirectly, by showing that nothing in the created world can partake of eternity in the sense of infinite being.[42] Since this is his objective, al-Kindī concerns himself only with showing that creation cannot be actually infinite; potential infinity presents no challenge to God's preeminence. For when al-Kindī says that God is "eternal," he means much more than just that God exists for an indefinitely long period of time. Indeed, given al-Kindī's insistence that time is a quantity always associated with moving bodies, God cannot be subject to time at all. Instead we find God described early in *On First Philosophy* as "the cause of time" (§I.5, AR 101, RJ 11).[43] The truly eternal is not just that which can last for an indefinite future time. It is the *actually* infinite, and thus the transcendent. This fact reemerges towards the end of *On First Philosophy*, as a way of recapitulating al-Kindī's argument for divine simplicity. Referring back to argument (1), he says, "we have already said that what has a genus is not eternal, and that the eternal has no genus. Thus the true One is eternal, and is never multiple at all, in any way" (§XIX.1, AR 153, RJ 83).

All of this helps to explain why al-Kindī included his eternity arguments in *On First Philosophy*. It is, however, somewhat less clear why he should repeatedly equate eternity with transcendence and simplicity. Perhaps he is here drawing on Neoplatonic sources. The idea that the eternal is not everlasting but in fact atemporal is introduced into Neoplatonism already by Plotinus, and becomes standard in the tradition. Both the Arabic Plotinus and the Arabic Proclus duly associate eternity with immaterial entities that transcend and cause our physical world. On the other hand, both of these texts at least sometimes say that God Himself is *beyond* eternity, with eternity belonging instead to His first effect, the universal intellect.[44] When these texts stress God's transcendence, they do so by saying that He is *not* eternal, rather than by saying, as al-Kindī does, that eternity implies simplicity and hence ineffability. This makes it awkward to explain his view by appealing to their influence alone.

A more promising approach would be to consider al-Kindī's immediate historical context. The most striking fact about intellectual life under the ʿAbbāsid caliphs al-Maʾmūn and al-Muʿtaṣim, with the exception of their support for the translation movement, was that they enforced acceptance of a fairly abstruse theological doctrine: the createdness of the Koran. In a ruthless inquisition or *miḥna*, the caliphs forced their subjects to profess that the Koran is not eternal, but created. As far as I know no one has thought to connect this with al-Kindī's insistence that God alone is eternal. But such a connection seems to me to provide a powerful explanation for several aspects of al-Kindī's discussion of eternity. For one thing, we have his composition of numerous treatises on the topic. It seems the eternity question was of particular interest to his contemporaries and sponsors, including the caliph's own family. The context of the *miḥna* would certainly explain this. More tellingly, the uniting themes of *On First Philosophy* as I have just outlined them bear a strong resemblance to the intellectual underpinnings of the dogma of the Koran's creation.

In order to show this I will need to give a quick summary of the history of this theological doctrine.[45] Those who said the Koran is created were reacting against literalist theologians, who were often scholars of *ḥadīth*, the sayings and actions of the Prophet. For the literalists the Koran was to be taken at face value when it speaks of God's having bodily parts, or sitting on a throne, for instance. They also took literally various statements made of God, such as that He is sometimes wrathful, that He is wise, just, etc. For them, these statements hold true much as they would for a wrathful, wise, or just man: in virtue of distinct attributes predicated of God. Another, more austere conception of God, associated with Mu'tazilite theology, was developed in reaction against this literalism. The Mu'tazilites and others held not only that God was incorporeal, but that God's attributes [*ṣifāt*] are not accidents distinct from or added to God, the way that attributes of created things are accidents distinct from those things. Rather, these attributes are identical with God or His essence.[46] All things other than God are furthermore incomparable to Him, since as the Koran itself says, "there is nothing like to Him" (42:11).

The controversy over the creation of the Koran resulted when these two sorts of theologians, the literalist and the austere, tried to explain how the Koran can be the word of God and yet not identical with God Himself. For the literalists, it was easy to maintain an intimate relationship between Koran and God while admitting that the two were distinct: the Koran, as God's word, was just one more attribute. Specifically, the most reknowned and stubborn defender of the Koran's uncreatedness, Ibn Ḥanbal, related God's word to His "knowledge [*'ilm*]," and said that he did not see how the Koran could be created if it was included within divine knowledge.[47] By contrast, theologians sympathetic to a more austere theology introduced the claim that the Koran is "created [*makhlūq*]," in order to emphasize the radical transcendence of their simple God over all other things, including His own revelation. For them the Koran's createdness follows immediately from the admission that it is distinct from God, because there are only two categories of thing: Creator and created. If the Koran is not the former, they argued, it must be the latter. But for the traditionalists this was a false dichotomy. They said the Koran is neither created nor Creator.

The austere theologians appealed to passages in the Koran itself to support their view, in particular 43:3, where God says "we have made it [*ja'alnāhū*] an Arabic Koran." They also accused the literalists of portraying the Koran much as the Christians portrayed Jesus, making God immanent in something distinct from the divine essence.[48] Both of these dialectical moves are made in letters written by the caliph al-Ma'mūn, in which he first imposed the dogma of the Koran's creation. These letters are preserved in the great *History* of al-Ṭabarī.[49] Al-Ma'mūn had already proclaimed the createdness of the Koran in 827 A.D., but he waited until 833 to require a "test" or "inquisition" (*miḥna*), in which literalists were forced to admit that the Koran is created. It is too simple to say that al-Ma'mūn did this because he embraced Mu'tazilite doctrine. I have already remarked (chapter 2) that "Mu'tazilism" is a rather ill-defined term for this early period. A good example of this is that the chief intellectual father of the doctrine of the Koran's createdness was one Bishr al-Marīsī. But he was no Mu'tazilite, as is clear from his affirmation of predestination.[50] On the other hand a central agent in the imposition of the *miḥna*, Ibn Abī Duwād, had more straightforwardly "Mu'tazilite" credentials. Rather than saying that al-Ma'mūn was imposing Mu'tazilite doctrine, it would be safer to say that the *miḥna* reflected the anti-literalist tendencies of a variety of theologians who disagreed significantly on other points. Al-Ma'mūn's political reasons for imposing the *miḥna* are also far from straightforward. He clearly wished to reinforce his position as a religious authority as well as a secular leader, but this does not explain why he chose this particular issue to make a stand.[51] In any case, al-Ma'mūn died soon after promulgating the *miḥna*, before full coercion could be brought against Ibn Ḥanbal, one of the only literalists to defy openly the caliphal decree. Ultimately Ibn Ḥanbal would, in a sense, prevail. Under al-Kindī's patron al-Mu'taṣim, he was flogged but then released, and his doctrine that the Koran is "uncreated" would soon become orthodox belief.

The central question in the controversy, as already mentioned, was usually put by asking whether the Koran is created or eternal. Wilferd Madelung, though, has shown that the literalists, at least early on, did not claim that the Koran was "eternal" (*qadīm*).[52] This was rather a polemical characterization of the literalist view by its opponents, found already in the first letter of al-Ma'mūn promulgating the *miḥna*.[53] The train of thought expressed by al-Ma'mūn seems to be the following: if the Koran is not created (*makhlūq*), then it is eternal. But then it would not be "made [*maj'ūl*]" or "originated [*muḥdath*]," and one could not say of it that "it was not, and then it was."[54] In that case, God would not be "prior" to the Koran. This would put the Koran on a par with God Himself, which is a violation of God's *tawḥīd* (His "oneness" or "uniqueness").[55] Al-Ma'mūn thus rejects all of these claims. He insists that God is prior to all things owing to His preeminence (*taqaddum bi-awwaliyyatihī*), that He cannot be compared to anything distinct from Him,[56] and that the Koran is created and hence "limited" or "finite" (*maḥdūd*).[57] Central to the doctrine enforced in the *miḥna*, then, was the contrast between that which is divine, prior, eternal, and infinite, and that which is created, posterior, temporally originated, and finite. The literalist view, on the other hand, required accepting a middle ground between the Creator and the created, and saying that God's attributes, including His "word," the Koran, were posterior to His essence and yet also "uncreated."[58] Eventually the literalists would describe their view by saying that the Koran is eternal, thus adopting the language of their opponents.

The central contrast made by al-Ma'mūn's letters, between the eternal and the created, is also a central contrast of al-Kindī's of *On First Philosophy*, expressed most clearly in argument (1) in the section on the eternity of the world. As we saw, this passage equates the eternal with the uncaused and simple. Hence, the only eternal thing is God, and God does not have a multiplicity of attributes, or indeed multiplicity of any sort. As we also saw, the passage does not actually argue for reserving eternity to God alone. It merely assumes, as had al-Ma'mūn, that all things are created or eternal, and that these are mutually exclusive. The rest of section 2, however, does try to exclude the possibility of anything eternal apart from a simple God. Obviously, al-Kindī does not explicitly mention the Koran as a candidate for an eternal object distinct from God's essence. But I think his readers could not have missed the relevance of his arguments for the most heated theological controversy of the day. This is, of course, not to say that al-Kindī is directly arguing in favor of the *miḥna* itself, especially as a political policy.[59] It is, rather, to say that al-Kindī is expressing his agreement with the general theological principles behind the doctrine of the

Koran's creation, and adding arguments in favor of these principles, especially the uniqueness of a simple God as the only eternal thing.[60]

The dispute over the Koran's createdness was an initial skirmish in a long-running battle between the austerity of Mu'tazilite theology and a variety of more literalist views, which would later find their most powerful and successful expression in the Ash'arite school of *kalām*. Al-Kindī's great insight was that Greek arguments regarding the eternity of the world, which he had from Philoponus, could be pressed into the service of an austere Islamic theology denying the eternity of anything other than God. An insistence on the Koran's createdness was the most prominent manifestation of this austere theology under the 'Abbāsids. But al-Kindī was right to see that the issue had always been broader than just the status of the Koran,[61] and had to do with whether anything other than an absolutely simple God can be "eternal," in the sense of actually infinite. As we saw (chapter 1), Ibn Ḥazm and Ṣā'id al-Andalusī would later refer to *On First Philosophy* by the title *Kitāb al-Tawḥīd*, suggesting that is a work devoted to proving God's oneness and uniqueness. Whether or not this is a title al-Kindī himself gave the work, it is a perfectly accurate description of the contents that have come down to us.

5

PSYCHOLOGY

Soul, Intellect, and Knowledge

Al-Kindī's psychology—his account of soul, the intellect, and how humans know about the world through soul and intellect—is among the more vexed areas of his thought. His statements on the subject are difficult to bring together as a coherent theory, and he is often elusive on matters of central philosophical importance. The good news is that we are in possession of a number of works dealing with psychological issues. Three works bear directly on the nature of the soul: *Discourse on the Soul*, *That There Are Incorporeal Substances,* and *Short Statement on the Soul*, which like *On the True Agent* looks like a fragment from a lost work. With regard to the intellect there is *On the Intellect*, which has attracted considerable interest as the first Arabic work to provide a four-fold taxonomy of intellect. We find similar accounts later in authors such as al-Fārābī and Avicenna. Finally, there are works dealing with two other psychic phenomena, memory and imagination: *On Recollection* and *On Sleep and Dream*. And of course there are relevant passages scattered elsewhere through the corpus, notably in *On First Philosophy*.

Al-Kindī's chief claim about the soul is that it is incorporeal, and hence immortal. This raises a problem, familiar from other dualist theories of human psychology: how exactly does the immaterial soul relate to the material body? A parallel problem arises in the epistemological sphere: is al-Kindī's theory of knowledge bifurcated in the way his account of human nature is bifurcated, or is our knowledge of material objects somehow related to our knowledge of immaterial objects? These are the two difficulties that will occupy us most in this chapter.

Soul and Body

The best place to start is *That There Are Incorporeal Substances*. As the title indicates, this epistle presents itself at first as a general study of the question of whether there are any incorporeal substances at all. But the actual purpose of the treatise is to show that the human soul is such a substance. To this end, al-Kindī deploys concepts from Aristotle's *Categories* to provide what looks to be a novel, though admittedly rather strange, argument for the soul's immateriality. The introduction to the treatise says that it "presupposes a knowledge of natural things" (§1, AR 265). In what follows, though, the only principle that looks remotely physical is the claim that the "quiddity [*mā'iyya*] of body" is "extension in three dimensions, namely length, width and depth" (§2, AR 265–6). And even this principle is never used explicitly in the subsequent argument.

Rather, al-Kindī makes use of a distinction between "univocal" and "equivocal" characterization (*na't mutawāṭa'* as opposed to *na't mutashābih*, §2). If A characterizes B univocally, then A gives B its name and definition; if it does so equivocally then A and B do not share a name and definition. For example, "human" characterizes me univocally, because "human" and I share a definition (rational, mortal animal) and a name ("human"). "Human" characterizes a picture of me equivocally, because a picture of me is not a rational, mortal animal, and though we might call the figure in the picture "human" we would do so only in an extended sense, meaning that it is a picture *of* a human. As some readers will have spotted, this distinction is the same as the one made by Aristotle in chapter 1 of the *Categories*. Al-Kindī wants to connect this idea of univocal characterization to the idea of substantial predication, which Aristotle raises in chapter 2 of the *Categories*. That is, if A gives B its name and definition, then A is the essence of B (§5, AR 267; in this treatise al-Kindī uses the terms *dhāt* and *'ayn* for "essence"). Conversely, if A is the essence of B, we may conclude that A and B share a name and definition; or, as al-Kindī puts it, they "share the same nature" (§5, AR 267). By contrast, if A is predicated of B but A is *not* the essence of B, then A and B do not share the same nature. This applies to accidental predication; for example I am bald, but I do not share a definition or nature with "bald."[1]

The heart of the treatise is an argument applying these distinctions to the soul. First, in §3 (AR 266), al-Kindī establishes that the body as such is not essentially alive. If it were, then when I died, my body would cease to be a body. (Perhaps the reader is meant to recall the aforementioned definition of body as what is extended in three dimensions: a corpse is still extended in three dimensions, and is therefore a body, though it is no longer alive.) Since body is only accidentally alive, it is not my having a body that explains my being alive; rather, it is my having a soul, which is the "quiddity of life in the body [*mā'iyya al-ḥayāt fī 'l-jism*]" (§4, AR 266). Al-Kindī then wants to establish that the soul is, first, a substance in its own right, and second, an incorporeal substance.

To prove that the soul is a substance, al-Kindī puts to use the conceptual equipment he has taken from the opening chapters of the *Categories*. Soul may be accidentally related to the body, but it is essentially related to the living being as such. In other words, soul gives the living being its name and definition, for the living being "is what it is through the soul" (§6, AR 267). That means that soul and the living being will share in the same nature. Therefore, given that the living being is a substance (this seems to be assumed as uncontroversial), the soul will also be a substance. We can generalize the point, though al-Kindī does not do so explicitly: the essential form of any substance will itself be a substance.

So far, so good. Al-Kindī's argument is perhaps forbiddingly technical, but its conclusion seems to be orthodox Aristotelianism. Now, though, al-Kindī strikes out in a rather surprising direction. He does not take himself to have shown yet that soul is incorporeal. His argument for this begins as follows:

> *Incorporeal Substances* §6 (AR 267): That through which a thing is what it is [*al-shay' alladhī bi-hī al-shay' huwa mā huwa*], is the form of the thing, be it sensible or intellectual. The substance is what it is through itself [*al-jawhar mā huwa bi-'l-nafs*]. The soul [*al-nafs*], then, is the intellectual form of the living thing [*ṣūra al-ḥayy al-'aqliyya*], and is its species.

Let us expand on this dense passage. First, he says that anything is what it is through its form. Something white, for instance, is white because it possesses the form *white*. But only substances are what they are through themselves. For example, a frog is a frog simply in virtue of being what it is, whereas a table is white not in virtue of being a table, but in virtue of the white paint that coats it. In Arabic this can be expressed, as al-Kindī expresses it here, by saying that the substance is what it is "through itself," *bi-'l-nafs*. But *nafs* also means "soul." Therefore in the case of the *living* substance, it is the soul (*nafs*) through which the substance is what it is, and that means that soul is the form of the thing. This argument seems, then, to equivocate on the term *nafs*. But arguably the equivocation is not vicious, insofar as the soul has already been explicitly identified as the "quiddity [*mā'iyya*]" of the living thing (§4, AR 266), and implicitly as its essence or self (*'ayn*, *dhāt*). With this in mind we might suppose that al-Kindī regards it as already proven that my soul is my essence; here he is just trying to explain that that means my soul is my form.

But there is still a problem. Note that al-Kindī calls soul not only the form of the living thing, but the *intellectual* form of the living thing, and hence the *species* of the living thing. He then goes on to argue in some detail that species are incorporeal, and it is this that shows that soul is incorporeal. This seems simply bizarre. Why should I think that my soul is itself the species to which I belong (the species *human*)? To understand why al-Kindī makes this move we need to remember that the text he is primarily using here is the *Categories* which, notoriously, makes no use of the notion of form. In the context of the *Categories*, what is predicated essentially of an object is not the form of that object, but the species to which that object belongs; for example, the species *frog* is predicated essentially of all frogs. Now, al-Kindī is being faithful to Aristotle when he says that such a species is itself a substance, though he suppresses the fact that a species is for Aristotle a *secondary* substance,[2] whereas (in the *Categories* at least) primary substances are the members of the species, for example individual frogs. But by claiming that the soul is itself the species of the living thing, al-Kindī has conflated the species universals of the *Categories* with the substantial forms of other Aristotelian works, like the *Physics*, *De Anima,* and *Metaphysics*. Of course scholars today disagree about how a human's substantial form relates to the universal species *human*, especially in the *Metaphysics*. Al-Kindī's implicit stance on the question is that the two should simply be identified. It is not clear whether he is aware of the potential difficulties of such a view. In the present context, there is at least one problem that should have been obvious to him, namely that there is only one species *human*, whereas there are many humans and, one would have thought, many human souls.[3]

In any case, all of this means that for al-Kindī to show that the soul is incorporeal, he need only show that species are incorporeal. He does so using the now familiar method of dichotomous argument. If a species is a body, he says, then it is either present in each member of the species as a whole or as a part. But neither option is possible, so species are incorporeal. The argument against the first of the two options is rather obscure:

> *Incorporeal Substances* §8 (AR 268): The species is composed of different things, for example "man" is composed of animal, rational, and mortal. Every one of its genera and specific differences are also composed of what defines them, i.e. of that from which its definition is assembled. Therefore, the parts from which it is composed are different from one another. Since the species is not made up of similar parts, if the species is completely present in one of its individual members, then how can it be completely present in another [member of the same species]?

I cannot claim to understand this with any confidence, but perhaps the point is as follows. If one body is wholly present in many things, then that body must be homogeneous. For example, every part of a body of water is wholly and completely water. Thus, if water saturates a sponge, then water is wholly present in every part of the sponge. But species are not homogeneous: rather they have parts that differ from one another (for instance the "parts" of the species *man* are *animal*, *rational,* and *mortal*). So if species is a body then it cannot be present as a whole in each member of the species. The argument against the second option (§9, AR 268–9) is clearer: the membership of a species is potentially infinite in magnitude. There can, for instance, always be more frogs. So if the species consists in parts that are present severally in the members of the species, it will never be fully actual—those parts of the species *frog* that would be in the frogs yet to come will be potential, and there will always be such potential parts.

Both options refuted, al-Kindī concludes that species cannot be corporeal. Since the soul has been identified as the species of the living thing, and since we already showed earlier that it is a substance, we now see that the soul is an incorporeal substance. When al-Kindī states this conclusion he phrases it in an ambiguous way: "so necessarily there are many incorporeal substances" (§10, AR 269). This may mean that every one of the many species is an incorporeal substance, by the dichotomous argument just given; so that for example, *frog*, *horse,* and *human* are distinct incorporeal substances. Or, it may mean that every soul is an incorporeal substance and there are many souls, one for each living being. As mentioned above, this would not sit well with the claim that the soul is itself the species of the living thing, because whereas three humans would have three souls, they all share in only one species. But al-Kindī seems to be unaware of this problem.

In any case, this concludes the argument of *Incorporeal Substances*. Though, as we have seen, al-Kindī's argument draws heavily on Aristotle's *Categories*, it is clear that the upshot of his argument is rather Platonic. Indeed the central thesis of the treatise is more reminiscent of the *Phaedo* than anything in the Aristotelian corpus. This takes us to another text of al-Kindī's, a brief passage found in the Istanbul manuscript labeled "Statement of al-Kindī on the soul, concise and brief [*Kalām al-Kindī fī 'l-nafs, mukhtaṣar wajīz*]." The lack of any introductory comments and the abrupt ending suggests that this may be a fragment taken from a larger Kindian work that is now lost. The content is also rather enigmatic, but it underscores our impression that al-Kindī's views on the soul were meant to combine the doctrines of both Aristotle and Plato. The text begins as follows:

> *Short Statement on the Soul* §1–2 (AR 281): Al-Kindī said: Aristotle says about the soul that it is a simple substance, and that it makes its acts manifest through bodies [*ajrām*]. Plato says that it is united to the body [*jism*], and likewise that the union with the body [*jism*] extends to the bodies [*ajrām*] and acts upon them. He distinguishes between *jirm* and *jism*, saying that *jirm* is those sensible substances which bear accidents in the world of generation, whereas a *jism* is, for instance, the celestial sphere.
>
> One might think that these two statements are contradictory [with what Aristotle and Plato say elsewhere],[4] for they both maintain elsewhere that the soul is a substance with no length, width, or depth. Both of them maintain that the soul is said to be conjoined to the celestial body only with respect to its acts, which are made manifest in the celestial body and through the celestial body. They do not maintain that [the soul] is conjoined to [the celestial body] the way that celestial bodies and sublunary bodies conjoin [to other celestial or sublunary bodies]. Both maintain, somewhere in their works, that the acts of the soul are manifest only in the sublunary bodies, which fall under generation, through the intermediary of the celestial sphere.

The first thing to notice is this passage's insistence on the agreement between Aristotle and Plato. In §2 we have a series of theses attributed to Plato and Aristotle together, including the claim, familiar from *That There Are Incorporeal Substances*, that the soul is not three-dimensional, that is, that it is not a body. This is a particularly striking example of al-Kindī's general tendency to present the Greek tradition as a single, harmonious whole (see above, chapter 2). He also shows himself concerned to stress that both Plato and Aristotle are internally consistent, that is, that the statements that begin the fragment do not conflict with their statements elsewhere.

Doctrinally, matters are more complex. For one thing we have a strange, and in al-Kindī unique, contrast between the terms *jirm* and *jism*. Normally he uses these as synonyms, but here *jism* is reserved for celestial bodies,[5] whereas *jirm* means sublunary bodies. Obviously the question arises as to whether this terminological distinction reflects any similar distinction in Greek. Possibly *jism* is meant to render *aether*, the so-called fifth element out of which Aristotle's heavens are made. But of course *aether* does not mean "body" and there is, as far as I know, no Greek text in which two synonyms both meaning "body" are distinguished as referring to heavenly and sublunary bodies. Possibly al-Kindī was simply misled by the use of two different, but synonymous terms in the Arabic translations he was reading. In any case, the view ascribed here to Plato is that the soul is associated in the first instance with celestial bodies: it is united to them, and its union "extends to [*yuwāṣilu*]"[6] the sublunary bodies and acts upon them (*yaf'alu fī-hā*). There is apparent agreement here with the Aristotle quotation, which likewise says that the soul's actions are made manifest through bodies. The term here for "bodies" is *ajrām*, which are sublunary bodies, if we should read the terminological distinction back into the Aristotle citation. Similarly, if we are to read the terminological distinction forward into §2,[7] then we have both Aristotle and Plato saying that the soul is conjoined to the *celestial* body, and making its acts manifest "in [*fī*]" and "through [*bi-*]" the celestial body.

This, it might be thought, is also pretty strange, as a reading of either Plato or Aristotle. However it was traditional in Platonism to hold that souls have, before birth and after death, a relationship with celestial bodies.[8] Al-Kindī apparently has at least a dim awareness of this doctrine, and is willing to go along with it to some extent. But he also wants to deny a Neoplatonic theory sometimes associated with this, according to which the human soul possesses a "soul vehicle [*okhêma*]" in which it primarily resides.[9] This comes out in section 3 of the fragment, where he denies that the soul "clothes itself with a celestial body by which it enters into and goes out of a sublunary body." He seems to find this simply ridiculous: "this is manifestly wrong, and is a view that would not be held even by someone below the rank of Plato." There follows a brief refutation of the view in §4 (AR 282).

There is one other issue raised by this brief text, which is the question of how the soul relates to the body—any body, whether celestial or sublunary. Al-Kindī is insistent, as we would expect from *Incorporeal Substances*, that the soul is completely distinct from the body. He denies that it is spatially extended, and that soul relates to body the way bodies relate to each other. He also says several times that, for Aristotle and Plato, the extent of the soul's relation to body is that it manifests its actions *(afʿāl)* through the body. And even this limited interaction between soul and body would seem to be a temporary affair, in the case of the sublunary bodies. All of this should be borne in mind as we turn to the longest of our three texts on the nature of the soul, the *Discourse on the Soul*.

In contrast to *Incorporeal Substances*, the *Discourse* seems to show al-Kindī at his *least* original. It consists almost entirely of putative quotes from Greek philosophers, namely Plato, Pythagoras (if this is the correct reading of the name, which is unclear in the manuscript), and Aristotle. It is just as much a work of ethics and eschatology as a work of psychology, and in fact offers little in the way of explicit doctrine about the nature of the human soul. Furthermore, it proceeds mostly by way of exhortation and colorful metaphor; even the section based on Aristotle (§VI) has nothing to do with *De Anima* or any other Aristotelian work familiar to us, but instead presents an anecdote about a visionary Greek king.[10] We are, then, quite distant from the technical considerations we have seen so far in this chapter, as well as those we will soon see in works like *On Intellect* and *On Sleep and Dream*. This invites the thought that the *Discourse* should be discounted in a detailed consideration of al-Kindī's psychology, especially if it is simply a recapitulation of a Greek source or sources with little or no input from al-Kindī himself. Certainly some works by al-Kindī do consist mostly of transmitted Greek material (for example *On Definitions* and the *Sayings of Socrates*, on which see chapter 6). On the other hand, al-Kindī is clearly quoting the Greek views with emphatic approval. In one instance (§II.4, AR 274) he explicitly asserts the truth of the views ascribed to Plato. So if we cannot square the teaching of the *Discourse* with the doctrines in al-Kindī's other works, we may just have to conclude that this is an area of al-Kindī's thought where he is inconsistent.

I think, however, that a closer examination of the *Discourse* will reveal that it is neither so discontinuous with the rest of his psychological writings, nor so fortuitous in the selection of its content, as we might at first believe. The most obvious unifying aspect is that al-Kindī begins and ends the *Discourse*, speaking in his own voice, with the blunt claim that the soul is a "simple substance [*jawhar basīṭ*]." At the end (§VII.3, AR 280), he presents this as the epitome of all that the ancients had to say about the soul. This suggests that the soul's status as an incorporeal substance is central to the *Discourse*, perhaps even its overarching theme—and if so, that would of course bring its concerns closer to the those of the two texts we've already examined. Let us see whether this is borne out by the rest of the treatise.

It begins with the assertion that the soul is not only simple, but also divine, being "from the substance of the Creator, like the light of the sun from the sun" (§I.2, AR 273). (Charles Genequand has suggested convincingly that this is an echo of texts found in the Greek Hermetic corpus.)[11] There follows a section of text which begins, "he has shown that [*wa qad bayyana*] . . ." (§II.1, AR 273). It is not clear who "he" is, but the argument that follows seems to derive from Plato, who is the first author to be named explicitly in what follows (§II.3). The first topic discussed (§II.2) is the phenomenon of self-restraint. For example, sometimes we have the urge to become angry, but we restrain ourselves, or we have a desire but refrain from acting on it. This, in a rather schematic form, is the argument of Plato's *Republic*, 436b and following, which is designed to show that the soul has multiple parts. For example, there is a part of the soul that desires drink, and a part of the soul that is capable of restraining this desire (439c): it cannot be the same part that both desires and restrains, because nothing can be opposed to itself. The three parts of the soul recognized by al-Kindī are also taken from the *Republic*: the intellective part, the *thumos* or spirited part (which feels anger, for instance), and the desiring part.[12]

Now, this tripartition of the soul is often thought to pose a problem for Plato: if the soul is a simple, incorruptible, and immaterial substance (as he seems to say in the *Phaedo*), then how can it have parts? But this problem does not arise for al-Kindī, as is clear from a closer look at his discussion of the soul's faculties:

> *Discourse on the Soul* §II.2 (AR 273): This soul is separated from this body and different from it, and its substance is a divine, spiritual substance, as is seen from the nobility of its nature and its opposition to the desires and irascibility that befall the body. This is because the irascible faculty moves man at some times, and incites him to commit a serious transgression. But this soul is opposed to it, and prohibits the anger from committing its act, or from pursuing rage and its vengeance, and restrains it, just as the horseman restrains the horse, when it is about to bolt from him or take fright. And this is a clear proof that *the faculty by which the man becomes angry is not this soul.* . . . As for the desiring faculty, it longs at certain times for certain desires, and *the intellectual soul* considers that it is a mistake, and that it leads to a deplorable state, and thus it prohibits this [state] and opposes it. And this is also a proof that each one of them [sc. the soul and the desiring faculty] is different from the other.

The doctrine being presented here is not that the soul has three parts. Rather it is that there is an opposition between the soul itself and its lower faculties. The intellectual soul (*al-nafs al-ʿaqliyya*), then, *is* the soul, rather than being one of the soul's parts. Anger, desire, and the like are not parts of the soul either, but "faculties" or "powers" (*quwan*). In the *Discourse*, it is not even clear that anger and desire have anything to do with the soul at all; one has rather the impression that they are powers of the body which are resisted by the intellectual soul. In another work, *On the Prostration of the Outermost Sphere*, al-Kindī does say that the rational, irascible and desiring faculty are "powers of the soul [*al-quwan al-nafsāniyya*]" (§VI.4, AR 255, RJ 193). But even there he adds that the irascible and desiring faculties "belong incidentally[13] to the living thing that is generated and corrupted, in order to set right a shortcoming in it [e.g. to supply it with food]. But the rational power is for the perfection of its excellence." So again, it seems that it is the rational or intellectual power that defines the nature of the soul.[14]

This goes some way towards solving the problem mentioned at the outset of the chapter: if soul is immaterial, how does it relate to the body? The answer is that some of the soul's activities, albeit activities that are not essential to it, are "made manifest through the body" (as the *Short Statement on the Soul* has it). I take this to be tantamount to the claim in the

Discourse and elsewhere that there are psychic powers or faculties that are realized in the body, though the soul as such is intellective and intellection is not realized in the body. It follows that the human soul can exist and fulfill its nature perfectly (by engaging in intellection) even without the body. So it comes as no surprise to learn that al-Kindī's Greek philosophers think that the soul can survive the death of the body, and that it is precisely when it is freed from the body that the soul has its best chance to come to its proper, intellectual realm. This realm, "the world of divinity," is said to be "behind the celestial sphere" (§V.1, AR 278), a claim that is explicated in the second section ascribed to Plato. According to al-Kindī's Plato, after the death of the body the soul comes to be associated with each of the heavenly spheres in turn, gradually being purified until it is freed from any association with the body (§V.1–2). Here one is reminded irresistibly of the *Short Statement on the Soul* and the idea that the soul acts through the celestial bodies as well as sublunary ones.

This brings us back to the problem of how well the *Discourse* fits with the rest of al-Kindī's psychology, and whether he has a consistent position on the relation of soul to body. Clearly the texts we have examined draw on different sources, with the *Discourse* in particular showing influence from the Hermetic and Neoplatonic traditions, which seem to serve as a filter for doctrines that originate in genuine Platonic works such as the *Republic* and *Phaedo*.[15] By contrast *Incorporeal Substances* is influenced chiefly by Aristotle's *Categories*. Yet one doctrine is consistently emphasized in all these texts: the doctrine that soul is a simple, incorporeal substance. What is striking is the lack of any attempt on al-Kindī's part to square this doctrine with Aristotle's *De Anima*, a source that is so far conspicuous only by its absence. We know that al-Kindī was, at least at some point in his career, able to read an Arabic paraphrase of the *De Anima*, which was itself influenced by Neoplatonic commentaries and probably based on an Alexandrian paraphrase of the work.[16] Why does it not exert a greater influence over his psychological teaching?

It is tempting to speculate that the works we have been examining might come from a phase of al-Kindī's career when he had not yet read this version of the *De Anima* (see above, chapter 1), or at least not yet integrated this work into his psychology. For example, nowhere in these texts do we find the formula that the soul is the form of the body in the sense that it is the body's *actuality*. We do find this formula in al-Kindī's *On Definitions*, which reports definitions of soul as the "perfection and completion" (*istikmāl, tamāmiyya*) of the body (§4, AR 165).[17] But in his other works al-Kindī seems to have avoided this conception of soul, either because he was not yet aware of it, or perhaps because it would imply that the soul depends on the body for its continued existence.[18] On the other hand, one should be careful not to confuse the Arabic paraphrase of the *De Anima* with the *De Anima* itself. For someone with the sort of dualist teaching we have found in al-Kindī, the paraphrase is more congenial than its ultimate source. It argues explicitly for the immortality of the intellectual soul (309), which is said to be a "simple substance [*jawhar mabsūṭ*]" (307), and avers that soul grasps intelligibles through itself but grasps sensibles through the instrument of sensation (311, cf. 323). If al-Kindī did already know the *De Anima* through this paraphrase when he wrote works like the *Discourse*, then he probably saw no conflict between Aristotle and the strongly dualist theory he associates with Plato and accepts as his own.[19]

Indeed, there are signs of this theory throughout al-Kindī's extant corpus, even elsewhere in *On Definitions*.[20] As we will see shortly it coheres with the epistemology of *On the Intellect*, *On Recollection* and *On Sleep and Dream*. It seems also to be at work in a passage from *On First Philosophy*, which argues that soul is not the true One. Here al-Kindī admits that emotions can affect the soul, as he must if the dire warnings in the *Discourse* about vice and the corruption of the soul are to be taken seriously. But his emphasis is largely on the intellective soul and its being subject to multiplicity, insofar as it engages in "thought [*fikr*]" (§XIX.5, AR 154, RJ 85; see further below). Finally, we can mention *On Dispelling Sadness*, which as we will see in chapter 6 is dependent on the dualist psychology we have seen in this chapter so far. In one passage, al-Kindī explains that we ought to care for the soul rather than the body, because it is our "essence [*dhāt*]" (§IV.1)—the language of this section is reminiscent of the argument in *Incorporeal Substances*. In the same section al-Kindī adds that our bodies are only the "tools" or "instruments" (*ālāt*) of our souls.[21]

It seems, then, that al-Kindī is consistent in maintaining that the soul is a self-subsisting substance, can survive the death of the body, and interacts with the body only by exercising certain "incidental" functions through the body (including sensation, presumably, as well as such things as anger and desire). Nevertheless the soul is somehow subject to the body's negative influence if it should become preoccupied with the sensible world. The soul's perfection is to occupy itself instead with things of the intellectual realm—that is, with immaterial objects of knowledge. Al-Kindī's strongly Platonizing psychology would thus lead us to expect him to provide a strongly Platonizing epistemology. If the soul is really to be so divorced from the sensible world and its objects, we will need an account of how it comes to know non-sensible things. For it does not look as though sense experience can provide any basis for intellectual knowledge. Indeed the body is an obstacle to such knowledge. To tackle this issue, we will need to understand in greater detail how al-Kindī understands the essential function of the human soul, namely rationality or intellectual thought. For this purpose we can do no better than to turn to his short treatise *On the Intellect*.

Intellect

With the exception of *On First Philosophy*, the enigmatic *On the Intellect* is al-Kindī's most famous philosophical work. This is because it inaugurates the Arabic tradition of interpreting Aristotle's theory of intellect by giving a classification of different "types" or "kinds" [*anwāʿ*] of intellect. This sort of classification will become central in the epistemologies of al-Fārābī, Avicenna, and Averroes. *On the Intellect* is also relevant for the Latin medieval tradition, having been translated in two versions by the twelfth-century translation circle in Toledo. As usual, al-Kindī looks back towards Greek sources even as he is anticipating these later developments. Unfortunately, in this case there is some doubt as to what those sources might have been. It is clear enough that *On the Intellect* is influenced by a Greek commentary (or commentaries) on Aristotle's *De Anima*, because these commentaries are the origin of the aforementioned classification of intellect into types. In a book-length study of *On the Intellect*,[22] Jean Jolivet has argued persuasively that the *De Anima* commentary of Philoponus is closer to al-Kindī's discussion than any other extant Greek commentary. But there is some doubt as to whether al-Kindī could have known this commentary directly, and as we will see, al-Kindī's epistemology is in sharp contrast to that of Philoponus on several crucial points.

On the Intellect is based on interpretations of Aristotle's treatment of intellect in *De Anima* III.4–5.[23] At the very beginning of III.4, Aristotle draws a parallel between intellection and sensation. Just as sensation is a faculty which is capable of receiving a sensible form, so intellection must be "some sort of being acted upon [*paschein*]" (429a14, cf. 429b26). And just as sensation is potentially what is sensible, so "intellect is the intelligibles potentially, in some way [*dunamei pôs esti ta noêta ho nous*]" (429b30–31; similarly intellect is said to be "not actually, but potentially, the forms [*ta eidê*]" 429a28–9). In short, sensation is potentially its object, and so is intellect. Whether sensation and intellect grasp different objects or the same objects is not clear. Aristotle says that intellect can grasp *all* things, as part of his proof that intellect has no bodily organ. This suggests that the objects of sensation are at least a subset of the objects of intellection. As we will see, though, al-Kindī believes that the domain of objects grasped by intellect is wholly distinct from the domain of objects grasped by sensation.

When the intellect actually becomes the intelligible, then thinking occurs. There is however a middle ground between the intellect in a state of absolute potentiality and the intellect in a state of actual thinking:

> *De Anima* 429b5–9: When [intellect] become the various things, as does one who is said to be a knower in actuality—this happens when one can actualize by oneself [*hotan dunêtai energein di' autou*]—then it is nonetheless potential in a sense, though not in the way it was before learning or discovering.

This passage applies the distinction between first and second actuality to thinking. When I have learned something but am not thinking about it just at the moment, I am in a state of first actuality. When I put that learning into use and actually think (which I can do "by myself") then I am in a state of second actuality. But how, precisely, is it that the potentiality of intellect is actualized, so as to produce thinking? Aristotle is less than clear about this in the present context. Famously, in *Posterior Analytics* II.19 he gives a broadly empiricist account of how *nous* ("intellect," though that may or may not be the best translation in the context of II.19) draws on sense-experience to grasp universals. But that sort of empiricist program is not obviously present in *De Anima* III.4, and as we will see it plays no role in al-Kindī's interpretation. Here, it is worth reiterating that al-Kindī would not have been able to read the *Posterior Analytics* in Arabic translation, though he may have known some ideas from it indirectly.

With some trepidation, we may now turn the page to the notorious *De Anima* III.5. This chapter begins by saying that in soul, "just as in all nature," there is something potential, like matter, and something else that is a "cause and maker [*aition kai poiêtikon*]" (430a10–12). So there is an intellect that "becomes all things [*panta ginesthai*]," and an intellect that "makes all things [*panta poiein*]," in the way that light makes potentially existing colors actual (430a14–17). This intellect, Aristotle declares, is "separate, impassive, and unmixed." It does not "sometimes think and sometimes not." Furthermore, "this alone is immortal and eternal, but we do not remember, because although this [intellect] is impassive, the passive intellect [*ho pathêtikos nous*] is corruptible" (430a22–25). Most, but not all, commentators agree that the "passive intellect" of this final passage is identical to the "potential intellect" just mentioned.[24] And they agree that this potential or passive intellect is distinct from the intellect that is the main topic of III.5, which comes to be called the "maker" or "agent" intellect (*nous poiêtikos*), a phrase never used by Aristotle himself.[25] The central challenge for commentators, then, was to integrate the potential intellect and maker intellect of III.5 into the account of III.4.

The classification of intellect we find in al-Kindī seems intended to do just that. He runs through the classification twice, briefly at the beginning of the treatise and in more detail at the end. The first type of intellect is described at first as being "always in act" (§2, AR 353), and later as "the cause and principle for all intelligible objects and secondary intellects" (§7, AR 357). It also plays the role of actualizing the intellect in the human soul, from which it is distinct (§6, AR 356). It would seem that this "first intellect" is the maker intellect of *De Anima* III.5. The claim that it is "always" thinking echoes Aristotle's statement that the maker intellect does not sometimes think, and sometimes not; like the maker intellect, it is referred to as a "cause"; it is "separate," in the sense that it transcends human soul; and it makes the potentially thinkable actually thought, which is reminiscent of the passage that compares the maker intellect to light. Finally, and perhaps most persuasively, if this "first intellect" were not the "maker intellect" of III.5, then al-Kindī's scheme would give no place to the maker intellect at all.

What of the remaining kinds of intellect? Here things are more straightforward: they are the human intellect in its various degrees of potentiality and actuality. In the first instance, prior to all learning, the human intellect is wholly unactualized yet able to take on the forms of all things. Thus, al-Kindī calls it "intellect in potency," which reflects the Greek *nous kata dunamin*, which is found in the commentary tradition. Next, we have the intellect that "is acquired by the soul," which the soul may "actualize whenever it wishes" (§8, AR 357). This is the intellect in the state described by Aristotle in III.4 as being actual, yet still in a sense potential. Al-Kindī's claim that it may be actualized at will picks up Aristotle's remark that one may put what one has learned into use "by oneself." There are two names we might give to this intellect. Following al-Kindī we might refer to it as "acquired intellect," though this is slightly confusing because al-Fārābī will later use this phrase to refer to something else. Alternatively, we could call it "dispositional intellect," since this is a term found in the Greek commentators (*nous kath' hexin*) for intellect in the state of first actuality. Finally we have the intellect that is actually thinking. This is our intellect when we are first "acquiring" an intelligible object, or when we actually think about such an object again later on. So to sum up, the four types of intellect are:

(1) The intellect that is always in act, and is outside the human soul
(2) The human intellect in a state of complete potentiality (first potentiality)
(3) The human intellect that has been acquired and may be actualized at will (second potentiality; first actuality)
(4) The human intellect that is actually thinking (second actuality)

Or, to give them proper names:

(1) The first intellect[26]
(2) The potential intellect
(3) The dispositional (or acquired) intellect
(4) The actual intellect

It is important to see that intellects (2), (3), and (4) are not distinct entities. Rather they are the same human intellect, but in different states. By contrast the "first intellect" is distinct from and transcendent above human intellect or soul. Ontologically speaking, *On the Intellect* recognizes two kinds of intellect, one human and one transcendent.

Like Aristotle, al-Kindī explains how we progress from potential intellect to actual intellect by drawing a parallel between sensation and intellection. The parallel rests on two points of similarity. First, intellect is potentially its object, just as the faculty of sensation is potentially its object. This is also the basis for the parallel in Aristotle. Second, the form that is taken on in sensation is *identical* to the sense faculty, which in turn is identical to the soul. There is no "otherness" between subject and object of sensation. And likewise for intellection:

> *On the Intellect* §5 (AR 356): When [the soul] unites with the intellectual form it and the intellectual form are not distinct, because [the soul] is not divided, such that it would undergo alteration. When it unites to the intellectual form it and the intellect are one and the same thing, subject and object of thinking [*ʿāqila wa maʿqūla*]. Therefore, the intellect and the intelligible object are one and the same thing with respect to the soul.

This stress on the identity of soul with the intelligible does not at first sight seem Aristotelian. But it may relate to Aristotle's worry in *De Anima* III.4 about whether and how intellect is "affected" or "acted upon," and to his claim that intellect has no bodily organ. Since intellect is immaterial, Aristotle did not want it to undergo alteration or motion, even though it is receptive of form: it is "acted upon" yet nonetheless "impassive [*apathes*]" (429a15). And needless to say it was at least as important to Neoplatonic commentators that the immaterial soul be immune to change. Al-Kindī betrays his own concern with this issue when he says that soul cannot be distinct from the form it grasps, because it is not "divided such that it would undergo alteration." I take this to mean that if soul were like a distinct substrate for the form it grasps, then a change from thinking about one thing to thinking about another thing would be just like any physical change where a material subject loses one form and takes on another. For similar reasons he rejects the idea that soul is like a "vessel" for the form it grasps, or like a body that takes on an image (§3, AR 354–5). Rather the soul *qua* intellect undergoes no process or transition when it thinks; it simply and all at once becomes identical with its object. The fact that the soul's simplicity is not compromised by its reception of a sensible or intelligible form thus preserves its immateriality and immutability. Al-Kindī's *On Sleep and Dream* also associates the simplicity of soul with its being identical to both sensible and intelligible objects (§VIII.1–2, AR 301–2; cf. also *On Recollection* §6).

But there is a puzzle about all of this, as we can see if we go back to the case of sensation. Does al-Kindī really want us to believe that when I look at a ripe apple, my sense-faculty becomes a ripe apple? The answer, fortunately, is no. Rather he wants us to believe that my faculty of vision becomes *red*: strictly speaking, what I sense is the sensible form, not the substance that has that form.[27] And in fact he even denies that my sense-faculty becomes identical with the *redness of the apple*. Rather, "the object of sensation belonging to the matter is distinct from the sensing soul [*fa-ammā 'l-hayūla fa-inna maḥsūsuhā ghayr al-nafs al-ḥāss*]. Therefore, with respect to matter [*min jiha al-hayūlā*] what is sensed is not what senses" (§4, AR 355). This does not, I think, exclude that the very same form has a relationship both to the apple (the "matter") and to my soul. When I see the apple and sense the form, my sense faculty does become identical with the form of red. But that need not be the same thing as becoming identical as the form of red *qua* belonging to this particular apple, since it is extrinsic to the color red that it belong to the apple. (If it were intrinsic, then it would be impossible for the very same color to belong to anything else.)

In light of the parallel between sensation and intellection already established, al-Kindī thinks these features of sensation will apply to intellect as well. Just as in sensation there is some external source or cause from which we take the sensible form—in my example, the source or cause is the apple—so in intellection there must be some external source or cause from which we take the intelligible form. An empiricist interpretation would say that this source is always a physical, sensible object. A particular apple could be the source not only of the sensible form *red* but also of such intelligible forms as *apple* and *fruit*. However, this is not the sort of interpretation al-Kindī adopts. Instead, it is here that he invokes the "first intellect" and gives it a role in explaining human intellection. Because the first intellect is, as already mentioned, always thinking all things, it is ideally suited to be the seat of all intelligibles. As al-Kindī says, using some rather odd terminology, it is the "species-ness of all things [*naw'iyya al-ashyā'*]" (§5, AR 356).[28] This doctrine is confirmed by *On First Philosophy*, which has the following to say about intellect:

> *On First Philosophy* §XIX.6 (AR 155, RJ 85): The soul is intellective in actuality when the species are unified with it. But before the species are unified with it, it is intellective in potentiality. Now, everything that belongs to something in potentiality is only brought into actuality by something else. This thing that brings something else from potentiality to actuality, is itself in actuality. So what brings the soul that is potentially intellective, to be actually intellective—i.e. that which unifies the species and genera of things, I mean their universals, with the soul—is the universals themselves. Through their union with the soul, the soul becomes intellective, that is, it comes to have a certain intellect,

> that is, to have the universals of things. Thus the universals of things, since they are in the soul, go from potentiality to actuality, and are the acquired intellect of the soul, which it had in potentiality. They are the intellect in actuality that brings the soul from potentiality to actuality.

This passage is remarkably similar in terminology to *On the Intellect*, even mentioning an "acquired intellect." And the point of the passage is the same: the soul is potentially the intelligibles, but can only become the intelligibles actually (i.e. can only think) by contacting something else that is already actually the intelligibles. This is the "intellect in actuality," the first intellect of *On the Intellect*.

We saw that al-Kindī wanted to maintain a distinction between a sensible form in matter and that sensible form in my sense-faculty. He makes the same sort of distinction in the case of intellection: "the intelligible object in the soul and the first intellect are not one thing, with respect to the first intellect. But with respect to the soul, the intellect and the intelligible object are one and the same thing" (*On the Intellect* §6, AR 357). In other words, just as red-in-the-apple is not the same as red-in-my-soul, despite both being instances of the same form *red*, so the intelligible-in-the-first-intellect is not in every respect the same as the intelligible-in-my-soul. This is important because the first intellect and my soul are both simple, and thus both absolutely identical to the intelligibles they grasp. So al-Kindī's move here is intended to prevent my soul from becoming absolutely identical to the transcendent first intellect. Because of this our intellect may be called "secondary" even when it is actually thinking,[29] although it has the same content as the first intellect. It can think of this content only intermittently and, presumably, partially, insofar as it thinks about one thing at a time instead of all possible intelligibles at once.

Although al-Kindī gets a lot of mileage out of the parallel between sensation and intellection, he also insists on a fundamental contrast between the two:

> *On the Intellect* §3 (AR 354): [Aristotle] says that forms are of two types. One of these two forms is material, and falls under sense. The other does not have matter, and falls under intellect; and these are the species of things and what is above [species, i.e. genera].

In what follows al-Kindī describes the intelligible objects as having "no matter and no *phantasia*" (§5, AR 356); this is why they are inaccessible to the faculties of sensation and imagination. One cannot, that is, see (or hear, smell, etc.) or imagine the species *human* or the genus *animal*. Rather one can grasp it only intellectually, perhaps by coming to know its definition. Now, this is on the face of it simply common sense: it would be a bold empiricist indeed who claimed that we actually *see* the species *human* when we look at Socrates.

What is more problematic is that al-Kindī, encouraged by the rigorous distinction between sensible and intelligible objects, has given sensation no role *at all* to play in the acquisition of intelligibles. Rather the intelligibles are acquired directly from the first intellect. Al-Kindī does not even claim (as Avicenna, for instance, will later do)[30] that the acquisition of intelligibles is somehow prompted or prepared by sense-experience. Nor, for that matter, does he rule this out. Indeed we are given no clue as to what occasions the bestowal of forms on the human intellect by the first intellect, with the possible exception of one ambiguous sentence. Very literally, it says: "as for the fourth, it is the intellect that is manifested from the soul whenever [the soul] actualizes [the intellect], so that from [the soul], something other than [the soul] has [the intellect] existing in actuality [*fa-kāna mawjūdan li-ghayrihā min-hā bi-'l-fi'l*]" (§7, AR 358). In other words, the soul makes this fourth intellect actual in something else. If we follow Gerhard Endress in seeing the "something else" as another human soul,[31] then al-Kindī's point here could be that one human who is already actually thinking brings another human from potentially to actually thinking. This could happen when, for instance, a mathematics teacher brings a student to grasp some mathematical concept or principle.

If this is right, then it would provide a link to Philoponus' commentary on the *De Anima*. For Philoponus also stresses the acquisition of new intelligibles through the good offices of a teacher. And, as already mentioned, in his extensive study of *On the Intellect* Jean Jolivet argued that Philoponus is the most likely Greek source for al-Kindī's treatise. I am, however, somewhat skeptical that it could have been a direct source. It seems to me more likely that al-Kindī's treatment of intellect is based on a subsequent, perhaps more summary, account that stemmed from the school of Ammonius at Alexandria and incorporated some ideas found in Philoponus but also departed from them in some respects.[32] This is shown by the fact that al-Kindī's account diverges from Philoponus' in several crucial respects.

The most obvious difference is in their handling of the maker intellect of *De Anima* III.5. While it is true, as Jolivet points out, that Philoponus and al-Kindī both have a four-fold classification of intellects, this is rather misleading. In fact Philoponus presents a three-fold classification, and then mentions more or less in passing that there is another "contemplative intellect" which is always in actuality. But this refers to God, not the maker intellect of III.5. For Philoponus the "maker intellect" is the human intellect *qua* active, in other words al-Kindī's intellect (4), not his intellect (1). The reason Philoponus thinks this is that he wants to see III.5 as Aristotle's promised discussion of whether any aspect of the human soul is immortal. It is here, according to Philoponus, that Aristotle proves that the human rational soul is immortal as well as immaterial. And although there are a couple of passing suggestions that God plays a role in actualizing human intellect,[33] in general Philoponus' epistemology in the *De Anima* commentary makes no use of any transcendent principle.

Rather, Philoponus sees the human soul as the source of its own intelligibles. For he ascribes to the Platonic theory of recollection, according to which every human soul has all intelligibles in it at birth, but in such a way that they are forgotten. When we seem to be learning, actually we are being prompted to remember these intelligibles, so as to bring them into full actuality. We are so prompted by another human intellect that is already actually grasping them, namely a teacher. And it is our soul *qua* actually thinking that survives the death of the body, which in fact will free the rational soul to engage in a life of purer intellection. When Aristotle, then, talks of a "maker intellect" that is "separable and immortal" and that is "always thinking," he means that the actually thinking human intellect makes other intellects think all things, that this intellect can survive bodily death, and that all things are always being thought of by active human intellects (though not necessarily by *my* active intellect).[34]

There is a difficulty for Philoponus in integrating the Platonic recollection theory with the Aristotelian distinction between grades of potentiality and actuality in intellect. Before an intelligible is remembered, it would seem that my intellect is not in a state of first potentiality with regard to that intellect, since after all I do know it. Nor is it in my dispositional intellect in a state of second potentiality, since I cannot think of it at will; rather I need to be prompted to remember by a teacher. And of course I am not actually thinking of these intelligibles either. Philoponus solves this problem in a characteristically clever and innovative fashion. He argues that the intelligibles are in the soul the way mathematical truths are in the soul of a *drunk* or *sleeping* mathematician, i.e. someone who does have the intelligibles in first actuality, but is somehow impeded from accessing them (39.12–15).[35] Of course the impediment is the fact of our embodiment, for the body gets in the way of intellection (cf. 20.74–6: "non enim cooperatur intellectui corpus, sed magis impedit naturales ipsius operationes").

In all this, Philoponus is staking out a position that is in stark contrast to al-Kindī's. Philoponus rules out any role for a sub-divine but still transcendent intellect. (In this respect al-Kindī's interpretation of III.5 is more like the one we find ascribed to Marinus, a student of Proclus.[36]) Philoponus does not need to posit such a transcendent intellect, because for him the intelligibles are always within the human soul, just waiting to be recollected and thus brought out into actuality. Nor does a transcendent intellect need to be invoked to explain how we achieve recollection. This is done in a more mundane fashion, by encountering another person who has already recollected, namely the teacher. By contrast, when al-Kindī says that the intellect "in potency is only actualized through something else which is that thing in act (§5, AR 356)," he goes on to make clear that the "something else" in this passage refers to the first intellect that is distinguished from any human soul. For al-Kindī we do not receive intelligibles from physical objects (as an empiricist would say), nor by discovering them within ourselves (as Plato and Philoponus would say). Rather we receive them from the first intellect, which is not God, but which is transcendent above us.

Recollection and the "Epistemic Gap"

One of the most striking features of the epistemology set out in *On the Intellect* is its stark contrast between the parallel processes of intellection and sensation. Of course these processes are closely associated with the separate soul and the body, respectively. I have already intimated that in ethical and psychological contexts, al-Kindī tends to portray the body as an obstacle to the soul's perfection, and the soul as something whose essential nature may be grasped without any reference to body or faculties exercised through the body. So one might expect his epistemology to minimize the role of such bodily faculties, and in particular sensation. We will now see that this expectation is well founded.

To see this it will be useful to distinguish between two ways of making intellection, and not sensation, the faculty through which we have knowledge. First, one might hold the relatively weak thesis that sensation and intellection have different objects, and that knowledge in the strict sense is only of the objects of intellection, i.e. universals. This would mean that we cannot have knowledge of a particular sensible object as such. But it would not necessarily mean that sensation makes no *contribution* to knowledge. One might hold, with Aristotle, that sensation somehow makes it possible for us to learn new intelligibles or universals, even though intellection and knowledge grasp universals, not sense-particulars.[37] A second, stronger thesis would be to say that sensation not only has different objects from intellection, but also makes no contribution to intellection. According to this thesis there would be an "epistemic gap" between sensation and intellection, with intellection operating on its own, and sensation serving only to distract us from the good function of intellect.

We have already seen that in *On the Intellect* al-Kindī explicitly adopts the weaker thesis, and at least implicitly the stronger thesis. Let us see whether this is borne out by his other works. A revealing text, which echoes the teaching of *On the Intellect*, is the following:

> *On First Philosophy* IV.4–5 (AR 107, RJ 19–21): Perception [*wujūd*] really consists in two things: sense-perception and intellectual perception, because things are either universal or particular. By the universal I mean the genera that belong to species, and the species that belong to individuals. By particulars I mean the individuals that belong to species. Particular individuals are material and fall under the senses [i.e. are perceptible to the senses]. On the other hand, genera and species do not fall under the senses, and are not perceived through sense-perception, but rather fall under one of the powers of the complete, that is human, soul, namely [the power] called "human intellect." Since the senses perceive individuals, all the sensibles that are represented in the soul are represented by the power that uses the senses. Conversely no concept of a species, or of what is above species [i.e. genera], is represented by the soul's using an image, because every image is sensible. Instead, it is confirmed in the soul and is perfectly certain, through the confirmation of the intellectual principles that are necessarily intelligible.

Here we have not only the familiar contrast between two kinds of cognition or perception (*wujūd*), but also a contrast between how we represent the cognized objects to ourselves. Sensation uses "images [*muthūl*]" whereas intellection does not; this will be of some importance below when we turn to a discussion of imagination. The passage certainly seems to support the weak thesis described above, but perhaps not the strong thesis. Indeed the strong thesis might seem to be contradicted by al-Kindī's consistent identification of the intelligibles as "universals." If I grasp the universal *man*, surely what I am doing is grasping a truth that applies to all particular men. In that case, it seems plausible that we learn the universal precisely through our experiences with various particulars that fall under that universal.

And in fact we have already seen (chapter 2) a passage in which al-Kindī seems to make sensation a means to intellection. This passage is in *On the Quantity of Aristotle's Books*, where al-Kindī insists that one can only achieve knowledge of "secondary substance," i.e. species and genera, through knowledge of quantity and quality. And it is *sensation*, not intellection, that grasps quantity and quality (§VI.6, AR 372). Is this not a clear-cut example in which we have knowledge of sensible objects? Indeed, is al-Kindī not saying that this knowledge of sensible objects is the basis for all further knowledge?[38] To answer this we need to remember the context: al-Kindī is defending the place of the mathematical, propaedeutic sciences as a prerequisite for all other knowledge. And these mathematical sciences (arithmetic, geometry, astronomy, and harmonics) are not studies of sensible particulars, but of numbers, lines, ratios, and the like. Sensation is only required for these sciences insofar as we first encounter number, line, ratio, and so on as inhering in a given sensible object.

We know this because, in what immediately follows, al-Kindī is very explicit that the sensible objects are *not* suitable objects of knowledge in their own right:

> *Quantity* §VI.7 (AR 372): Sensory knowledge is the knowledge of primary substance, and is in flux due to the uninterrupted flux of what is known (this ends only when the [object of knowledge] itself ends, which means that it is wholly destroyed in its substance), or because of the multiplicity of sensible substance and the multiplicity of number. For if all that is numbered is finite, and it is always possible to multiply any number, then what is numbered is potentially infinite in magnitude—if not in the number of the individuals, then in the number of multiples. But what is infinite cannot be comprehended by any knowledge.

This passage confirms al-Kindī's commitment to the weak thesis, that one cannot have intellectual knowledge of particulars as such, but only of universals. He gives two arguments for the thesis here. The second of these is that, since sensible objects are potentially infinite (there can always be more individual men, for instance), there can be no knowledge of them; for no one can know what is infinite.[39] The first argument is that particular objects are in constant change, so they do not have the stability required for objects of knowledge. Al-Kindī makes the same point elsewhere:

> *On First Philosophy* §IV.2 (AR 106, RJ 19) [Sensation] is not stable because our contact [with the sensible] can cease; [the object of sensation] flows and is in constant change, through one sort of motion or another. Its quantity is subjected to a contest between the more and the less, the equal and the unequal. Its quality varies, being similar or dissimilar, and more or less intense. Thus it is constantly passing away and unceasingly changing.

Here flux undermines not only the stability of sensible objects, but the stability of sensation itself. Note that sensible objects are in flux with regard to quality and quantity, the very features that are indispensable in the sketchy epistemology of *Quantity*.[40]

Now, these references to flux are important, since they could provide support for the strong thesis: the thesis that sensibles cannot even be a basis for the knowledge of intelligibles, and that sensation therefore has no direct role to play in the acquisition of knowledge. In the *Phaedo*'s famous argument that sensibles cannot be the source of concepts like equality, the crucial claim is that supposedly equal sensibles like sticks and stones suffer from compresence of opposites. Any stick is both equal and unequal, or no more equal than unequal. By this Plato seems to mean that stick A is equal to stick B, but unequal to stick C. However readers of Plato often conflate this problem with the problem of flux, encouraged in part by Aristotle's claim (*Metaphysics* A.6) that the flux theory led Plato to postulate Forms. From the claim that for any sensible object is always changing from F to not-F (flux), it is a short step to the claim that no sensible object is any more F than not-F (compresence of opposites). One need only add the premise that something that is changing, say, from white to not-white is, at the moment of change, in some sense both white and not-white. And in fact, in the passage just quoted from *On First Philosophy*, al-Kindī speaks of a "contest" between equality and inequality. This suggests that the sensible objects suffer from compresence of opposites. We have already seen him insist on particular examples of this, for instance that all sensibles are both one and many, acting and acted-upon (see chapter 3). So al-Kindī may well have the strong thesis in mind as well as the weak thesis in the epistemological section of *On First Philosophy*, even though he presents no explicit argument for the strong thesis here.

This interpretation gains support from a different treatise by al-Kindī. The work in question was discovered by Gerhard Endress, and discussed by him in two articles.[41] A heading or lengthy title identifies the subject of the treatise: "what the soul remembers of the things which it possessed in the world of the intellect when it comes into the world of sense-perception, and what it remembers of the things in the world of sense-perception when it comes into the world of the intellect." *On Recollection*, as I will call it, responds directly to some of the Arabic Neoplatonic works produced in his circle. As the heading just quoted indicates, it engages with two questions: first, given that the soul will survive the death of the body, what will it remember of its bodily existence? This question is taken from Plotinus, *Enneads* IV.4, via the second chapter of the so-called *Theology of Aristotle*. The second question is in a sense the converse: Platonists hold that the soul existed *before* it was in the body, but then why do we not remember anything from its non-bodily existence? This question is raised in a short *Treatise on the Soul* which is, falsely in my opinion, ascribed to Porphyry. I believe it to be rather an independent, early work composed in Arabic and based in part on the Arabic Plotinus.[42]

Though the way these questions are posed (and some of the terminology used) connects *On Recollection* to these Neoplatonic works, al-Kindī also shows a more direct awareness of the theory of recollection as it is found in Plato's *Phaedo*.[43] Unlike the *Theology* or pseudo-Porphyry, al-Kindī lays all his emphasis on Plato's claim that when we think we are learning, we are actually remembering what the soul knew before birth but forgot when it came to be in the body.[44] It seems that al-Kindī was acquainted with at least a summary of the *Phaedo*, which may also have given him some of the ideas we find in *Discourse on the Soul*. In fact, an example used by al-Kindī in *On Recollection* looks to be drawn directly from a version of the *Phaedo*. He mentions the case in which we know, by recollection, about *istiwā'*, meaning "planarity," that is, the nature of a geometrical plane. It is clear from the context that al-Kindī has geometrical planes in mind, because he also talks about an individual plane, *mustawā*. But *istiwā'* also means "equality," and of course equality (*isotês*) is the example used in the *Phaedo*'s discussion of recollection (74a–75e). Al-Kindī seems to have misunderstood the intended sense of *istiwā'* in an Arabic version or summary of the *Phaedo*, and expanded the example for use in his own *On Recollection*.[45]

This treatise accordingly emphasizes the original Platonic theory of recollection. It also depends heavily on the contrast, familiar from *On the Intellect*, between objects of intellection and objects of sensation. After the death of body, soul will remember nothing about sensible objects, "which can only be grasped and comprehended by corporeal organs"—it will have neither sense organs nor imagination, which is what we use to remember sensibles during our bodily life (§3). Likewise, the soul remembers only intelligibles from before it entered the body, because there is nothing else to remember. Now, when we recollect these intelligibles we do not realize we are remembering, but think we are learning them for the first time. Why is this? Al-Kindī's answer to this question (§4), which seems to be original with him, is rather clever. When I remember something sensible, I always imagine the particular circumstances that attended it: the place, time, and causes for that thing. (As it is said that Americans of a certain generation all remember where they were when they heard President Kennedy was shot.) But when I remember something intelligible learned before my bodily existence, there are no sensible circumstances with which to associate it; there is only the intelligible itself. We are so used to remembering things of the sensible world that when sensible circumstances are not associated with a memory, we do not realize we are remembering at all.

This is all very well, you might say, but why shouldn't I believe that things are as they seem, and that I am indeed learning intelligibles for the first time as I progress through my education? Al-Kindī's argument against this (§5) turns on the notion of "sensible differences [*fuṣūl ḥissiyya*]." These would seem to be the features belonging to a particular sensible object that my sense faculties can in fact grasp. Now, al-Kindī says, I may see a geometrical plane (suppose I am looking at a flat table top), and of course I may say that this is a plane by virtue of planarity. But I cannot use sensation to learn *what planarity is*, that is, to grasp the essence of plane figure. All I can do is sense the instance of planarity before me. To grasp the essence, the sensible "differences" that are true of this or that plane (e.g. the brown of the table top as opposed to the blue of the wall) are not helpful. I must instead "perceive [the essence] not differentiated, but known in a primary way; by 'primary,' I mean without the intervention of any intermediary at all," in other words without using sensation. Al-Kindī gives us another example, which depends on a linguistic sleight of hand. The Arabic word *nāṭiqa* means both "rational" and "speaking." So I can use sensation to notice that someone is "rational," *nāṭiqa*, because I hear him "speaking," *nāṭiqa*. (This could be based on a Greek example, since *logos* similarly means both "language" and "reason.") This is not, I think, merely wordplay. In fact a human's ability to speak really is a valid, and sensibly accessible, indication of rationality. But of course speaking is not the same thing as rationality, and to grasp what rationality is I must use my own reason, not sensation.

We finally have an answer to the question of how sense-experiences relate to intellection. Sensation merely prompts the soul to uncover the intelligibles that are already within it, by reminding it of those intelligibles. The intelligibles cannot be somehow gleaned afresh from sensation. This text is al-Kindī's clearest endorsement of the strong thesis I described at the beginning of this section. We should however be wary of simply integrating the theory of *On Recollection* into the epistemology of *On the Intellect* and *On First Philosophy*. After all, it was Philoponus' use of the theory of recollection that led us to contrast his interpretation of *De Anima* III.5 to that found in *On the Intellect*. And there is a similar tension in al-Kindī's own two accounts. *On the Intellect* says that before the soul unites to the "first intellect" it "acquires" what was previously only potentially present in it. By contrast, *On Recollection* says that "we do not know anything outside ourselves; we only remember within ourselves those things that are left to us from the beginning of our existence, that is to say, the existence of our souls" (§4). (Al-Kindī, unlike Philoponus, makes no effort to explain how something we have only temporarily forgotten could be in us "potentially but not actually.") And whereas *On the Intellect* explicitly contrasts the soul's intellect to the first intellect, *On Recollection* emphasizes the identity of soul and intellect (§7), recognizing no intellect that transcends soul.[46]

More broadly, however, *On Recollection* shows that al-Kindī did incline towards, and at least in this treatise explicitly endorse, the strong thesis that sees an "epistemic gap" between sensation and intellection. Though he does not argue so explicitly for such a gap in the other texts we have examined, neither does he set out any means by which sensation could in fact contribute to intellection. In particular he never discusses the notion of "abstracting" universals from sense-experience. He seems unaware of, or unconvinced by, Aristotle's strong empiricist commitments, at least in the texts we have examined so far. This represents a significant point of overlap between al-Kindī's works on psychology and epistemology, underwriting the strong contrast between the rational soul and the lower psychic faculties that we found in works like *Discourse on the Soul*.

There is a fly in this dualist ointment, however. The beginning of a work I have not yet mentioned, namely *On Rays* (*De Radiis*), lays out as explicit a theory of abstraction as anyone could wish for:

> *On Rays* §I: All men who perceive sensibles through sensation grasp them in a certain form. Through this grasping, and by a motion of the reason [*motu rationis*], they find that individuals perceived by sensation agree with certain forms yet differ from others. Also, when each man employs sensation through the ruling faculty, this is in agreement with the use of reason, which grasps things individually in a common form by removing those things that are not common. This grasping of the mind is intellect [*comprehensio mentalis intellectus*] which, because it grasps things in this way, is called "universal."

What is particularly striking here is the lack of any distinction between sensible and intelligible forms. To the contrary, al-Kindī seems to be saying that the intellect or reason (*ratio*) grasps the very same forms as sensation, but is able to compare two particulars and see that they do or do not share a given form. Al-Kindī does go on to argue that reason has access to notions that are not directly accessible to sense (e.g. fire's ability to heat) but even these are posited only on the basis of their sensible effects (e.g. the warmth we feel in things placed near the fire). This passage, then, seems a radical departure from the epistemology we have found in other Kindian treatises, where he relies so heavily on a sharp contrast between sensible and intelligible forms.[47]

But this may be the exception that proves the rule, if I was right to suggest (see chapter 1) that *On Rays* was written late in al-Kindī's career. The fact that *On Rays* embraces abstraction would be far easier to explain if we suppose that it was written at a different period from *On First Philosophy*, *On the Intellect,* and *On Recollection*. This would also fit well with my tentative hypothesis that al-Kindī's interests shifted away from Neoplatonizing metaphysical considerations and towards mathematically oriented, "scientific" research. Both of these developments could have been encouraged by, or caused, a shift towards empiricism (although we will see in chapter 7 that even al-Kindī's scientific output is only minimally "empiricist"). And of course it is also possible that after writing his extant psychological works, but before writing *On Rays*, al-Kindī became acquainted with new sources indicating to him the abstractionist empiricism of the Aristotelian tradition.

Imagination and Prophetic Dreams

In this discussion of al-Kindī's epistemology, I have so far looked at only two cognitive faculties belonging to humans, sensation and intellection. I have suggested that al-Kindī sees these as radically opposed to one another, and that this opposition corresponds to his dualist position on the relation of soul to body. Al-Kindī allows, however, that there are other faculties that are neither sensation nor intellect, but like sensation in some respects and like intellect in others. Most prominent among these is *phantasia* or imagination. Al-Kindī explores imagination most deeply in a treatise devoted to the phenomenon of prophetic dreams, entitled *On Sleep and Dream*. This treatise will give us a chance to see how al-Kindī deals with psychological phenomena that, so to speak, fall into the gap between intellection and sensation.

We saw above that in *On First Philosophy*, al-Kindī says that our grasp of universals does not involve "images [*muthūl*]," and that "all images are sensible." This suggests that imagination, insofar as it works with images, is to be associated with sensation more than intellection. To some extent this is confirmed by the definition of imagination provided in *On Definitions*:

> *On Definitions* §21 (AR 167): Imagination [*tawahhum*]: it is *phantasia* [*fanṭāsiyyā*], a power of soul that perceives sensible forms in the absence of their matter. And it is said: it is *phantasia*, that is, imagination [*takhayyul*], and is the presence of the forms of sensible things in the absence of their matter.

As remarked above (chapter 2), al-Kindī uses a striking variety of terms for the imaginative faculty. To the three on offer in this definition (*tawahhum*, *takhayyul*, and a transliteration of the Greek *phantasia*) *On Sleep and Dream* adds *quwwa muṣawwira*, very literally the "formative faculty."

This term must be partly intended to bring out the connection between imagination and sensible "forms [*ṣuwar*]." This sorts well with the definition just quoted, which emphasizes that even if imagination is a faculty "intermediate between sensation and the intellect" (*On Sleep and Dream* §II.2, AR 294), it nonetheless grasps only sensible forms, not intelligibles. Imagination differs from sensation primarily in that it can do this even when the sensible objects that bear these forms are no longer present (§III.2, AR 295). Another difference is that imagination is able to combine sensible forms, so as to imagine things that have not been sensed, like a man with feathers (§V.1–2, AR 299–300). However, even here al-Kindī emphasizes that it is *sensible* forms that are being combined by imagination, and thus that when we imagine "we perceive sensible forms that sensation does not perceive at all" (§V.3, AR 300).[48]

In light of this one might wonder why al-Kindī thinks imagination is intermediate between sensation and intellect, rather than putting it on a par with sensation. Al-Kindī does draw numerous distinctions between sensation and imagination, all of which at least imply the superiority of imagination. First, he says that sensation uses "secondary organs," such as the eyes, ears, and so on. These are subject to vicissitudes "due to both internal and external factors" (§III.6, AR 297)—in other words, we see poorly if disease befalls the eyes, or if external conditions impede sight (as when it is foggy, for instance). By contrast:

> *On Sleep and Dream* §III.7 (AR 297): This imaginative power grasps its object without a secondary organ that is subject to [variation in] strength and weakness. Rather, it grasps it through the separate soul. Thus it is subject to neither impurity nor corruption, even if it is in the living being that [the form] is received, through a primary organ that partakes in sensation, intellect, this imaginative power, and the other powers of the soul—namely the brain. For this member [sc. the brain] is the location for all these powers of the soul.

Because the faculty of imagination has to do with a "primary organ," namely the brain, "the imaginative power is mostly safe" from the accidents that might befall the sense faculties in the secondary organs, which are more exposed (§IV.3, AR 298).

Still more significant is the fact that, in this passage, imagination is said to grasp its object "through the separate soul," or perhaps "through nothing but the soul": *bi-'l-nafs al-mujarrada*. The faculty of imagination is "received" in the brain, but it is the immaterial soul that actually engages in imagination. This seems to be an application of the doctrine we found in *Discourse on the Soul*, according to which the faculties of soul are realized in (or "made manifest by") bodily organs, even though the soul is the subject or agent of the acts associated with those faculties.[49] To some extent, of course, one may say the same for sensation: it is not the eye that is the subject that experiences vision, but the soul.[50] But al-Kindī means more than this when he says that we imagine *bi-'l-nafs al-mujarrada*. He means that we do not need any external stimulus in order to engage in imagination. For imagination, unlike sensation, can grasp sensible forms when the "bearers" of those forms are absent. If I want to imagine a rhinoceros, I can do it at will, whereas if I want to see one, I have to go to the zoo. This feature of imagination, mentioned also by Aristotle,[51] should be compared to our ability to actualize the potential intellect; as Aristotle says, intellect can become actual "by itself [*di' autou*]" (*De Anima* 329b7).

On the other hand, imagination can only use images that have been originally taken from sensation. If I have never seen a rhinoceros, I can't imagine one. Sensation is the source on which imagination draws. Yet it is also inimical to the good function of imagination. Just as bodily desire distracts us from intellection, so use of the senses impedes the imagination. Al-Kindī refers to the phenomenon of daydreaming or being lost in thought; when one is sufficiently preoccupied with imagination, what is imagined is so lively as to be indistinguishable from forms present to sensation (§III.3, AR 295–6). Those with highly developed souls, though, are able to engage in vivid imagination even while keeping track of their sensible surroundings (§III.4, AR 296). Such people are described as being skillful in "mind and intellect [*al-dhihn wa 'l-'aql*]." I take this to mean not that imagination is actually a use of the intellective faculty, but rather that the sorts of people who are good at intellection are also good at imagining, because they are not overly influenced by sensation.

A final respect in which imagination is unlike sensation is that it need not grasp any *particular* sensible object. Any given sensible form, according to al-Kindī, will be realized only imperfectly in any given material substrate. Since imagination grasps sensible forms without their matter, and since it is not affected by any variation in the sensible organs themselves, it is able to imagine the forms as refined and uncontaminated (§IV.4–6, AR 299). This means, I think, that it is possible to imagine a human without imagining any particular person we've met; rather one can imagine a human in a more generic, or perhaps idealized, sense. But again, we should not be misled by any of this into thinking that imagination is a type of intellection or a source on which intellection may draw. It was right to say at the outset that, in the context of al-Kindī's bifurcated epistemology, imagination falls on the side of sensation. For there are two fundamental respects in which imagination is very like sensation: its objects are sensible forms, and it is realized in a bodily organ. By contrast the intellect grasps intelligible forms (universals) and is not realized in the body at all.

Now let us see how al-Kindī applies this theory of imagination to the topic at hand, namely sleep and the prophetic dream or dream-vision (*ru'yā*). As usual, al-Kindī says that the topic has been chosen by one of his sponsors, and not by himself. But it is hard to avoid the suspicion that it was in fact composed because the *Parva Naturalia* of Aristotle had just become available to al-Kindī. The *Parva Naturalia* include Aristotle's three linked treatises *On Sleep*, *On Dreams*, and *On Prophecy in Sleep*. Al-Kindī's own *On Sleep and Dream* is compelling evidence that he knew these texts in some version. Unfortunately the origins of the Arabic version of the *Parva Naturalia* are to some extent cloaked in obscurity.[52] But a manuscript discovered by Hans Daiber contains a translation of the *Parva Naturalia* that may have been produced in al-Kindī's circle, or at least at a sufficiently early date for al-Kindī to have known this translation.[53]

Of the three Aristotelian treatises on sleeping and dreaming, it is *On Sleep* that seems to have influenced al-Kindī most deeply. Aristotle believes that we become sleepy, usually after eating, because hot vapor rises to the upper parts of the body, where it is cooled by the brain and then forced back into the inside of the body. Thus when we sleep our extremities are cold, but the area around the heart is warm (see esp. 457a33–b6). The physiological purpose of sleep is to encourage digestion and growth (455a2). This is, as it were, the physical definition of sleep. Aristotle also gives what one might call a more functional definition of sleep: it is a certain kind of cessation from using the senses. This is why only creatures with sensation, but not plants, sleep (454a15–17). Sleep is thus a condition of the "primary sense organ" (see 455b10, 456a21, and 458a28–9), in which this organ is not actualized. For Aristotle this "primary organ" is, famously, the heart.

Al-Kindī's account in *On Sleep and Dream* follows Aristotle by invoking the same physiological processes to explain sleep, but it departs from Aristotle by making the brain the "primary organ" and adapting

Aristotle's theory accordingly. Rather than invoking the brain simply as the cause that cools the vapor, he introduces the idea that the brain may vary in its own degree of heat and coldness. For al-Kindī, sleep occurs when the brain is made cool and moist (§X.1, AR 306), for the brain is primary not only in imagination but also in sensation (§III.7, AR 297). Presumably this is because it is the brain that houses the "common sense faculty" that gathers together sensations from the various "secondary organs," like the eyes and ears.[54] Al-Kindī (or his source) thus reverses the causal story found in Aristotle, and claims that the brain gets colder *because* heat concentrates in the chest, producing cold vapors that rise to the brain. It is this cooling of the brain that then stops sensation, and causes sleep. It is clear from these changes that Aristotle's account has been altered to fit a theory like that of Galen, where most psychological faculties are realized in the brain, rather than the heart. But in other respects al-Kindī's account is faithful to Aristotle: sleep is intended to encourage digestion (§X.7, AR 308–9), and is defined functionally as the cessation of sensation in the primary organ of sense (§X.2–4, AR 307).

What al-Kindī has to say about dreams is likewise a modification of Aristotle. Both agree that dreams are realized by the imaginative faculty, which remains active while the senses cease to function.[55] In *On Dreams* Aristotle is much clearer than al-Kindī in associating *phantasia* with sensation and contrasting it to intellection, rather than making it an intermediary faculty.[56] But the real difference between al-Kindī and Aristotle comes in their respective discussions of prophetic dreams. For Aristotle dreams are either residual motions left over in the sense-organs from previous experiences, which are too subtle to be noticed except when we are asleep (he compares them to the spots we see after looking at bright lights), or impressions received from outside the body and barely perceived (as one might dream about a feast and wake to find that the smell of cooking food has been wafting into the bedroom). Having given this straightforwardly physiological explanation of dreams, Aristotle has some difficulty explaining the widely accepted phenomenon of prophetic dreams when he comes to write *On Prophecy in Sleep*. He dismisses the idea that such dreams could be sent by the gods (462b20–22, 463b12–15), and suggests that they often come true simply by coincidence (have enough dreams about the future, after all, and some are bound to come true). In some cases we may foretell one of our own actions, because the thought leading to that action has already been formed (463a27–30). The most robust theory Aristotle considers plausible would be one like that of Democritus, in which external events and objects somehow produce some "motion" that comes to us and is too subtle to be detected except while we are asleep (464a5–19). But even this is not really prophesying future events; it is sensing motions that are contemporaneous with the dream.

Al-Kindī, by contrast, is an enthusiastic believer in prophetic dreams, and invokes no physical mechanism to explain them. As we saw, al-Kindī believes that imagination is realized in the brain, but that we imagine "through nothing but the soul." The soul causes the physical process that goes with imagination, not the other way around. Consistently with this, he says that it is the soul that grasps future events and then "announces" these to the brain, i.e. causes a dream that shows how the future will be (§IX.4, AR 303–4).[57] A passage in *Discourse on the Soul* confirms that the separate soul sees truths when our bodies are asleep and our senses are inactive: "this soul does not sleep at all, because in the time of slumber it abandons the use of the senses and remains restricted, not freed by itself, and it knows all that is in the worlds, and everything manifest and hidden" (§IV.3, AR 276–7). Immediately following this al-Kindī speaks of the soul's "seeing marvellous dreams" so long as it has "attained purity" (§IV.4, AR 277).

In neither *Discourse on the Soul* nor *On Sleep and Dream* do we find a good explanation as to why the soul is able to foretell the future. In *On Sleep and* Dream we are told only that the soul is the "place of all sensible and intellectual things," including, apparently, things that are yet to occur (§VII.2, AR 301). Those with pure and well-prepared souls, and organs able to receive the dream well, are most likely to have accurate dreams (§XI.1–2, AR 303). (Aristotle, by contrast, implies that the wise are *less* likely to have predictive dreams, since the emptier your mind, the better your chances of receiving a useful motion from outside; 464a22–24.) If one's organ is in a less receptive state, then one can still have a prophetic dream, but it will be distorted in some way. Rather than simply seeing what will happen, one may see it symbolized—for instance a dream about flying could symbolize a journey (§IX.4, AR 304)—or even backwards, so that a dream about a man being poor could prophecy his having great wealth (§IV.8, AR 306). So although al-Kindī does not give any detailed suggestions for interpreting dreams, he does provide a theoretical basis for this practice.[58]

What follows from all of this for al-Kindī's psychology? First, we have learned that there is at least one faculty that is neither sensation nor intellection, but something in between, namely imagination. In *On Sleep and Dream* al-Kindī says explicitly that there are more faculties like this (he uses the plural *quwan* for intermediate faculties at §II.2, AR 294), but he does not name them. However we can infer from *On Recollection* that memory (at least of sense-experiences) would be one such faculty. Another possibility is suggested in *On Sleep and Dream* by the close association al-Kindī makes between imagination and "thought [*fikr*]." As we saw, he opposes thought to sensation, saying that when we undergo "preoccupation with thought [*al-shughl bi-fikrihī*]" or are "lost in thought [*mufakkir*]" we may almost leave off use of the senses entirely (§III.3, AR 296). He then says:

> *On Sleep and Dream* §III.5–6 (AR 296–7): When thought is preoccupied with its object to the point that it does not use any of the senses at all, then thought may thereby come to the point [where it is as if one were] sleeping. Then one's imaginative power is able to manifest its activity in the highest degree. For nothing distracts one's soul from giving the sensible form of the concept of his thoughts [*sūra ma'ānī afkārihī al-ḥissiyya*], so that one would "see" it as if one were sensing it. . . . But rather, while one is only thinking of something, the form of [the object of] one's thought appears to one sensibly, in a more immaculate, clear, and pure way than the sensible [form].

If we assume that al-Kindī is not speaking loosely here, then he would seem to be telling us that there is a faculty called "thought [*fikr*]" that is able to occupy itself with sensible forms, and not just intelligible universals.

If this is right then it would be of help in explaining several psychological phenomena that al-Kindī acknowledges, but that cannot be accounted for within his strict bifurcation of human cognition into sensation and intellection. For instance, in *On Sleep and Dream* itself, he compares dreams of varying accuracy to opinions of varying accuracy (§IX.5, AR 304–5), even saying that an inaccurate dream yields a thought (*fikra*) that has the status of mere opinion.[59] Given the potential weakness of opinion and thought, and the fact that they grasp sensible particulars, it is tempting to say that the faculty of thought is distinct from the faculty of intellection, which unerringly grasps universals. This temptation is encouraged by the fact that, in *On First Philosophy*, al-Kindī describes "thought [*fikr*]" as a function of soul that falls short of pure intellection, insofar as it "makes a transition from certain forms of things to others"

(§XIX.5, AR 154, RJ 85). Here al-Kindī seems to be following the Arabic Plotinus texts, which also use *fikr* for discursive thought that is inferior to intellection—what Plotinus himself called *dianoia*. But the evidence of *On Sleep and Dream* suggests that al-Kindī is aware of a more elaborate theory of the "internal senses."[60] In that case he may suppose that thought, like imagination and perhaps memory, is a faculty higher than sensation yet still located in a bodily organ, namely the brain.[61] This would help him to explain why we are able to think about sensible things, and to have opinions that fall short of knowledge. (Knowledge would of course remain the privilege of intellection, since as we have seen, al-Kindī emphasizes that objects of knowledge must be stable universals.)

Surprisingly, the one text that provides strong evidence of such a theory in al-Kindī is a work on music, *On the Informative Parts of Music*.[62] This treatise, which will be discussed further below (chapter 7), associates the four strings of the *'ūd* with other things arranged in four, like the elements, the seasons, and the bodily humors. One of the points of comparison is the "powers of the soul that are situated [*munba'itha*] in the head."[63] There are four such powers: the "cogitative power" or "power of thought" [*al-quwwa al-fikriyya*], "*phantasia*, that is, imagination" (reading *al-fanṭāsiyyā wa-hiya al-takhayyul*, as in *On Definitions*), the "retentive power [*al-quwwa al-ḥifẓiyya*]" and the "power of memory [*al-quwwa al-dhikriyya*]."[64] We have, then, thought, imagination, and what look like two alternative terms for memory—it is not clear whether al-Kindī really wishes to differentiate between two functions here, or just wants to expand the theory of three internal senses to fit his numerological scheme.[65] Later on in the same treatise al-Kindī adds that "rational utterances [*al-alfāẓ al-manṭiqiyya*]" are identified with "intellect [*'aql*]," but only once they have undergone critical examination (*intiqād*) by thought (*fikr*).[66]

Unfortunately this tantalizing claim is never expounded at greater length. And as we have seen, al-Kindī never makes any serious attempt to integrate the theory of internal senses into his chief works on psychology and epistemology. But even in these works, he recognizes the need for something to fill the gap between sensation and intellection. He recognizes, that is, the role that imagination and other intermediate faculties might play in accounting for the complexity of human cognition. On the other hand, imagination, the only intermediate faculty discussed at length by al-Kindī, is associated much more closely with sensation than with intellection. He never tries to use the intermediate faculties to compromise his bifurcated epistemology, for instance by saying that imagination or memory serves as a basis for abstraction or by discussing in detail the relationship between intellection and *fikr*.

Nor does he compromise his commitment to dualism. As we saw in *Discourse on the Soul*, some psychic faculties like sensation and imagination perform their acts in the body, but the soul itself remains wholly immaterial and distinct from body. Likewise, in the account of prophetic dreams, the separate soul is what grasps the future. The dream produced by the faculty of imagination does require the body (since imagination is seated in the brain), but the dream is only a by-product of the soul's independent prognostication. It is, we might suppose, a way for us to gain access to what the soul could see clearly if it were not impeded by the body. In chapter 6 we will see that al-Kindī had good reason to be so resolute in his dualist theory of soul, and in his separation of intellectual knowledge from the faculties of soul that are tied to the body. For his ethics, too, minimizes the importance of bodily things, and makes our immaterial souls the locus of our identity and perfection.

6

ETHICS

Socratic, Stoic, Platonic

From a philosophical point of view, al-Kindī's ethical writing is on the whole less impressive than his works on metaphysics and psychology. Much of it takes the form of pointed anecdote and moral exhortation, rather than argument or analysis. To be fair to al-Kindī, though, the relative poverty of deep reflection on ethics in his extant corpus may be simply a matter of bad luck. Ibn al-Nadīm's *Fihrist* tells us that he wrote a dozen works on ethical and political topics, most of which are lost. Despite these losses and the occasional banality of what remains, there is at least one respect in which al-Kindī should be recognized as a pioneer: his anticipation of the standard genres of ethical writing in Arabic. In a very helpful survey of Arabic ethical literature, Dimitri Gutas has grouped relevant works into three categories: (1) gnomological collections, (2) "popular-philosophical" works, and (3) *Fürstenspiegel* ("mirrors for princes").[1] Al-Kindī can be argued to have contributed to all three genres:

(1) A gnomological collection is a list of memorable sayings and brief anecdotes, often concerning Greek figures, intended to bring home moral lessons to the reader. These collections represent an important, though often overlooked, legacy of Greek thought in Arabic.[2] Al-Kindī wrote what may be the earliest such collection in Arabic, the *Sayings of Socrates*. Socrates regularly features in later

gnomological works, which often repeat material found in al-Kindī's *Sayings*.[3]

(2) "Popular-philosophical" works: there are numerous later Arabic works that popularize ideas from the Greek ethical tradition, especially by means of catalogues of the virtues. Both Miskawayh and Yaḥyā b. 'Adī wrote treatises titled *Tahdhīb al-Akhlāq* (*Refinement of Character*), which include such catalogues. Although al-Kindī did not write any freestanding work of this kind, there is an excursus about "the human virtues" in *On Definitions* (§91, AR 177–9). Unfortunately the passage has suffered from textual corruption. What remains is little more than a garbled list of virtues and vices, relying on the Aristotelian understanding of virtues as means between extremes.[4] Still, this should be recognized as a forerunner of works in the popular-philosophical genre, especially in light of the general aims of *On Definitions* as I have explained them, namely making Greek ideas and terminology accessible to speakers of Arabic (see chapter 2). Here we should also mention *Discourse on the Soul*, which focuses as much on ethics as on psychology, and which uses anecdote and exhortation in the manner of a "popular-philosophical" work.[5]

(3) *Fürstenspiegel* are texts supplying practical and moral advice to high-ranking recipients. Al-Kindī's work of consolation, *On the Method of How to Dispel Sadness*, might fall into this category, though it is certainly a sort of popular ethical treatise as well. The recipient of the epistle is not specified, but as we have seen many Kindian writings are addressed to a member of the caliph's family, and this may well have been the case here.[6] This is suggested by the use of anecdotes dealing with ancient kings in the text: Alexander the Great and Nero. The Nero anecdote (§IX.6–7) impresses upon the reader that royalty would do well to listen to their court philosophers, a message al-Kindī was no doubt happy to put across to his patrons.

A surprising feature of al-Kindī's ethical writings is that, with the exception of the passage from *On Definitions*, they so consistently ignore Aristotelian ethics. Al-Kindī is indeed mostly unconcerned with the practical, virtuous actions that are the focus of the first nine books of Aristotle's *Nichomachean Ethics*. Instead, his emphasis is on a rigorous asceticism that will turn us away from the transient things of this world to contemplation of intelligible things. For al-Kindī Socrates is the exemplar of such an ascetic, philosophical approach to life. To this extent he follows Cynicism and Stoicism in disvaluing what Aristotle called "external goods," and in idolizing Socrates. But as we will see, his ethical teaching is ultimately grounded in the Platonist psychology and epistemology just explored in chapter 5.[7]

The Socratic Paradigm

The *Fihrist* indicates al-Kindī's keen interest in the figure of Socrates.[8] Ibn al-Nadīm mentions no fewer than five works about Socrates, at least two of which seem to have been in dialogue form:

(1) *Account of Socrates' Virtue*
(2) *Sayings of Socrates*
(3) *On a Dialogue That Passed* [*muḥāwara*] *between Socrates and Arshījānis*[9]
(4) *Account of the Death of Socrates*
(5) *On What Passed between Socrates and the Ḥarranians*[10]

Item (2) is extant, and will be discussed presently. First, though, a moment of reflection on these five titles, which constitute valuable evidence about al-Kindī's knowledge of Plato's works. Item (4) looks as though it had something to do with the *Phaedo*. Gutas has gone further and suggested that (1), (4), and (5) refer respectively to the *Crito*, *Phaedo,* and *Apology*. The nature of the works may be very tentatively inferred from another scrap of evidence about al-Kindī's knowledge of Plato, in which al-Kindī is named as the transmitter of a summary of passages from the *Symposium*.[11] The summary is not in dialogue form; instead it offers a compressed paraphrase of the content of the Greek original. So it seems likely that at least some of these "Socratic" works by al-Kindī were little more than reports summarizing the gist of Platonic dialogues. If this is right, then their loss doesn't deprive us of much insight into al-Kindī's own philosophy, however useful they would have been as evidence for the transmission of Plato into Arabic.[12]

On the other hand, we have already seen that *Discourse on the Soul*, which explicitly claims merely to repeat ideas from various Greek thinkers, is in fact very revealing for al-Kindī's theory of soul. And while the *Sayings of Socrates*,[13] a collection of anecdotes and sayings, might seem unlikely to tell us much about al-Kindī's own views, in fact it makes a good departure point for studying his ethics. Al-Kindī refers to *Sayings* §4 in his longest ethical treatise, *On Dispelling Sadness* (at §IX.5 and 9), precisely because the Socrates of these *Sayings* stands as the hero of the rigorous asceticism al-Kindī espouses whenever he treats ethical topics. *On Definitions* (§70C) also repeats a Socratic maxim (*Sayings* §15) in the midst of defining philosophy as "preparation for death," another reminiscence of the *Phaedo*.

A further indication of al-Kindī's abiding interest in Socrates is to be found in a report of al-Kindī's own sayings, included in *Muntakhab Ṣiwān al-Ḥikma*, which are at least partly, and perhaps entirely, authentic.[14] Not only are these sayings clearly styled on the aphorisms reported in the *Sayings of Socrates*, but one of al-Kindī's sayings (108) is a near quotation of *Sayings* §38. These sayings of al-Kindī serve to remind us of his literary ambitions and activities. They aim more at pithiness and wit than philosophical depth, sometimes relying on wordplay. (For example saying 55 says that "worry [*hamm*]" is worse than "poison [*samm*].") The similarity of these sayings to the *Sayings of Socrates* is, then, a reminder of al-Kindī's penchant for blurring the distinction between *adab* and *falsafa*.

In light of all this, it would be unwise to leave the *Sayings of Socrates* out of any discussion of al-Kindī's ethics; it is with some justice that several commentators have seen al-Kindī's ethics as fundamentally Socratic.[15] On the other hand, the *Sayings* shows how little al-Kindī knew about the historical Socrates, or the Socrates of Plato's dialogues. There are a few scraps of accurate information about Socrates here: that he did not write books (§1), that he was married (§8), and that he was put to death (§10). But most of the sayings could be attributed to any sage ("God created for man two ears, but only one tongue, so that we might listen more than we speak," §23). Several do have more biographical specificity, but are based on the wrong biography: they conflate Socrates with the Cynic philosopher Diogenes of Sinope, a confusion widespread in Arabic gnomological writings.[16] For example this Socrates lives in a jar (§4) and has a penchant for insulting passersby (he tells a well-dressed woman "you go not to see the city, but in order that the city may see you," §25). One of the longer anecdotes has Socrates being impudent to a passing king, and lets him deliver a put-down that, according to Greek legend, Diogenes aimed at Alexander the Great. ("The king said, 'What is it that you need?' Socrates replied, 'I need you to stop casting your shadow on me, because it is blocking the sun,'" §6).

To the extent that there is any dominant theme running through the *Sayings*, it is Socrates' attack on material possessions and pleasures like food and drink, which we might call external "goods" (using scare-quotes to indicate that they are only supposedly good). Like Diogenes, al-Kindī's Socrates is repeatedly portrayed as being destitute (§§2, 5, 34). And like the Socrates of Plato's dialogues, this Socrates insists that wisdom or virtue is the only thing of intrinsic value: "the fruits of wisdom are peace and calm, but the fruits of gold and silver are suffering and drudgery" (§29; cf. §32: "the wealth of the sage is with him wherever he goes"). In fact this Socrates goes even further. Whereas Plato's Socrates seemed to admit that wealth and other external "goods" could be genuinely good as long as they were used wisely, the Socrates of the *Sayings* repeatedly says that external "goods" are in fact always bad, because they are disgusting, or because their acquisition brings unhappiness (§§6, 16, 17, 18, 28, 29). Perhaps the most telling of these is §17: "[Socrates] said, 'possessions are the wellspring of sorrows; do not take possession of sorrows.'" According to this Socrates, external "goods" are not even neutral in value, but are actually negative in value. They are never to be pursued, not even by the wise man. For it is inevitable that they will lead us astray as soon as we desire them.

Having rejected these spurious goods, does al-Kindī's Socrates have any positive characterization of the good to offer? On the whole, he restricts himself to extolling wisdom and various virtues (especially justice), without explaining what constitutes virtue or wisdom. There are traces, though, of several theories of happiness familiar from Greek ethics. For example, some sayings suggest that happiness lies in self-sufficiency (§6: "what Socrates needs is with him, wherever he turns," cf. §4: "I own nothing whose loss would make me sad"; also §§24, 28, 32). Others emphasize "lack of disturbance," or *ataraxia*, the common goal of all schools of Hellenistic philosophy. For instance, §34: "A man from the wealthy set said to him, 'Socrates, of what use to you is your wisdom, and are you not distressed by your poverty?' He said, 'it is of use to me in keeping me from the suffering you feel on my behalf.'"[17] For this Socrates *ataraxia* is chiefly to be had by not fearing death (§§7, 8, 12, 18, 21), a theme that brings us closer to the real Socrates, or at least the Socrates of the *Phaedo*.

Also familiar from the *Phaedo* is the reason we should not fear death: "take death lightly, that you may not die; for in dying your souls become immortal. Adhere to justice and salvation will belong to you" (§18). This is of a piece with the generally Platonic emphasis on perfecting the soul through justice (§§37–39, cf. §19). But though there is one saying that identifies the just man as "the one who commits no injustice" (§37), al-Kindī's Socrates is more concerned to turn us away from the physical world than he is to encourage virtuous action. When we turn away from the physical world, we do so first, Platonically enough, through the study of mathematics (§§13–14). But the ultimate goal is considerably more exalted: "wisdom is the ladder to exaltation; he who has it is not far from his Creator" (§20). This is one of several Islamicizing passages in the *Sayings*, which speak of *tawḥīd* (§1), praise the one who has no need of idols because of his "true knowledge of God" (§9), and make justice the *mīzān*, the "scales" or "balance," of God (§38). Of course the very nature of the *Sayings* means that it offers no overarching argument or theory of happiness. But is not hard to bring together the dominant themes of the collection into a coherent ethical outlook: external "goods" are to be avoided because they turn us towards the physical and away from the knowledge of immaterial things, namely our own immortal souls and God Himself.

The most dramatic confirmation that Platonist metaphysics and psychology lurks amidst the barbed wit of the *Sayings* is an entry I have not yet mentioned:

> §27: [Socrates] said, "nature is the maid for the soul, soul is the maid for the intellect, and the intellect [is the maid] for the Creator, because the first thing created by the Creator [*mubdiʿ*] was the form of the intellect."

Here the metaphysical system of Plotinus is put into the mouth of Socrates. Two features of the saying indicate that it is an invention originating in al-Kindī's circle. The reference to the intellect as the "first created thing" comes from the Neoplatonic translations made in his circle (see *Liber de Causis* §4). And the Plotinian hierarchy includes, following God, intellect, and soul, the fourth hypostasis of "nature": this four-fold emanation scheme is based on *Enneads* V.2.1 and found in the Arabic Plotinus. It turns up in both the Prologue to the *Theology of Aristotle*, which I believe to be by al-Kindī himself, and in the opening sequence of entries in *On Definitions* (§§1–4). So *Sayings* §27 may well be the invention of either al-Kindī himself, or a member of his circle. In any case al-Kindī clearly saw the asceticism of his Socrates as fitting neatly together with the Neoplatonizing psychology and metaphysics familiar to us from his own theoretical works.[18]

The Eclecticism of *On Dispelling Sadness*

From a literary point of view, *On the Method of How to Dispel Sadness* is probably al-Kindī's most attractive surviving work. Full of vivid anecdotes and persuasive rhetoric, it provides genuinely useful advice on how to cope with loss and sorrow. Unsurprisingly it was one of al-Kindī's most popular works, frequently cited by later authors.[19] The literary polish of *On Dispelling Sadness* is not necessarily matched by its philosophical heft—Thérèse-Anne Druart has called the work "pleasant if somewhat pedestrian."[20] But in fact I believe that one can tease out of *On Dispelling Sadness* a coherent argument against the rationality of valuing external "goods," and in favor of a thoroughly intellectualist ethics.

The modern interpretation of *On Dispelling Sadness* got off to a bad start, when the otherwise excellent edition and translation of Richard Walzer and Helmut Ritter proposed that it was just an Arabic version of some Greek work of consolation, with al-Kindī adding little or nothing of his own.[21] Their guess was that it is a translation of Themistius' lost *On Sadness*; they went so far as to include this speculation as a subtitle on their title page. This hypothesis was already rejected in a 1938 review of Walzer and Ritter's work by Max Pohlenz. Pohlenz pointed out, though, that there was a Greek source for one passage, in which al-Kindī compares our earthly lives to a sojourn made by people temporarily disembarking from a ship.[22] This metaphor appears, in a much less elaborate version, in the *Enchiridion* of the Stoic philosopher Epictetus. Now, in general one needs to be very cautious when speaking of Stoic influence on Arabic philosophy; there is very little evidence of any actual textual transmission that could have made this possible.[23] But the parable of the ship provides a rare definite link between a Stoic author and an author writing in Arabic.

It is appropriate that we should find an echo of Epictetus in *On Dispelling Sadness*, because Epictetus' writings make similar use of aphorisms and moralistic exhortation (this is especially true of the *Enchiridion*, but also a feature of his *Discourses*). And like al-Kindī, Epictetus venerates Socrates as a philosophical hero.[24] There is also a more general resonance between the central argument of *On Dispelling Sadness* and Epictetan Stoicism. To oversimplify, Epictetus' fundamental teaching is that to be happy, we must value only that which is "up to us" or under our control. Insofar as our continued happiness requires our having external "goods," our happiness is vulnerable and indeed certain to be fleeting. For no one can control or guarantee the permanence of his material possessions, his health, the well-being of his family, and so on. We should instead value only the rational use of our *prohairesis*—our ability to make choices. For one may choose to be virtuous no matter what one's external circumstances might be. Happiness, then, is choosing a life of reason and virtue, and valuing nothing but this.

The parable of the ship is the only borrowing from Epictetus in *On Dispelling Sadness*. The borrowing is presumably indirect, and there is no strong reason to think that al-Kindī knew more Epictetus than this, or that he even knew Epictetus was the source of the ship parable. Nevertheless *On Dispelling Sadness* is very much in the spirit of Epictetus when it argues that unhappiness is the inevitable result of valuing what is vulnerable and transient. Sadness, says al-Kindī, is "a pain of the soul occurring because one loses what one loves or is frustrated in obtaining what one seeks out" (§I.2). Most people seek out and value sensible things, like money, power, or things that provide pleasure. But they are foolish to do so, because sensible objects suffer from two sorts of vulnerability. First, "stability and constancy do not exist in the world of generation and corruption," so sensible things are by their very nature transitory (§I.2). Second, sensible possessions can be "seized by any power; it is impossible to protect them" (§I.4). Indeed such things are really the common property of all: "we are no more entitled to them than someone else; whoever takes them, keeps them" (§VII.1, cf. §I.5). These considerations show that, if one wants to be happy, one should not make one's happiness contingent on the acquisition of sensible things, that is, external "goods." As al-Kindī says in the concluding sections of the epistle, "he who does not acquire things external to himself is master of the things which turn kings into slaves, i.e. anger and desire which are the source of vices and pain" (§XIII.3).

Al-Kindī furthermore says that it is not "natural" for sensible things to endure permanently. If we do want to acquire and keep sensible "goods" without them perishing, "we want from nature something which is not natural; and he who wants something unnatural wants something which does not exist" (§I.5). Al-Kindī thus suggests that a life lived "in accordance with nature," in the famous Stoic phrase, would be a life lived without any desire for sensible things at all. At one point al-Kindī goes so far as to say we should actually try to "minimize our possessions" (§IV.4). Here he strikes a world-denying note worthy of the Socrates of the *Sayings*. But his considered view in *On Dispelling Sadness* would seem to be that external "goods" are to be neither rejected nor pursued. Thus he says we should treat sensible "goods" as royalty treats visitors: accepting them graciously when they arrive, but never deigning to go to meet them or making a fuss when they depart (§II.3).

Though all of this is reminiscent of a Stoic author like Epictetus, there are non-Stoic elements in al-Kindī's argument as well. We have, in fact, just seen al-Kindī disagree subtly with one orthodox Stoic position. The Stoics held that only virtue is absolutely choiceworthy, and only vice absolutely to be avoided. But they admitted that external "goods" like health could sometimes be rational objects of choice: a sage could pursue bodily health so long as this pursuit did not conflict with virtue. The Stoics thus spoke of "preferred indifferents," things that were choiceworthy (*proêgmena*) even though happiness may be attained without them (the Stoic sage, notoriously, is happy even on the rack).[25] Al-Kindī never seems to consider this position, which is something of a compromise between the Peripatetic acceptance of the need for external goods in the best life, and the more thorough rejection of such "goods" associated with, for instance, the Cynics.[26] On the whole al-Kindī seems to incline more towards the Cynic view, perhaps under the influence of the Socratic materials he collected in the *Sayings of Socrates*. Even bodily health, which is choiceworthy if any external "good" is choiceworthy, is mentioned only by al-Kindī in a relatively unfavorable light: he says that the health of the soul is much more important than the health of the body (§§IV, XIII.3).

A more obviously non-Stoic element in al-Kindī's position is that he does not identify virtue as such, or the virtuous and rational use of our power of choice, as embodying happiness. Rather, he says this:

> *On Dispelling Sadness* §I.2–3: Necessarily, stability and constancy only exist in the world of the intellect, which we can contemplate. Therefore if we do not want to lose the things we love and do not want to be frustrated in obtaining things we seek out, we must contemplate the intellectual world and form our conceptions of what we love, possess and want from it [sc. the intellectual world].

Like Epictetus, al-Kindī urges us to value only what is invulnerable to loss due to circumstances outside our control. But he draws a Platonist conclusion from this Stoic line of argument. The conclusion is already implicit in al-Kindī's critique of external "goods," when he refers to them as "sensible things" (§§I.4, II.1, III.6), which are distinguished from intelligibles by their corruptibility (§§I.2, 5, II.1, 5, IV.1). If we are to be happy, we must instead pursue things in the "world of the intellect,"[27] because these intelligible things are not subject to corruption, and cannot be taken away from us. Thus the fundamental distinction al-Kindī's epistemology between sensible and intelligible objects turns up here in *On Dispelling Sadness* as the fundamental distinction in his ethics. The stability that allows intellectual objects to be suitable objects of knowledge also makes them appropriate objects of value. Conversely, the transient nature of sensible things makes them not only unknowable, but also undesirable for one who is wise.

Here one is inclined to say to al-Kindī that his conception of human happiness is too narrow. After all, humans do have faculties other than intellect, such as sensation, and the power to seek nutrition and reproduce. Is he really telling us that the use of these faculties plays no role in human happiness? The answer is yes. And this should be no surprise, given that (as we saw in chapter 5) al-Kindī thinks the rational or intellective soul is the true nature or essence of the person, and that the lower faculties are mere projections of this soul's power into the body. We will return shortly to the consequences drawn from this in *Discourse on the Soul*. But it is worth noting that he reiterates the doctrine in the present treatise as well:

> *On Dispelling Sadness* §IV.1: For it is through our souls that we are what we are, not through our bodies, because what all bodies have in common is corporeality, whereas every living thing has life in common, and this is through the soul.[28] Our soul is essential to us; and the welfare of our essence is more incumbent upon us than the welfare of things alien to us. Our body is an instrument for our soul, through which its [i.e. the soul's] activities are made manifest.[29] Improving our essences is much more befitting for us than improving our instruments.

In this same section al-Kindī points out that "the soul remains while the body is obliterated," which not only underscores soul's greater importance but also indicates the affinity between the soul and the "world of the intellect."

These psychological claims conclude the core argument of *On Dispelling Sadness*, which runs from §I to §IV. This argument is that, given the vulnerability of sensible things and the inevitability of their loss, as contrasted with the stability and permanence of intellectual things and the soul itself, happiness resides in intellectual contemplation and not the attainment of external "goods." Al-Kindī seems to have made his case, and from here on out little will be added in the way of further argument. Nevertheless, we are not even halfway through the epistle. From §V onwards, al-Kindī offers numerous "remedies" for sadness, which are of a more practical nature. For example, he counsels us to remember that others have undergone similar losses to those we must endure (§VI.4). And he supplies various anecdotes about the ancients—Socrates, Alexander, Nero—as well as the lengthy elaboration of Epictetus' parable of the ship. However, al-Kindī does not allow us to lose sight of the fundamental premises of the argument of §I–§IV. In the later sections, al-Kindī continues to refer dismissively to "sensible things" (§§VI.4, XII.1, 3, 6–7, XIII.1–2), and to emphasize their transitory nature and their susceptibility to corruption (§§V.7, VI.8, XI.1). He refers to those who are able to resist grief over the loss of sensible things as "men of intellect" and those who do grieve as "men of no intellect" (§§II.3, V.1, VI.6–8, IX.4, X.3, XI.10, XII.7). He concludes the letter by praying that God will allow the recipient to "harvest the fruits of the intellect, and . . . keep you from the baseness of ignorance."

What, then, does the second part of *On Dispelling Sadness* add to the argument of the first part? It would seem that the "remedies" are given in order to make it easier to accommodate ourselves to the rigorously ascetic and intellectualist conclusion of that argument. Grasping the fact that sensibles must all pass away, and that true happiness would consist in contemplation of the intelligibles, is not necessarily enough to prevent us from being pained at the loss of our external "goods." For that, we need to be ***habituated*** to greet the loss of sensible things with cheerful acceptance:

> *On Dispelling Sadness* §III.6–7: It is therefore clear that the sensibles which one loves or hates are not something determined by nature, but rather by habit [*bi-'l-'ādāt*] and frequent use. Since . . . finding solace from what we have lost is easily and clearly achieved by way of habit as we have explained, we ought to apply ourselves to bringing our souls to this [state] and to educating ourselves so that this becomes our necessary habit and acquired character ['*āda lāzima wa ḫhulqan mustafādan*].

The idea of habituation is the only discernible inheritance from Aristotelian ethics in *On Dispelling Sadness*.[30] But it does not represent a departure from al-Kindī's previous conclusion: what we need to be conditioned or "molded" (§III.7) to do is precisely to reject sensible things and embrace the intelligible world. Still it is a significant concession that this will only be possible for us if we condition our characters well.

Even by al-Kindī's standards, *On Dispelling Sadness* is a remarkably eclectic work. It blends together arguments, themes, and gnomological materials beholden to several ancient ethical traditions—Stoicism, Cynicism (we find Socrates conflated with Diogenes at §IX.9), and Aristotelianism. But the argument of the work stands or falls with the Platonist claims made at the outset, about the stability and attainability of what is intelligible, in contrast to the vulnerability of the sensible, and about the incorporeality and immortality of the human soul. For this reason I disagree, to some extent, with the interpretations of two previous commentators on the work, Thérèse-Anne Druart and Charles Butterworth. Both of them have provided very useful overviews of al-Kindī's contributions to ethics; I take issue with them here simply because their readings of *On Dispelling Sadness* serve as useful foils to my own.

Druart points out that in *On the Quantity of Aristotle's Books* al-Kindī makes ethics the capstone of the philosophical syllabus, following after psychology and metaphysics. As we will see below, she is right to say that *Discourse on the Soul* embodies this view of ethics by presupposing al-Kindī's psychological and theological doctrines.[31] In my view the same can be said of *On Dispelling Sadness*. Druart, though, thinks that *On Dispelling Sadness* is meant to persuade us to *begin* philosophical study. She proposes that it should be classified as a work of "prephilosophical ethics," which does not invoke metaphysical doctrines to ground its ethical teaching.[32] Of course Druart is right to see *On Dispelling Sadness* as trying to help the reader to live in a more philosophical way, for it gives advice on how to condition oneself to disdain external "goods." But any reader unconvinced by the opening arguments given in §I–§IV will have no reason to attempt to condition himself in the way al-Kindī recommends. In particular, the reader must be persuaded that our true nature is our rational soul, that this soul is able to grasp intelligible objects, and that only these objects are stable. All of these crucial premises are asserted without argument in *On Dispelling Sadness*, and as we have seen al-Kindī refers back to them in the later, hortatory sections of the text. So if the reader is to follow and accept al-Kindī's argument, he will need at least a passing familiarity with the doctrines of works like *On the Intellect*, section 2 of *On First Philosophy*, and *Discourse on the Soul*.

My interpretation departs more widely from that of Butterworth, who starts from the assumption that al-Kindī wants to provide "a human science that presupposes neither metaphysical knowledge nor divine inspiration—one, that is, on the order of the practical reasoning presented here [i.e. in *On Dispelling Sadness*]."[33] Because Butterworth worries that, for al-Kindī, intelligible truths are in fact unattainable without revelation, he does not think that the opening sections can provide the grounding for the epistle as a whole.[34] For Butterworth *On Dispelling Sadness* instead points to the need for a properly *political* philosophy, but fails to provide this itself.[35] Butterworth is right to say that, in the extant corpus, al-Kindī makes no effort to situate his ethics within a political context. (The *Fihrist* shows that al-Kindī did write on the topic of political governance, but this dimension of his thought is lost to us.) Yet this very lack of attention to politics, and indeed practical philosophy in general, renders highly suspect the notion that *On Dispelling Sadness* was ever intended to offer a basis for virtuous *actions* in the sensible world, or an argument with no basis in psychology and metaphysics. To the contrary: al-Kindī is drawing an ethical conclusion from theoretical principles about the immortal soul and the intelligible world. The conclusion is that we must turn away from this world and look to the world of the intellect. The only thing about the epistle that is intended to be "practical" is the advice he gives for habituating oneself to live in accordance with this challenging conclusion.

Discourse on the Soul Revisited

The *Discourse on the Soul* is even more explicit in situating al-Kindī's ascetic and intellectualist ethics within the context of his metaphysics and psychology. The *Discourse* presents itself as a doxography of Greek psychological theories. But as we saw in chapter 5, it sets out the principles of al-Kindī's own psychology: the soul is intellective in its proper nature, the lower faculties being mere projections of this soul's power into the body. The soul is a "simple substance" that can survive the death of the body and go on to live the life that is best for it, namely one of pure intellectual contemplation. We have also seen that in other works dealing with epistemology, al-Kindī gives the body and the soul's lower faculties no role to play in the acquisition of knowledge. But it is in the *Discourse* that we find his most robust polemic against bodily things. Pythagoras is cited (§IV.1–2, AR 276) as comparing the soul to a mirror, which can perfectly reflect the forms of what is known if it withdraws away from bodily desire, but which becomes rusted and non-reflective if it gives in to bodily vices. Earlier, in his own voice, al-Kindī enthuses about the beneficial effects of ignoring sensible things and withdrawing to a life of contemplation, in which the "knowledge of the invisible" and "secrets of creation" become available to us (§II.3, AR 274).

The *Discourse* also adds another, more theological dimension to this teaching. As Druart has pointed out,[36] al-Kindī is under the influence of the ubiquitous ancient maxim, derived from Plato (*Theaetetus* 176b), that our good is to achieve "likeness to God." Al-Kindī refers to this ideal in *On Definitions* (§70B, AR 172), and also in the *Discourse*, saying that if the "the intellectual soul achieves knowledge of [the] noble things" in the intelligible world, it will "attain imitation of the Creator" (§II.4, AR 274). However, neither *On Definitions* nor the *Discourse* hold out the prospect of a complete union or identity with God—al-Kindī is no Sufi. In *On Definitions* al-Kindī speaks only of making our *actions* like those of God.[37] And the *Discourse* only goes so far as to say that the man of intellect can become "close [*qarīb*] in similarity" to the Creator (§II.5, AR 275).[38]

Al-Kindī explains this proximity to God by returning several times to the analogy of the sun, which of course derives ultimately from *Republic* 508a–509b. At the very outset of the treatise (§§I.2–II.1, AR 273) al-Kindī asserts that the soul is a "divine, spiritual substance" which is "from the substance of the Creator, like the light of the sun from the sun." The man who "prefers the truth and the beautiful" can thus "become of a species whose power and ability are part of the species of the Creator . . . because [the soul] acquires from His light, and in it is a power similar to His power" (§II.6, AR 275). As in the *Republic*, the analogy is also used to make an epistemological point. Just as sunlight makes things visible in the sensible world, so in the "world of the intellect" it is being in God's light that enables the soul to know all things.[39] Though the soul is called "divine" insofar as it flows directly from God, it is no more to be identified with God than sunlight is to be identified with the sun. The soul's proper abode, then, is the now familiar world of the intelligibles, which can apparently be known directly and completely so long as the soul is wholly separated from body. Al-Kindī quotes Plato (§II.3, AR 274) as claiming that some philosophers achieve this intellectual vision even during their earthly existence, by "attaching no importance to sensory things." But for most souls the path to the intelligible world is a long and arduous one. It is not automatically reached even when we die. Rather (again, supposedly according to Plato), the soul that is free of its earthly body comes to reside in each of the heavenly spheres in sequence, until it is fully "cleansed and purified" of the "stains of sensation [*adnās al-ḥiss*]" (§V.1–2, AR 178).[40]

The *Discourse* ends with a passage that is reminiscent of *On Dispelling Sadness*, though it adopts a tone of mockery instead of sympathetic advice towards those who are saddened by the travails of this sensible world:

> *Discourse on the Soul* VII.1–2 (AR 279–80): Say to those who weep, whose nature is to weep about grievous things: it is necessary to weep, and to do more weeping, for him who neglects his soul, and goes too far in pursuing vulgar, base, unclean, false desires, which bring wickedness, and incline his nature to the nature of beasts. He stops attending to the contemplation of this noble concern and dedication to it, and purifying his soul in accordance with his ability. For true purity is only purity of the soul, not purity of the body.

Here al-Kindī speaks *in propria persona*, showing himself to be as demanding in his expectations as any of the Greek thinkers quoted in the *Discourse*. In fact we rarely seem to be far from al-Kindī's own voice in the *Discourse*, so much so that it is hard to see where the supposed citations of his sources end and his own interjections begin.[41] As mentioned above (chapter 5), some specific elements from Hermetic and Neoplatonic works in the *Discourse* have been identified, and we have seen there are also clear, if imprecise, reminiscences of certain Platonic dialogues. Yet it has been difficult to trace the main sources al-Kindī used in writing the *Discourse*. I suspect this is in part because al-Kindī is engaging in loose and creative paraphrase rather than direct quotation. He thus manages to portray a psychology, ethics, and eschatology that is substantially his own as if it were the unanimous view of the Greeks. (And he could hardly have chosen more authoritative figures for this project than those named here: Plato, Pythagoras, and Aristotle.) This is not to say that al-Kindī would necessarily endorse every claim made in the *Discourse*. In particular, we do not find the idea of the soul ascending through the heavenly spheres, so as to be gradually purified, anywhere else in the Kindian corpus.[42] Still, the treatise brings together in one place al-Kindī's most characteristic teachings on psychology—that soul is an immaterial substance, immortal, and essentially intellective—with his most characteristic ethical teachings. These are that happiness is to be had in a life of intellectual contemplation, and that the body, the faculties that tie us to the sensible world, and above all physical pleasure, are hindrances and snares that prevent us from living the life of the mind that is our ultimate reward.

7

SCIENCE

Mathematics and Methodology

From the scarce remains of al-Kindī's writings on ethics, we now turn our attention to the relatively vast corpus of his scientific works. As we saw in chapter 1, al-Kindī wrote about a bewildering array of topics in the physical sciences. Though most of this material is lost, a great deal has fortunately survived to us. Indeed one may almost speak here of an embarrassment of riches. This presents difficulties of its own, however. A thorough survey of al-Kindī's scientific work would require a book, not a single chapter, and to write such a book one would need to be an expert in the history of disciplines as diverse as medicine, chemistry, optics, music, astronomy, and astrology. Unlike al-Kindī himself, I cannot claim such wide-ranging expertise. But since the present volume is intended as a study of al-Kindī's philosophical thought only, we can content ourselves with a fairly brief tour of the scientific treatises, highlighting those aspects that are most relevant to what we would now consider to be philosophical issues. It should be remembered, though, that al-Kindī himself recognizes no firm dividing line between "science" and "philosophy." I have had occasion to point this out above, but it will become especially clear in the course of this chapter.

The most obvious "philosophical" question that arises from the scientific works is that of al-Kindī's methodology. This question is particularly pressing given his epistemological commitments. Given his downplaying of the role of sensation in the acquisition of knowledge, what account can al-Kindī give of the physical sciences, which would seem to depend so fundamentally on empirical observation? As we will see, al-Kindī does take sensible experience seriously in the process of confirming scientific theories, but the theories themselves are not reached by making empirical observations and then generalizing from these observations. Most frequently, Kindian science is instead driven by abstract mathematical reasoning. Indeed the role of mathematics in al-Kindī's scientific works is so central that it makes sense to organize the extant material in accordance with al-Kindī's own division of the mathematical sciences. As explained above (chapter 2), he follows tradition in recognizing four mathematical sciences: arithmetic, geometry, music, and astronomy. In this chapter we will study works that draw on the first three of these sciences. Al-Kindī's astronomy, and more generally his cosmology and account of how the stars influence life in our lower world, will be the subject of chapter 8.

The Arithmetic of Medicine

Like many later Arabic philosophers, al-Kindī devoted significant energy to the study of medicine. The *Fihrist* lists about two dozen titles on medicine, many very narrow in scope (for instance treatises on specific maladies like rabies). We have, in the Istanbul manuscript, two such narrowly focused treatises, on coitus and on lisping.[1] There is also a work on the days of crisis in acute illness,[2] and an extensive handbook or *Formulary* of recipes for drugs.[3] The most important surviving work, though, is one that provides the theoretical basis for the recipes we find in the *Formulary*: extant in both Arabic and Latin, *On Degrees* expands on Galenic pharmacological theory to give an account of how to produce compound drugs.[4]

According to Galen, the reason that drugs affect us is that they are, to varying degrees, hot, cold, dry, and moist. These four Aristotelian contraries are fundamental not only to Galenic medicine but also to nearly everything al-Kindī wrote about the physical world; as we will see they play a key role in his account of celestial influence. On the authority of Galen al-Kindī takes it as uncontroversial that certain "simple" ingredients have known degrees of the four contraries, and that there are only four such degrees of each contrary.[5] For example, in a recipe given in *On Degrees* mastic, a kind of tree resin, is said to be "hot in the second degree," and cardamom "hot in the first degree." Presumably, we originally discover the degree to which a simple ingredient is hot, cold, dry, or moist by observation and experience. Suppose, however, that we want to produce a drug that is between the first and second degrees of heat. Or, suppose that some compound drug is already in use, and we want to calculate its degree of heat on the basis of the qualities of its ingredients. (For instance, suppose I have a drug that consists of equal parts mastic and cardamom: can I just assume it is halfway between the first and second degrees of heat?) To do either of these things requires knowing the rules of proportion between two simple ingredients. This, says al-Kindī at the beginning of his treatise, is something the ancients failed to discuss (1–2 [269]); here his project is not just to recover and explain Greek science, but to expand upon it.

Al-Kindī begins with compounds that are neither hot nor cold,[6] but rather in a state of "absolute equilibrium [*i'tidāl bi-'l-iṭlāq*; *equalitatis absolute*]." Though one might suppose that such a compound is neither hot nor cold, al-Kindī instead claims that it is both hot and cold, but without either of these contraries outweighing the other (2 [269–70], cf. 8 [274]). Mathematically one can express this by saying that it is half hot and half cold. Equilibrium is the "origin, root, and principle [*al-aṣl wa-'l-rukn wa-'l-mubdi'*, *origo et principium et elementum*]" for all compound drugs, which are produced by adding hotter and colder ingredients to take the compound out of equilibrium (2 [270]). The question, then, is how something hot in the first degree relates to something in equilibrium. While one might expect that this is a question to be settled by observation, this is not how al-Kindī proceeds. Instead, he launches into the mathematical discussion that constitutes the theoretical basis of *On Degrees*.

Al-Kindī assumes that the relationship between the equilibriated compound and compounds of the first, second, third, and fourth degrees must be some arithmetic progression; otherwise, it would be impossible to quantify. But of course there are an infinite number of increasing numerical series. Which one governs the proportions of heat and cold in the simple ingredients? The crucial assumption that drives *On Degrees* is that it must be the most "natural" arithmetic progression (3–4 [270]). There are, says al-Kindī, five types of natural progression for numbers,[7] and of these the most natural is the progression of doubling, which yields the set {2, 4, 8, 16,...}. This may come as a surprise. Surely the most natural progression is simply that of the integers, which yields the set {1, 2, 3, 4,...}? This would later be the view of Averroes, who criticizes al-Kindī on this issue.[8] Averroes maintains that the progression of drug intensities is just 0 for equilibrium, followed by 1, 2, 3, and 4. Thus something hot in the third degree is three times as hot as something hot in the first degree, and 1.5 times as hot as something hot in the second degree.

The reason al-Kindī denies this is that, for him, the naturalness of a progression has to do with the ratios or proportions between consecutive members of the set. He speaks repeatedly of the "relation" or "proportion" (*nisba*) between numbers, and indeed says that "relation" and "increase [*ziyāda*]" are synonyms in this context (4 [270]: the Latin has *proportio* and *augumentum*). Al-Kindī shows that we can "reduce the members of the set to equality" with a very simple formula: subtract from each member of the set every preceding member, and the result will be the first member of the set (for example: 16 – 8 – 4 – 2 – 1 = 1; and 32 – 16 – 8 – 4 – 2 – 1 = 1).

The four other types of natural progression require much more complicated manipulation to reduce their members to the first member of the set. For al-Kindī this shows that double is the "first relation" in arithmetic, and that the progression that results from doubling is the most natural and "proportional [*mutanāsiba*, *proportionalis*]" (8 [274]). Though the argument about reducing progressions to equality is rather technical, intuitively it is easy to see why al-Kindī prefers the progression that results from doubling to a progression like the one that produces the integers. In the latter case, the ratio between consecutive members is always changing (2 is the double of 1, but 3 is not the double of 2), whereas with the doubling relation the ratio is always the same (4 relates to 2 just as 8 relates to 4).[9]

Having shown this, al-Kindī goes on to show how the doubling relation can be applied to the case of drugs. If we take the "smallest part" of the equilibriated compound, which is half hot and half cold, and double the heat, then we will have something hot in the first degree. We could write this formally as follows:

Equilibrium: 0.5 H, 0.5 C
First degree: 1 H, 0.5 C

To produce something hot in the second degree, we must double the heat of the compound hot in the first degree, and so on:

Second degree: 2 H, 0.5 C
Third degree: 4 H, 0.5 C
Fourth degree: 8 H, 0.5 C

Thus something hot in the fourth degree is 8 times as hot as something hot in the first degree and 16 times as hot as an equilibriated compound.

At this point the modern reader will probably start to wonder what in the world al-Kindī is talking about. Clearly these degrees of heat do not have to do with a perceptible heat in the drugs or ingredients themselves. Not only does mastic not feel twice as hot to the touch as cardamom, but in fact neither feel hot to the touch at all. Still, there is apparently some connection between the degrees of heat and what we can perceive. He says that what is hot in the first degree is the first thing whose heat has an effect that is "evident to sense [*ẓāhir li-'l-ḥiss*, *sensui manifeste*]" (11 [278]). This must mean that the first degree is the least amount of heat that will produce a noticeable effect in the patient who takes the drug. Yet al-Kindī does not say that, for instance, a drug hot in the third degree produces four-fold the healing effect in the patient that a first-degree drug would. And for good reason, since it is unclear how would we even go about quantifying such a perceptible effect in the patient.

It seems to follow from this that the mathematical proportions al-Kindī has in mind are not directly sensible at all. Although a fourth-degree drug is 8 times as "hot" as a first-degree drug, this does not mean we can perceive qualities in the two drugs, or effects the two drugs have on a patient, that would stand in a ratio of 8 to 1. Al-Kindī indeed says explicitly that the arithmetic progression has to do with the *quantity* of heat and cold in the compound, and not with any quality, perceptible or otherwise (9 [274]). Rather, the ratios al-Kindī discusses simply govern the chemical interaction of various substances. This explains why al-Kindī does not appeal to experience in order to settle the question of how much hotter a second-degree ingredient is than a first-degree ingredient. From the point of view of experience, the four-degree system is simply a rank ordering: we can perceive that second-degree drugs are stronger than first-degree ones, and third-degree ones are perceived to be stronger still. But this provides us no basis for understanding their chemical relationships, which are what matter when we are making compound drugs.

On the basis of his arithmetical theory of drugs, al-Kindī is able to produce complex calculations for drugs provided as examples. For instance, he calculates that a certain drug composed out of 8 different ingredients has 35 parts hot, 7 parts cold, 37 parts dry, 5 parts moist. Such a drug would have a ratio of 5 parts hot to 1 part cold, making it slightly hotter than something hot in the second degree. Now, obviously these compound drugs are supposed to be useful. So it must be possible to perceive the difference between the medicinal effect of this drug and that of a simple second-degree drug—otherwise why not just use the simple drug? For the same reason we must be able to notice that it is weaker than a simple third-degree drug, and for that matter weaker than some other compound drugs that are between the second and third degrees (for instance a drug with a ratio of 6 hot to 1 cold). This means that, although al-Kindī's chemical system is not derived from experience or observation, it is possible to use observation to *check* the system. Al-Kindī exploits this fact when he criticizes a rival arithmetical pharmacology.[10] Though al-Kindī has a technical argument against the rival theory, he begins his critique with the blunter claim that the theory is shown to be false "on the basis of experience [*min ṭarīq al-tajriba*, *modum experimenti*]" (26 [284]).

Observation of particular cases, then, has two roles to play in Kindian pharmacology. First, it establishes whether a given simple ingredient is equilibriated or has a certain degree of hot, cold, moist, or dry. Second, observation supposedly bears out the accuracy of the mathematical system al-Kindī defends, while showing the falsehood of rival systems. Yet al-Kindī's theory is in a sense non-empirical, insofar as it rests on the assumption that if the doubling relation is the most basic or "natural" arithmetic relation, then the proportions between chemical properties must be governed by this relation. Thus Léon Gauthier, the first to study this text, remarked that al-Kindī's theory is to some extent "a priori."[11] Al-Kindī does not pause to wonder whether the ideal proportions of arithmetic do in fact govern physical relationships, and he certainly gives us no argument to persuade us that they do so. In this regard, perhaps the most revealing passage in *On Degrees* is one in which al-Kindī says that musicians, too, confirm that the doubling relation is "the most excellent" (22 [282]), presumably because we achieve an interval of one octave by doubling the length of a string. This observation, which Averroes will later complain is irrelevant,[12] is a sign of al-Kindī's conviction that mathematical proportion and harmony governs all things in the natural world—it is a conviction so deep that he does not think to defend it. We will see below how he develops this point in other contexts.

In other medical works, meanwhile, we can see how strong are the ties between the theoretical principles of *On Degrees* and the practical concerns of the doctor confronted with specific ailments. For example, in *On Coitus*,[13] al-Kindī gives an anatomical explanation of the function of the male sexual organ (§1). On this basis he argues that sperm production is encouraged by heat and moisture, and impeded by cold and dryness (§3). So to treat the insufficient production of sperm, we need medications that will increase heat or moisture. Al-Kindī duly mentions a series of simple ingredients that perform this function, and then supplies complete recipes of compound drugs for specific ailments. This treatise does not explicitly evoke much of the theory found in *On Degrees*, but equally it depends upon that theory. For it shows that we cure illnesses by administering compound drugs that will induce the right degree of heat, moisture, and so on. And it is *On Degrees* that tells us how to make such drugs. Still more practical is al-Kindī's *Formulary*, which consists entirely of drug recipes, without any theoretical or anatomical account. As Charles Burnett has pointed out, the *Formulary* is one of several practically oriented "handbooks" written by al-Kindī, which consist mostly of applied science, and which often appeal directly to al-Kindī's personal experience.[14] The interrelated *On Degrees*, *On Coitus,* and *Formulary* show that al-Kindī was capable of approaching a single topic like pharmacology from a theoretical perspective, a practical perspective, or a perspective halfway in between.

The Geometry of Vision

In the case of optics, too, al-Kindī applies his expertise in mathematics to understand a physical phenomenon.[15] Here he is able to follow in the footsteps of Greek mathematicians, who had already used geometrical diagrams and demonstrations to model the phenomena of vision. His most important work in geometrical optics, titled *On Perspectives* (*De Aspectibus*),[16] is a reworking and expansion of Euclid's *Optics*, probably mediated by (Pseudo?) Theon of Alexandria, who passes on some ideas from Ptolemy. (Al-Kindī may also have known an Arabic version of Ptolemy's own *Optics* but this is uncertain.) In *On Perspectives*, al-Kindī makes some key conceptual advances that will later be taken up by the great Ibn al-Haytham, the first person to provide a broadly correct theory of how vision works.

There are two ways that one might try to explain the mechanism of vision. One might suppose, as we now know to be the case, that something comes from the seen object to the eye, so that sight occurs by "intromission." Alternatively one might hold that something goes out of the eye to make contact with the seen object; in this case we may speak of an "extramission" or "emission" theory. Within these two broad approaches several more specific positions were defended within the Greek tradition. The best-known intromission theory is Aristotle's. According to him, a sensible form is communicated to the eye through a suitable medium; the eye is potentially identical with that form and upon becoming actually identical with the form, it sees the object. Light is needed to make the suitable medium actually able to communicate the form, which is why we can't see in the dark. Another intromission theory is that upheld by the atomists, who believe that material objects constantly shed layers of atoms, which enter the eye and allow us to see their source. (Other, similar views invoke other sorts of effluences from the visible object.) No one in the ancient world, though, believed that we see because *light* goes from the object to the eye.

Al-Kindī rejects these intromission theories and instead follows the theory defended by Euclid and Ptolemy. According to this theory, we emit a "visual ray" from the eye, which allows us to see when it strikes the surface of a visible object.[17] One advantage of this sort of theory is that it can be represented using the methods of geometry. (It is no accident that the chief proponents of this theory, such as Euclid and Ptolemy, were also mathematicians.) A good example of why the visual ray theory is so powerful is that it can explain what happens when we see something in a mirror. Al-Kindī, who wrote several works on mirrors, argues in *On Perspectives* (§16) that the mirror is able to reflect the visual ray, which leaves at an angle equal to the angle of incidence (e.g. if it comes in from the left at a 45-degree angle to the surface of the mirror, it will be reflected off to the right at a 45-degree angle to the surface). One can even explain the various effects obtained by changing the shape of mirrors. For example a concave mirror will obviously reflect the visual ray differently from a flat or convex mirror (§18).

As al-Kindī points out, though, one does not need to appeal to this sort of special optical problem to show the inadequacy of rival visual theories. Borrowing an argument from Theon, he points out that a circular object would transmit a circular form or effluence into the air; so on a theory like Aristotle's, one should see such a thing as circular from any angle. Instead, we find that a circle seen from the side looks like a straight line or is not seen at all (§7). One might add that a circle seen from an oblique angle will look like an oval. Here the visual ray theory is in a much stronger position.

It can predict how something will be seen by modelling it geometrically, i.e. imagining lines drawn from the eye to each point on the visible object. These lines all fall within a "cone" of vision extending from the eye to the object; anything outside the cone will lie outside our peripheral vision and remain unseen. Notice that this also allows us to explain the directionality of vision, in other words why I have to look *towards* something to see it (§10).[18] On a theory like Aristotle's, it is hard to explain why we cannot see behind ourselves (cf. §15). For, if there is an illuminated medium between touching both my eye and a visible object situated behind me, then why don't I see the object?

Furthermore, the propagation of light itself clearly occurs along straight lines. Al-Kindī demonstrates this by discussing, for instance, the fact that a smaller light source will illuminate a larger object, but with a still larger shadow beyond it, whereas a larger light source will produce a shadow smaller than the object that is illuminated (§§2–3). He also considers the case of light illuminating something through an aperture in a wall (§6). It should be noted that al-Kindī tends, in *On Perspectives*, to demonstrate that rays of *light* have certain features (e.g. being propagated along straight lines in all directions), and then assume without explanation that these same features apply to *visual* rays. This does not, I think, need to mean that visual rays are themselves literally rays of light, but only that the two kinds of rays operate in the same way.[19]

So far, this departs but little from the geometrical optics of Euclid. Yet al-Kindī is strikingly critical of Euclid when it comes to the physical realization of geometrical optics. (He wrote a further optical work on *The Rectification of Euclid's Errors*, which is still preserved in Arabic.)[20] In fact Euclid had hardly anything to say about the physical nature of light or the visual ray, but contented himself with geometrical formalizations of these rays. Al-Kindī believes that Euclid's treatment of vision is thus misleading in several ways. Most importantly, the visual ray is not actually a line, because lines have no width. If the visual ray were a line, it would contact the object only at an extensionless point; and this means we could not see anything (§11). One might retort that we will in fact see, since there is a line between the eye and *every* point on the surface of the object. But if this means claiming that an *infinite* number of discrete visual rays going from the eye, it will fall afoul of al-Kindī's arguments elsewhere against the possibility of an actual infinity. In any case the suggested response would not be available to Euclid. For Euclid explains our inability to see distant objects as clearly as we see near ones by supposing that there are "gaps" between the visual rays. Al-Kindī protests that there are no gaps in the visual field, but rather we see the objects before us as continuous.

For al-Kindī, then, the visual ray is a continuous cone. It can be formalized as lines, but there are not literally individual rays wherever one can draw a line from eye to object. Still, al-Kindī too needs to explain why we do not see every object within the visual cone equally well. Rather, we see something best when it is in the middle of our field of vision, which is why we focus on certain letters when reading a book, even though the whole page is visible. We also see things better when they are closer. Why is this? At first (§12) al-Kindī tries invoking the "strength" of the visual ray: the ray is strongest near the center of the visual field and loses strength at greater distances from the eye. But he then gives an improved version of the answer, and in so doing makes his most important contribution to the history of optics. First, al-Kindī makes the move of thinking of the visual ray as proceeding from the surface of the eye (strictly speaking, the cornea over the pupil), rather than from a single point at the center of the eyeball.[21] Then, he assumes that the ray goes in *all* directions from *each* point on the eye. We see something better when lines can be drawn from more points on the eye to more points on the object. This lets us explain both the problem of peripheral vision and the problem of distance (§14). Regarding peripheral vision, an object in the center of the visual field is connected by straight lines to every point on the eye's surface. The further from the center of the field an object is, the fewer points on the eye lie along a straight line to the object. Conversely, a distant object subtends a smaller angle within the visual cone than a closer one of the same size, so that less of the visual ray strikes it. This is why closer things are seen more clearly.

This idea that the visual ray goes straight in all directions from every point on the surface of the eye is important, especially in a context where light and visual rays are assumed to work in the same way. For it will be crucial in Ibn al-Haytham's theory that *light* is propagated in all directions along straight lines, from every point on the surface of the light source.[22] Al-Kindī is unable to exploit this the way Ibn al-Haytham does, because he does not consider vision to require the propagation of light from the visible object to the eye. But this raises an obvious question: what is al-Kindī's explanation of why light is needed in the visual process? After all, the eye still emits visual rays in the dark, and these should still strike their objects. Al-Kindī's answer to this question is that the visual ray will only allow us to see an object when the object is also being struck in the same place by a light ray (§12). To some extent al-Kindī is thus able to agree with Aristotle's idea that light is a first actuality. In the dark, objects are only potentially visible, but once illuminated they are actually visible, and we need only direct our visual ray at them to see them.

Al-Kindī also has a story to tell about why some things, like apples, are potentially visible whereas others, like air, are not. Another way of putting this is to ask what makes things *colored*, for to be visible is to have a color. While we're at it, we might also want to know why different things have different colors. The problem of color is addressed by Aristotle in *On Sense and Sense-Objects*, albeit in a rather unsatisfactory way. He says (459b8–10) that the color in an object depends on the amount of "the transparent [*to diaphanes*]" in that object, and that color is in fact the limit of the transparent in a visible thing. The reason this is unsatisfactory, or at least puzzling, is that in *De Anima* II.7 the notion of transparency is instead applied to the visual medium. For the medium to be transparent is for it to be able to take on the actuality of light, so that it can then transmit sensible forms to the eye from the visible object. But of course transparency in the medium does not make the medium itself visible. The commentator Alexander of Aphrodisias brought together these two apparently conflicting ideas about transparency, though. He says that when transparency is in a body that has distinct limits, then it produces color at those limits. But when it is in an "indefinite" body with no limits, like air, then it does not produce color, but is merely the ability to take on light.[23]

Al-Kindī's treatment of color is clearly influenced by these or similar discussions, but his own view is diametrically opposed to that of the Aristotelians. He takes up the issue in *On the Body That Is the Bearer of Color* (AR^2 64–8), by asking which of the four elements are responsible for making things colored. Three of the four elements, as it turns out, are "transparent [*mushiffān*]." Transparency is not, however, what makes visible things colored, or makes it possible for light to be present. Rather the transparent is simply what allows vision to pass through unimpeded, so that we can see what is on the far side of it (§5, AR^2 65). Of the four elements, only earth is "dense" enough to "block" or "intercept" vision. So anything visible must have earth in it (one might suppose that fire is colored, but the colors seen in flames are actually due to the earthy parts of what is being burnt; §12, AR^2 67–8).[24] The various colors are apparently produced by the various sorts of earthy matter present in visible bodies.[25]

Al-Kindī never explicitly mentions the visual ray in *On the Body That Is the Bearer of Color*, and it would seem to be Aristotelian texts that led him to discuss the question of which element causes color. Yet his explanation of color fits well with the explanation of vision we find in *On Perspectives*. Only an emissionist theory of vision would require that the visible be dense, on the basis that it must "block vision." Similarly, al-Kindī's negative understanding of the transparent, according to which the transparent is merely that which does not intercept vision, is a departure from the positive theory of the transparent found in Aristotle and Alexander. But it fits with *On Perspectives*, because the Euclidean and Ptolemaic theory of optics requires no positive role for the transparent medium (the medium just needs to let the visual ray through). This does not necessarily mean that, when he wrote about the cause of color, al-Kindī had already begun the systematic research on optics that resulted in *On Perspectives* and other treatises. But he does seem to have accepted at least a rudimentary version of the emissionist theory, which suggests that he is already aware of the Euclidean and Ptolemaic account of vision.

Al-Kindī's theory of vision and color, then, gives us a good example of how his reading of "scientific" or "mathematical" works, like Euclid's *Optics*, informed his engagement with "philosophical" works, like the parts of the Aristotelian psychological corpus having to do with sensation. This process could go in the other direction, as well. As I have shown elsewhere,[26] *On Perspectives* §15 draws on a passage from the Arabic version of the *De Anima*, which in turn is derived from Philoponus' commentary on the *De Anima*. But it is clearly the tradition of geometrical optics, and not the Peripatetic tradition, that al-Kindī found most fruitful in his attempts to understand vision. We have already seen that there are good practical reasons for this: the visual ray theory explains phenomena that Aristotle's theory leaves mysterious. And given al-Kindī's mathematical proclivities, he was no doubt in any case predisposed to prefer a theory that explained vision using the laws of geometry.

On the other hand, optics is not a purely mathematical or abstract science, as is made clear in the preface of *On Perspectives*. Here al-Kindī says that the demonstrations he will supply are indeed geometrical and use geometrical principles. But we must also take principles from natural things (*ex rebus naturalibus*), to ensure that the demonstrations actually apply to the way things are "naturally." I take this to mean that the demonstrations must correspond to observable phenomena such as reflection in mirrors and the way objects are illuminated by light rays. True to his word, throughout *On Perspectives* al-Kindī appeals to physical observation as well as the laws of geometry. Observation can be used to refute incorrect visual theories—consider for instance the example of a circle viewed from the side. More importantly, al-Kindī's positive demonstrations invoke observable facts about physical phenomena. For example we can *see* that a straight line, drawn from a light source to the edge of an object illuminated by it, will then meet the edge of the shadow cast by that object. What this shows is that light is propagated in straight lines. And that, in turn, means that the behavior of light can be formalized using geometrical constructions. Empirical observation checks that the rules of geometry do in fact govern vision, much in the way that in *On Degrees* empirical observation checks that the rules of arithmetic govern chemical composition.

The Harmony of the Cosmos

So far we have seen that mathematics can provide the resources to understand specific physical processes like chemical interaction and vision. But al-Kindī's ambitions for the mathematical sciences are much broader than this. His boldest claims for any mathematical science are reserved for the study of harmony or music. The fundamental concept in al-Kindī's theory of music is "relation [*nisba*, *iḍāfa*]." In his overview of the Aristotelian corpus he says:

> *Quantity* §VII.2 (AR 377): The science of harmony [*'ilm al-ta'līf*] discovers the relation [*nisba*] or combination of one number with another, and the knowledge of what is and is not harmonious. The object of inquiry here is thus quantity insofar as one [quantity] is related [*muḍāf*] to another.

He goes on to add that this is the most comprehensive mathematical science: it "is composed from arithmetic, geometry, and astronomy. For there is harmony in everything [*fī 'l-kull*], though it is most obvious in sounds, and the composition of the universe [*tarkīb al-kull*] and of human souls" (§VII.3, AR 377–8). The claim that there is harmony in *all* things suggests that the science of harmonic relations, very broadly construed, would be a science of everything, or at least everything that has quantity.

Al-Kindī's attempt to make good on the promise of a musical theory of all quantitative nature shows how deeply he was influenced by the Greek Pythagorean tradition. His main source was the *Introduction to Arithmetic* of Nicomachus of Gerasa,[27] a second-century Platonist and mathematician, whose work inspired the later Neoplatonic tradition, especially Iamblichus and his successors.[28] As I have mentioned (chapters 2, 5), the opening sections of the *Introduction* are the basis for al-Kindī's idea that physical objects are subject to constant flux, and for the treatment of the mathematical sciences in *On the Quantity of Aristotle's Books*. Indeed, Nicomachus is a source for the definition of music as the study of relative quantity, just cited above.[29] Al-Kindī also drew on the *Introduction* for more technical purposes: notably, the five types of mathematical progression discussed in *On Degrees* are taken from Nicomachus.[30] More generally, reading Nicomachus would have encouraged, if not inspired, al-Kindī in his project of finding correspondences between musical phenomena and (seemingly) non-musical phenomena, including the structure of the cosmos itself.[31]

This project is realized in five extant works devoted to music, which have been edited but unfortunately only rarely studied.[32] Here I will concentrate mostly on *The Informative Parts of Music*.[33] As we have already seen (chapter 5) this includes al-Kindī's only clear mention of the internal senses. It also vividly illustrates his conviction that musical relationships are fundamental to a wide range of physical and psychological phenomena. After a promise to adhere to the teachings of the ancient philosophers, rather than the modish customs of modern musicians (95.7–9; 95.15–18), *Informative Parts* begins by explaining the eight different types of rhythm, which should be used appropriately with certain poetic recitations and at certain times of day. Al-Kindī then moves on to discuss the four strings of the *'ūd*[34] and the various four-fold groupings with which they share a "similarity [*mushākala*]" (100.7). The four strings are "related [*munāsib*]" to the four seasons, the quarters of the heavens and of the zodiac, the elements, the humors of the body, the phases of the moon, the directions of the winds, the ages of man, and several psychic and bodily faculties.[35]

Unfortunately the crucial word "related" is rather vague, so it is not immediately clear what al-Kindī means.[36] In another work, *On Stringed Instruments*, al-Kindī discusses the fact that different nations have used different numbers of strings on their musical instruments. In each case the number of strings corresponds to fundamental features of the cosmos and philosophy discovered by each nation. The one-stringed instrument of the Indians represents the fact that 1 is principle of the numbers, and that there is a single cause for the entire world (73.6–13). But the people of Khurāsān have a two-stringed instrument, because of the many dualities in the world (night and day, sun and moon, substance and accident, etc., 73.14ff). And so on, through instruments of up to 10 strings. All this might suggest that the number of strings is only "related" to other phenomena in a loose, perhaps symbolic sense. In which case it is hard to see how a study of musical harmony could help us to understand those natural patterns.

A very different impression, though, is given by al-Kindī's claims about the influence of music on those who hear it. For instance, he says that playing on the various strings of the *'ūd* will summon up particular kinds of actions and states of the body in those who hear the music, because the strings act directly on certain bodily humors.[37] The highest-pitched string, the *zīr*, excites the yellow bile and thus induces cheerfulness, whereas the second string, the *mathnā*, excites the blood, which is perhaps why it induces digestion. In these cases the "relation" is thus actually a *causal* relation. Al-Kindī goes even further than this by saying that just as we can produce various effects in soul and body using music, so we can use colors and perfumes to provoke moods and actions through the senses of vision and smell. Most effective of all will be the musician who uses music, color and scent all at the same time to affect his audience. Nor need this be a simple, mechanical process, a matter of plucking the *zīr* string repeatedly while thrusting pink roses at someone. Combining different rhythms, playing multiple strings, and blending multiple colors and scents will all produce more subtle, complex effects, and increase the efficacy of the individual components. Potentially, then, what al-Kindī is describing is a sophisticated art, which goes far beyond what we normally associate with music.

The contrast between individual strings, colors, and scents, on the one hand, and the combinations of these elements, on the other, is reminiscent of the contrast between simple and compound drugs in *On Degrees*. This is a more apt comparison than it might at first seem. Given that the *'ūd* strings are associated with the four elements as well as the bodily humors, it seems likely that music changes the state of the body with respect to the four Aristotelian contraries much in the way that drugs do: by increasing heat, cold, moisture, and dryness. A legend handed down about al-Kindī tells of his temporarily curing a boy's paralysis by having his students play the *'ūd* to him,[38] which suggests that he was known for using music in medical contexts. Nor should one forget al-Kindī's mention of musicians, and their appreciation of the doubling relation, in *On Degrees* itself.

Still, it is hard to see what sort of causal relationship al-Kindī might have in mind when he compares the strings of the *'ūd* to things like the seasons or the phases of the moon. And in any case we have as yet no explanation of why the different strings might affect things like the bodily humors. We can answer both questions, I think, by returning to the notion of "relation [*nisba*]." In the context of mathematics, a relation is a ratio: for instance, the ratio of *double* which relates 1 to 2 (as we saw, in *On Degrees* al-Kindī uses the word *nisba* for this). Furthermore we can say that 1 stands to 2 as 2 stands to 4—they have, that is, the same ratio or relation. We can write this in shorthand as follows: 1:2::2:4. Similarities like this can also obtain between things that are not numbers. For instance, imagine a 1-foot-tall statue of a man. Obviously its head will be much smaller than that of a real man. Yet the height of its head will be, let us say, half the length of its arm, if this is also true in the case of the real man. Thus:

head-of-statue:arm-of-statue::head-of-man:arm-of-man

We are accustomed to say that this is a similarity of "proportion [*tanā-sub*]," a word which in al-Kindī's discussions of music is closely related to the word "relation [*nisba*]," in part because the two share the same root in Arabic (*n-s-b*).[39]

In our example, there are in fact two kinds of relation: the internal proportions of the statue or the man, and the similarity or correspondence between the statue's proportions and the man's proportions. This second kind of relation can serve as a part of a causal explanation—it is precisely *because* a real man's arm is twice as long as his head is tall that this is also the case for a statue. Of course a complete explanation would need to go further than this, for instance by invoking the sculptor's intention to produce a realistic statue. But it is clearly plausible to think that similarity of proportion is sometimes relevant in causal explanation. I propose that when al-Kindī talks about the musical resonances throughout nature, and thinks of them as a basis for causal relationships, he has in mind this type of *relation between relations*: similarity of proportion. In other words, he thinks that yellow bile has the same quantitative relationship to blood that the *zīr* string has to the *mathnā* string:

zīr:*mathnā*::yellow bile:blood

It is for this reason that the *zīr* affects yellow bile and the *mathnā* affects blood. And even when there is no direct causal influence between the musician's song and the things compared to the strings of the *'ūd*—for instance the four parts of the zodiac, the ages of man—still there is a correspondence, and this correspondence has to do with similarity of proportion. This has far-reaching consequences for the study of the physical world. For if there is such a correspondence, understanding the proportions between the four strings of the *'ūd* could help us understand quantitative features of the four winds, the four bodily humors, and so on.

Al-Kindī invokes this sort of correspondence even, or rather especially, with regard to the structure of the entire cosmos. We know from *Quantity* that the study of music is followed by astronomy, which suggests that there are harmonic proportions that govern the quantitative aspects of the heavens (their size, speed of rotation, etc.). And in *The Informative Parts of Music* al-Kindī says explicitly that "the string of the musician . . . lets the particular souls know that the motions of the celestial spheres and the stars also have proportionate [*mutanāsiba*], harmonious and pleasant melodies"(110.19–21). But the most important treatise for this topic is *On Why the Ancients Related the Five Figures to the Elements* (AR^2 54–63, hereafter *Five Figures*). Already in the title, and then throughout the treatise, we have the notion of "relating [*nasaba*]" five "figures [*ashkāl*]" or polyhedra to the four elements and the celestial sphere, as follows:

pyramid	fire
cube	earth
octahedron	air
icosahedron	water
dodecahedron	the celestial sphere

This association between the geometrical figures and the elements has its source in Plato's *Timaeus* which, as we have seen, al-Kindī may have known in the translation of Ibn al-Biṭrīq. The *Timaeus* was central in late ancient, Neo-Pythagorean interpretations of Plato, because it makes extensive use of mathematics in setting out its cosmology. Most famously, at *Timaeus* 53c and following, Plato gives an analysis of the four elements in terms of triangles. The elements are, at the "atomic" level, polygons whose faces are combinations of triangles. This makes it possible for three of the elements to transform into one another, as the triangles are pulled apart and rearranged to form the faces of a new polygon. The case of earth is an exception (55e), since it is the only element made of isosceles triangles. (Earth's polygon is a cube, so its faces are squares made up of two triangles with angles of 45, 45, and 90 degrees. The other elements are made of triangles with angles of 30, 60, and 90 degrees.) Plato then assigns the various polygons to the four elements: pyramid to fire, cube to earth, and so on, as al-Kindī repeats. Plato does not assign the dodecahedron to the celestial sphere. This is however an association made later in the Platonic tradition, possibly in reaction to Aristotle's identification of aether, the matter of the heavens, as a fifth element.[40]

Since we do not know al-Kindī's direct source for the Pythagoreanizing interpretation of the *Timaeus* supplied in *Five Figures*, it is a matter for speculation how much of the numerological analysis is original with him. But the general strategy of the work is based on the notion of proportional similarity I have outlined above. To give a relatively simple example, al-Kindī says (AR^2 56) that the ratio of 12 to 6 is a "relation of the whole [*al-nisba alladhī bi-'l-kull*]," that is, the relation of "the first simple multiple." In other words, this is an example of the doubling relation. This is relevant here because the 12-sided dodecahedron, which is "related" to the heavens, is being compared to the 6-sided cube, which relates to earth. Earth is the element furthest from the heavens, since earth is at the center of the physical cosmos; so it is appropriate that the relation between these two polygons should be a complete or "extreme" ratio. We have, then, what I have called a similarity of proportion via the doubling relation, as follows:

earth:heavens::6:12::cube:dodecahedron

As Carmela Baffioni has pointed out,[41] this is somewhat easier to understand in light of Pythagorean musical theory. The phrase "relation of the whole" corresponds to the Greek phrase for the relation between two notes that are one full octave apart (*dia pasôn*)—as mentioned already, the lower note is produced by a string double the length of the higher. So here the octave, or double, is compared to the magnitude separating the heavens from the element that is furthest from them, namely earth. The intermediary elements would then be at intervals of distance that correspond to the intervals that separate the intermediate notes in a scale from the tonic.[42]

Unlike Plato, who makes use of the intuitive physical properties of his elemental polygons (saying for instance that fire cuts because it is made of sharp pyramids instead of other, rounder polygons), it is not even clear that al-Kindī thinks the elements are literally *made up* of polygons. Rather he seems to take the whole scheme to be an extended analogy.[43] But it is an analogy that genuinely reveals or explains features of the elements and the heavens, because thinking about the mathematical properties of the polygons allows us to grasp the proportional relations between the elements and the heavens.[44] These proportions are the same as those that govern music. It is in this sense that the study of harmony is the study of all things. Al-Kindī would seem to have thought that this sort of inquiry could be applied to almost any physical system, to judge by his musical treatises and the programmatic statements of *Quantity*. So again, we see the primacy of mathematics in al-Kindī's understanding of the physical world, this time in its entirety.

Let us now turn back to *The Informative Parts of Music*, and in particular to its concluding section (106–10). This section falls into the genre of gnomological literature (discussed in chapter 6), though the focus is on music rather than ethics: al-Kindī presents "sayings [*nawādir*]" about music ascribed to anonymous philosophers gathered at a banquet. As with the reports about Socrates and *Discourse on the Soul*, we need to proceed carefully here, since al-Kindī is not speaking in his own voice. On the other hand he seems to present the sayings with approval, and some of the sayings allude to philosophical views we know he accepted.[45] For example, several connect the theory of recollection with the effect mournful music has on the soul:

> *Informative Parts of Music* 109.8–10: Another [philosopher] said that when the souls are purified of bodily desires and renounce physical pleasures, spurning material distractions, they sing mournful songs, and remember their spiritual, sublime, higher world, and desire it.[46]

While this passage is welcome additional evidence for al-Kindī's use of the recollection theory, it also raises a problem. If I have been right to say that music affects things by means of similarity with respect to *quantitative* proportion, how can the *immaterial* soul be affected by music?

But this question assumes, incorrectly, that only physical objects can exhibit quantitative or numerical features. Remember that according to *On First Philosophy* everything other than God, including soul and intellect, is characterized by both multiplicity and unity. Thus some sort of quantity or number must apply to soul. In fact, al-Kindī's musical sayings suggest that the soul is by nature even closer to number than physical things. Al-Kindī quotes another philosopher as saying that "the substance [*jawhar*] of the soul is being in harmony [*al-ta'līfiyya*], because it is of the same genus as, and similar to, numbers" (110.5–6). The close association of number and soul is standard Neoplatonic doctrine, and indeed goes back to Plato himself (*Timaeus* 35b–36d); Xenocrates of the Old Academy even defined soul as a "self-moving number."[47] In this context we should recall that al-Kindī wavers in his identification of the science intermediate between physics and metaphysics, which studies immaterial things connected somehow to body. Is it psychology, as he says in *Quantity*, or mathematics, as he says in *On Stringed Instruments*? As I suggested in chapter 2, al-Kindī might want both psychology *and* mathematics to be intermediate, insofar as these two disciplines study soul and number, which are intimately linked and on the same ontological level.

This would give an additional rationale for al-Kindī's mathematical approach to physical science. Just as the beauty of the natural world is an effect of the soul's power (*Informative Parts of Music*, 110.11–19), and can therefore only be understood once we know something of the soul's nature, so the phenomena studied in al-Kindī's scientific works are manifestations of mathematical quantities and qualities,[48] realized within matter. Thus it is also with good reason that, in *Quantity*, al-Kindī emphasizes the need to study mathematics *before* progressing to physics, even if mathematics in other contexts is treated as a higher science on account of its objects. For physical phenomena (like the natures of drugs, the mechanism of vision, and the effects of music) are knowable precisely insofar as they instantiate mathematical features, like lines, angles, arithmetic progressions, and harmonic proportions.

On the other hand, Kindian science does give a role to empirical observation. The physical sciences are not *purely* axiomatic, demonstrative sciences like geometry and, indeed, metaphysics. For they draw on the evidence of the senses in asserting, for instance, that shadows in fact fall in such-and-such a way, that a given drug in fact has such-and-such an effect.[49] So al-Kindī has not run afoul of his own strictures against using a purely axiomatic "mathematical investigation" to study natural things.[50] Yet the study of nature does proceed chiefly by *applying* the truths of sciences like geometry to the physical world; observation is used chiefly to license and check the accuracy of this application. Perhaps because his use of mathematics makes his science so intellectualist, al-Kindī finds it natural to incorporate considerations taken from psychology and metaphysics into treatises on scientific and mathematical topics. The sayings gathered at the end of *Informative Parts of Music*, with their allusions to the purifying and recollection of the soul, are a good example. Another example is the end of *Five Figures*, which ends with a disquisition on the sphere that echoes the central theological argument of *On First Philosophy*.[51] But al-Kindī's most extensive fusion of themes from metaphysics, psychology, and physics is to be found in the works he devoted to the heavens and their influence.

8

THE HEAVENS

Prediction and Providence

Unsurprisingly, al-Kindī broadly follows Aristotle in his cosmology.[1] His main Aristotelian source is *On the Heavens*, which was available to him in the translation of Ibn al-Biṭrīq.[2] Al-Kindī also knows the *Physics*, as we have seen, and he makes extensive use of Aristotle's *Meteorology* in his account of how the heavens cause sublunary phenomena. According to Aristotle and al-Kindī, the terrestrial world is at the center of the universe. It is composed of the four elements, earth, water, air, and fire, which have natural motions "up" and "down," that is, towards or away from the midpoint of the universe. Al-Kindī explains that the four contraries, hot, cold, moist and dry, account for these motions. The two "active qualities" are hot and cold, and these determine whether an element moves up (fire and air) or down (earth and water). The two "passive qualities" are moist and dry, and these determine the "speed" of the motion: since fire and earth are dry they move more "quickly" than the moist elements, meaning that earth precedes water in going down and fire precedes air in going up.[3] The region of the four elements—the "sublunary" world, that is, the world below the sphere of the moon—is surrounded by a series of celestial spheres, in which are embedded the sun, moon, planets, and, in the outermost sphere, the fixed stars. As we have seen (chapter 4), al-Kindī follows Aristotle in thinking that the spheres are made of a "fifth element" which does not have the four contraries, and can only move with perfect, circular motion. There is nothing outside the sphere of the fixed stars, not even empty space.

This cosmology, then, envisions the world as a series of concentric spheres, with the lowest spheres being those of the four elements. Al-Kindī in fact devoted a short treatise to showing that the elements and heavens are all spherical in form.[4] But of course the sublunary world does not consist of four separate spheres of pure fire, air, water, and earth. Rather the four elements are mixed, and this mixture is the generation and corruption of compound bodies and, ultimately, the bodies of plants, animals, and humans. Given that the elements would naturally take up unmixed spherical regions, due to their natural motions,[5] the mixing process that makes the sublunary world so eventful calls out for an explanation. For al-Kindī there is both a proximate and a remote explanation. The proximate explanation or cause is the motion of the heavens; the remote cause is God, who brings it about that the heavens move in the first place.

The Cause of Heavenly Motion

Al-Kindī explains the reasons for heavenly motion most fully in *On the Prostration of the Outermost Sphere and its Obedience to God* (hereafter *Prostration*). As we have seen (chapter 2), this treatise was written at the request of a patron for an exposition of the Koranic verse which says that "the stars and the trees prostrate themselves" before God. This provides al-Kindī with an opportunity to expound his theory of the heavens and their relationship to God. He begins by pointing out that since the stars cannot literally "prostrate" themselves physically, here "prostration" must have the figurative sense of "obedience" (§II.4, AR 246, RJ 179). And "obedience" means the following of someone's command:

> *Prostration* §II.5 (AR 246–7, RJ 179–81): Thus it is clear that [the stars] carry out the command of someone, great be His praise. For they follow one proscribed motion without alteration, and this has existed for them in former ages until the present. Through their motion exists the alternation of the seasons, and through this alternation of the seasons every cultivation and reproduction, every generation and corruption, is brought to completion. They follow one command from which they do not depart, as long as their Creator, great be His praise,

> maintains them. And everything generated is generated through the generation of what He wants to be generated.

Here al-Kindī sketches the account he has given much more fully in another work, *On the Proximate Agent Cause of Generation and Corruption*; I will return to this earlier treatise below.[6] According to this account, God wishes that there be generation and corruption in the sublunary world, and He "commands" the heavens to move in such a way as to bring this about. However, "following a command" implies "choice [*ikhtiyār*]," and only something that has a rational soul can choose (§II.4, AR 246, RJ 179). So to explain how the heavens can be "obedient" in this sense, al-Kindī must now show that the heavens are rational. This is the chief task that will occupy him in the rest of *Prostration*.

In order to prove that the heavens have rational souls, al-Kindī needs first to undertake the more basic task of proving that they have souls at all. He needs, that is, to show they are alive.[7] Al-Kindī has two arguments for this. The first (§III.4–8, AR 248–51, RJ 183–7) is an extended dichotomous argument, of the sort he so often favors, which proceeds from the fact that the heavens are the cause of all generation, and thus all life, in the sublunary world. Any cause must bestow either that which it has by its own nature (as when fire heats), or not (as when a builder makes something into a wall). If the heavens bestow life in the first way, then they are of course alive. But whatever imparts a property that is not in its own nature does so "by means of an animal organ"; in other words, inanimate causes can only impart what is in their nature. So if we tried to suppose that the heavens bestow life without themselves being alive, we would have to assume that they did so by means of an animal organ, and hence that they were alive after all. The second argument (§IV.1–3, AR 251–2, RJ 187–9) is that the heavens have an orderly, stable motion that is unaffected by generation and corruption. Even in the sublunary world, orderly, stable motions belong only to what has soul; therefore the heavens are ensouled.

It must be said that neither of these arguments are particularly impressive as they stand. The second argument would be stronger if we interpret it as implicitly appealing to the idea of *self*-motion. Since, as al-Kindī does say here explicitly, the heavens are not moved by any body external to them, we could conclude that they must be self-movers, and what moves itself must be alive. Perhaps he does not want to argue in this way, though, because even though no other *body* moves the heavens, they are somehow moved by God. We can shed further light on this issue by returning to the first argument. That argument is somewhat confused in its presentation, because al-Kindī introduces the idea of final causation without really making clear how this relates to the main thread of the argument. A final cause imparts motion by inducing desire in what is moved. Such a cause can cause a property that it does not, itself, have: for instance a magnet can induce motion in iron, and the beloved can induce love in the lover. This is problematic, since if the heavens cause life in this way, they could do so without being alive. Al-Kindī seems to think that final causes must actually be what their effects are potentially, but that must be wrong, as is clear from his own examples of the magnet and beloved. So his own examples suggest a problem he does not adequately solve. Yet he may have good reason to introduce the notion of final causation in this context. Nowhere in *Prostration* does al-Kindī indicate the immediate mechanism by which God moves the heavens. The treatise simply argues that God commands them to move, and that the heavens obey, exercising their capacity for rational choice. I suspect, though, that al-Kindī believes the heavens do move themselves, as I just suggested, and that they do so out of desire or love for God, as Aristotle argues in the *Metaphysics*. If this is right, then al-Kindī will have brought final causation into the discussion here to leave room for God's causing of motion in the heavens, rather than for the heavens' causing of life in the sublunary world.

In any case, al-Kindī has shown to his own satisfaction that the heavens are alive. He now adds that being alive and capable of motion, the heavens must at least have sensitive souls, like animals (§V.1–2, AR 254–5, RJ 189–91). However, the senses of touch, smell, and taste are for the sake of nutrition and growth, so the heavenly bodies will not need these. Al-Kindī concludes that the heavens do, however, have the senses of hearing and vision, the "two noble senses."[8] More importantly for the present purposes, the heavens have the power to reason. This is obvious, according to al-Kindī, for several reasons. First, hearing and vision are for the sake of either nutrition or discernment (*tamyīz*), which implies reason. Again, the heavens need no nutrition, so if the heavens can hear and see they must be able to reason (§VI.1, AR 254, RJ 191). Second, the heavens are our cause and must therefore be nobler than us; if we are rational, we can hardly deny reason to these more exalted beings (§VI.2, AR 254–5, RJ 191).[9] Third, there are three powers of the soul, desiring, irascible, and rational—note the sudden inclusion of the tripartite Platonic soul, which also appears in al-Kindī's *Discourse on the Soul*—and the heavens would have no need for a desiring or irascible soul. So if they have soul at all, as we have shown they do, they must be rational (§VI.4, AR 255–6, RJ 193).

The most striking feature of these arguments, I think, is the application of principles of human psychology to the heavens. Al-Kindī is happy to assume that the Aristotelian division of the soul's powers into nutritive, sensitive, and rational, and also the Platonic tripartition of soul, exhaust all the possible psychic capacities. He does not allow the possibility that the heavens could have souls of a wholly different kind from ours. The ending sections of *Prostration* suggest one reason why he might have thought this was a reasonable assumption. On the one hand, says al-Kindī, the entire sublunary world is insignificant in size compared to the cosmos as a whole, and humans are much smaller still, so much so that they "are almost as if they do not exist at all" (§VII.2, AR 256, RJ 193). It would demean God's providence to suppose that humans, in their puniness, are the only rational beings. On the other hand, the entire universe is reflected in the nature of man, both at the anatomical level (our intestines, for instance, are comparable to mines), and at the level of the nutritive and sensitive powers, which are like those possessed by plants and animals. Our rational faculty, meanwhile, is a power shared with the heavens (§X.2–3, AR 260, RJ 197–9). This idea of man as microcosm may have encouraged al-Kindī to apply human psychology to the case of the heavens. Conversely, the idea of the entire universe as a living thing ("a single, articulated animal, a body with no void in it") gives al-Kindī the opportunity to enthuse about the wondrous nature of divine providence, who has made the world a single well-ordered organism, with the heavens as its most noble part.

The Cause of Sublunary Motion

Now let us return to the question of how the heavens make the sublunary world into something more interesting than a set of concentric elemental spheres. In answering this question al-Kindī's most important guide was the great Peripatetic commentator, Alexander of Aphrodisias. Al-Kindī's circle translated three relevant texts by Alexander into Arabic: two short treatises or *Quaestiones* (2.3 and 2.19), and the longer *On Providence* (*Peri Pronoias*), which would later be re-translated by Abū Bishr Mattā. As

Silvia Fazzo and Hillary Wiesner have shown,[10] al-Kindī drew especially on *On Providence* in writing *Proximate Agent Cause*. Conversely, the three Arabic translations reflect some of al-Kindī's own preoccupations, for instance his interest in astrology. Alexander expanded upon a few stray remarks in Aristotle to provide an Aristotelian account of divine providence, in which God directly causes the motion of the heavens, and the heavens then mix the four elements to produce compound bodies of increasing complexity, culminating in man. Alexander even believed that matter receives soul and intellect due to the heavenly bodies, since soul supervenes on bodily mixture.[11] It is hard to see how al-Kindī could have accepted this last point, given his strict dualism about the soul. But he is keen enough to emphasize the power of the heavens that he is willing to admit at least that "the *actions* of the soul follow on the mixtures of bodies" (*Proximate Agent Cause* §VII.1, AR 224, my emphasis).

How exactly do the heavens mix up the elements? An answer was suggested by remarks of Aristotle's, such as at *On the Heavens* II.7, 289a19–21, where he says that heat and light are produced by the rubbing of the heavenly bodies against the sublunary realm.[12] Alexander and al-Kindī latch onto the idea that the heavens produce sublunary motion by being in *contact* with the sublunary world as they are themselves moving. In particular, al-Kindī says, the heavens produce heat. Since they are not hot themselves, the heavens must do this by means of the friction between themselves and the elements as they move over the sublunary world (§VI.1, AR 223).[13] While this simple mechanism may not sound like a very promising explanation for the bewildering complexity of the sublunary world, al-Kindī immediately shows how it can yield an immense variety of effects. For one thing, there are many heavenly bodies, of different sizes, speeds, and distances from the earth. This means they will all produce different degrees of heat (§VI.2, AR 224). Also, a heavenly body directly above us in the center of the sky will have a greater effect on our region than one that is at an oblique angle to us, because the distance is less. Hence, a heavenly body at the zenith will have the greatest heating effect (§VI.5, AR 224). The heavens also affect the other three contraries indirectly: when the heavenly bodies are not directly overhead, there is less heat and so things cool down. Moisture and dryness, meanwhile, are "concomitant on heat and cold," which I take to mean that heat dries things out and cold moistens them.

Of the heavenly bodies, the one with the most obvious effect is the sun, because it is the largest (§VIII.2, AR 227).[14] Because the sun travels along the ecliptic, its latitude relative to the earth changes, which leads to the change of seasons. Al-Kindī points out, depending here on Ptolemy's *Tetrabiblios*,[15] that people of different climates are shaped both in their bodies and their characters by the sun (for instance people from the colder north have white skin and, being dominated by cold and moisture, are sober and restrained; §VII.2, AR 225). The moon too has obvious effects, as we can see especially from the tides—which are not mentioned here, but are discussed at length in a separate treatise.[16] Further, it must be the case that the planets and fixed stars have an effect on the sublunary world as well. Otherwise, every time the sun and moon were in the same positions, we would see the same effects here (§X.1–2, AR 233–4). Also providential (literally) is the fact that all these bodies move at an inclination to the earth, rather than on paths parallel to the equator. This maximizes the amount of variation in the sublunary effects at different times of the year, and in the case of the sun results in the yearly seasonal cycle. To some extent, we can also explain variety based on the conditions of bodies that result from earlier mixture. For instance if my body is particularly moist already, then the heavens will affect it differently than if it had been dry (§XII.1–2, AR 234).

The heavenly motions can thus be invoked to explain how we could get from four separate elemental layers to the complex world we now see. For instance earthen and watery bits will be heated and thus made to go up, contrary to their nature, so that they mix with the air. (As we will see later, this particular phenomenon is particularly important to al-Kindī.) But presumably neither Alexander nor al-Kindī think that the elements were ever actually separated. Rather the world has always been, or was created, in its current complex form, and the heavenly motions simply ensure that the cyclical motions that produce compound bodies will continue, and that the elements will not separate by following their simple natural motions. Alexander seems, for reasons I will explain below, to be happy with the general (and genuinely Aristotelian) claim that the heavens produce generation and corruption in a regular fashion—as shown by the yearly seasonal cycle, and its effect on crops and animal reproduction. But as we have seen, al-Kindī wants to use heavenly motion to explain even very detailed variation, from year to year, place to place, and person to person.

His emphasis on the complexity of celestial influence suggests that al-Kindī, unlike Alexander, wants to claim that the heavens are the cause for *all* sublunar events. This would make it possible for him to develop the theory in two ways. First, it would give him a theoretical basis for the science of astral prediction, which claims to be able to predict specific events, and ideally at least to predict events of any sort. Second, it would allow for a more robust account of divine providence than the one Alexander had offered, insofar as God would now be credited with bringing about everything that happens in the physical cosmos, whether directly (in the case of heavenly motion) or indirectly (in the case of sublunary motion). This raises obvious philosophical questions, though, especially the question of whether al-Kindī is a thoroughgoing causal determinist. Would he trace all celestial and sublunary events back to God's agency, even human actions?

These two further developments of al-Kindī's cosmological account—the possibility of astral prediction and the question of determinism—will occupy us in the last two sections of this chapter. But before we can turn our attention to those issues, we need to look briefly at a very different cosmological work ascribed to al-Kindī.

On Rays

As we have seen there are several works ascribed to al-Kindī that survive only in Latin, one of which is *On Rays* (*De Radiis*).[17] The interpretation of this work is a delicate matter, because it is of doubtful authenticity, but so interesting that it will have a major impact on our assessment of Kindian philosophy if we decide it is really by him. I incline towards the view that it is authentic, for reasons given below. Yet there are significant departures in *On Rays* from doctrines set out clearly in works we know to be by al-Kindī. I have already suggested (chapter 1) that this can best be explained by taking *On Rays* to have been written at a later stage of al-Kindī's career than most of his extant cosmological and philosophical works. We should also bear in mind that, even assuming *On Rays* goes back to an original Kindian treatise, there is no telling what doctrines or ideas may have been subsequently added (or removed!) as the work was copied and translated.

If it is authentic, *On Rays* is al-Kindī's most ambitious treatise on the physical world. It attempts nothing less than a comprehensive explanation of all physical interaction by means of a single mechanism, namely "rays" (*radii*, presumably rendering *shuʿāʿāt*). After a methodological introduction (§I, already discussed in chapter 5), *On Rays* shows how we can explain the influence of the stars (§II) and the interaction of the elements (§III) by means of rays. After this, there is a chapter which bids fair to be one of the most interesting texts ascribed to al-Kindī, a stunningly forthright affirmation of universal causal determinism (§IV). I will return to this at the end of this chapter. *On Rays* then goes on to apply the ray theory to various "magical" phenomena: prayer and magical utterances, including the names of God (§VI, the longest chapter in the work), magical "figures," i.e. diagrams and symbols (§VII), talismans (§VIII), and sacrifices (§IX). Perhaps unsurprisingly, the Latin version of this work provoked its share of outrage amongst Christian authors, leading to al-Kindī's inclusion in Giles of Rome's *Errors of the Philosophers*.[18]

Given our present purposes, we can mostly focus here on the sections dealing with astral and elemental causation, which in any case present the clearest account of how "rays" function. The main advantage of rays as an explanatory device is that they can account for action at a distance, for example the fact that heavenly bodies have an influence on the sublunary world. There is no sign here of the idea that astral causation is by means of contact and friction. Instead *On Rays* takes it as axiomatic that "every star has a proper nature and state, which includes among other things the projection of rays" (§II, 219). Each star has a special place within the celestial harmony (*stellarum armonia*, *celestis armonia*—a favorite phrase in *On Rays*) and its own special effect on the sublunary world. The stars' different effects, and their constant motions, give rise to the variation of things in the world of the elements. This is, according to *On Rays*, evident even to the senses, for instance from the illuminating and heating effects of the sun (§II, 220). The same goes for elemental rays, whose existence is obvious from such phenomena as the heat that radiates from fire and the sound that radiates from colliding bodies (§III, 224). Although such action at a distance is the clearest proof that causation occurs by rays (other examples include magnets and images reflected in mirrors, §III, 226), *On Rays* also claims that rays explain interaction between things that are in contact (§III, 225–6). At one point, *On Rays* introduces an important qualification: although we can speak loosely of the elements acting on one another by means of rays, in fact only the celestial harmony has any real efficacy. What we call "acting" and "being acted on" (*actionem et passionem*) is really only a "concomitance" produced by the genuine actions of the stars (§IV, 228–9). If we are to take this seriously,[19] then the points made in section III about the rays of the elements are true only in a loose or convenient sense.

On Rays is a remarkable work, indeed one that merits a much longer discussion than I can provide here. But is it really by al-Kindī? There is only one piece of evidence external to the text that could help us decide. The list of al-Kindī's works includes the title *Risāla fī shuʿāʿāt*, which means "Epistle on Rays," and this title appears in the section on astronomical treatises.[20] This is encouraging evidence in favor of its authenticity. However the internal evidence of the text is troublesome in several respects. Most obviously, the central account of astral causation in *On Rays* differs sharply from that of *Proximate Agent Cause* and other Kindian treatises. There are other major doctrinal divergences as well. As we have already seen, the methodological introduction fits badly with al-Kindī's epistemology. The text speaks frequently of a "ruling unity [*unitas regitiva*]"[21] in man, which doesn't correspond to anything found in his psychology elsewhere. A section on religious language and knowledge of God, while broadly corresponding with the negative theology of *On First Philosophy*, goes much further than al-Kindī does elsewhere, saying flatly that "God cannot be known by man [*Deum enim nullus homo cognoscere potest*)" (§VI, 246, cf. 249). The same passage also introduces the idea of negative predication "in the infinite mode," for example by calling God *not* finite, *not* created, *not* mortal, and so on (§VI, 245). This whole development, interesting as it is, seems foreign to the sort of negative theology we find elsewhere in al-Kindī. And one could multiply further divergences on points of detail.[22]

However, there are also respects in which *On Rays* fits quite well into al-Kindī's thought. For one thing, it supports the broader aims of *Proximate Agent Cause*. Though the mechanism that explains astral causation is different, the fundamental idea that sublunary events can be traced to celestial influence is of course Kindian, as is the emphasis that *all* sublunary events are caused by the heavens. It is clear that both *On Rays* and works like *Proximate Agent Cause* emphasize this in order to ground the science of astrology. *On Rays* makes other points that fit with al-Kindī's astrology, for example that the different heavenly bodies have different natures and hence different effects (see further below). *On Rays* also resonates with al-Kindī's attempts elsewhere to explain how heavenly influence could produce sufficiently varied effects to yield the world we see around us. It invokes not only the differences in heavenly motion and speed, but also the differences in the places on the earth that are affected (§II, 223). All of this gives the impression that the ray theory is being pressed into the service of a cosmology and astrology that is at least very like al-Kindī's.

Furthermore, the ray theory itself resonates strongly with al-Kindī's *On Perspectives*.[23] As we saw, the optical theory given there is that the eye emits visual rays which strike objects and thus allow us to see them. *On Perspectives* and al-Kindī's works on color also invoke the idea of light rays coming from the sun, which is mentioned in *On Rays*. We even find a parallel regarding the question of why rays have effects of varying strength: both *On Perspectives* (§12) and *On Rays* (§II, 219) say that a perpendicular ray is stronger than an oblique one. One might speculate, then, that al-Kindī was so impressed with the usefulness of the ray theory in the context of vision that he decided to apply it to all other physical phenomena. Insofar as the rays of *On Rays* are also susceptible to geometrical analysis (as is suggested by his point about the stronger, perpendicular ray), this would allow in principle for a "geometricization" of all physical interaction, a prospect al-Kindī would no doubt have found appealing.

The one major difficulty with this developmental account, according to which *On Rays* exports the ray theory from the optical context, is that *On Rays* does not seem to share the visual theory of *On Perspectives*. Nothing is said about visual rays, and at one point colored objects are said to be visible because *they* emit rays ("omne coloratum radios suos emittit quibus videtur," §III, 224) which of course is not at all al-Kindi's view. Still, the parallels both with Kindian cosmology and the ray theory in his optical works are encouraging signs for the authenticity of *On Rays*. In the next section I will provide an argument that should encourage us further, drawing on al-Kindī's meteorological works. There are also numerous other, more detailed bits of evidence internal to *On Rays* in favor of its authenticity.[24] If we accept its authenticity, though, I think we must also accept that it was written at a different time (according to me, significantly later) from a work like *Proximate Agent Cause*, because the doctrinal divergences are so striking. *On Rays* should therefore be considered separately from the treatises on philosophical cosmology I discussed above.

The Theory Applied: Astrology and Meteorology

Let us return then to the theory of *Proximate Agent Cause*, which stands behind numerous extant works by al-Kindī dealing with astral prediction. Al-Kindī's contributions to the astrological tradition won him lasting fame in both the Arabic- and Latin-speaking worlds.[25] The *Fihrist*, if anything, seriously underestimates the extent of al-Kindī's astrological output when it lists only a dozen titles under "his books on judgments of the stars [*aḥkām al-nujūm*]," i.e. astrology. (The undercount is partly because some works on astrology appear under other headings.) We are in possession of a good number of his technical astrological works. These deal with such topics as predicting the duration of the reign of the Arabs,[26] predicting the point at which an illness will reach its crisis point,[27] finding buried treasure,[28] choosing the best time for a journey,[29] and knowing when to expect God to answer prayers.[30] Al-Kindī also made a different kind of contribution to astrology, when he won over an enemy of his by getting him interested in the mathematical sciences.[31] This erstwhile foe, Abū Ma'shar al-Balkhī, went on to become one of the greatest figures in the history of astrology. As I have shown elsewhere, he follows al-Kindī in his own attempts to show that astrology is an empirically grounded Aristotelian science.[32]

To see how al-Kindī's astrological thought is connected to the cosmology of *Proximate Agent Cause*, we can do no better than to turn to his works on meteorology. The Istanbul manuscript containing most of al-Kindī's philosophical works also includes six treatises on weather and related phenomena: why it rains in some places more than others; about fog; why there are snow, hail, lightning, and so on; why the higher atmosphere is colder than the air near the earth; why the sky is blue; and about the increase and ebbing of the tide.[33] These treatises show the impact of Aristotle's *Meteorology* on al-Kindī; as with *On the Heavens*, he knows it in the translation of Ibn al-Biṭrīq.[34] All of these texts discuss the heating influence of the heavenly bodies on the terrestrial world.

Central to most of these texts is the fact that, as Aristotle explained in the *Meteorology* (e.g. at I.3), heated water and earth rise up into the atmosphere as "exhalation" (*bukhār*, translating Greek *anathumiasis* and *atmis*). This is why we see clouds: these are exhalations that have clustered by becoming colder as they rise into the chilly upper air. A wide range of other meteorological phenomena can be explained in terms of exhalations. Fog is cloud that has been pushed to the surface of the earth by wind; rain and other precipitation happen when watery particles become cold and fall back to earth. A particularly ingenious use of the exhalation theory is al-Kindī's *On the Blue Color of the Sky* (hereafter *Blue Color*). As we saw in chapter 7, al-Kindī thinks that the only element that can cause color is earth. This claim seems to have provoked one of al-Kindī's readers to wonder how the sky could be colored. In answering this question al-Kindī admits that only "dense" bodies can take on illumination so as to be seen, and that air is not dense. So in reality the sky has no color of its own. But the air is full of watery and earthy particles (§4, AR^2 105), which can be illuminated by the heavenly bodies and by the light reflected from the earth's surface (§9, AR^2 107).[35] The blue that we see is a color between the inherent "darkness" of the air and the light intercepted by the exhalations in the atmosphere.

In one of the treatises found in the Istanbul manuscript, *On Why the Higher Atmosphere Is Cold and the Atmosphere Closer to the Earth Is Warm* (hereafter *Higher Atmosphere*), al-Kindī confronts an obvious objection to the account of *Proximate Agent Cause*: if the heavenly bodies produce more heat when they are closer, why is the higher air, which is closer to the heavens, colder than the air near the earth's surface? After admitting that some see this as a devastating objection (AR^2 91), al-Kindī says rather tetchily that a solid grounding in the physical sciences is needed to avoid falling into such misapprehensions. He sets out the basic principles of his cosmology: the Aristotelian contraries, the motion of the elements, and the heating effect of the sun's rays on the earth's surface (AR^2 93–6). By nature earth is cold and air is hot, but earth is "dense," which means it is more susceptible than air to being heated by the sun, so that it rises up as smoke. Water is also heated and rises as vapor.[36] Furthermore, the heating effect of the sun thins the air near the earth, making it easier for the exhalations to rise. But then the exhalations reach the upper atmosphere, where the sun's heat has had less effect; here they cool and congeal as cloud or precipitation, sometimes causing wind because they push the air downwards as they gather and fall (AR^2 96).[37] Crucial to this account is that the elements can accidentally take on contraries they do not have by nature. Indeed for al-Kindī's explanation to make sense, it must be possible for a naturally cold particle of earth or water to become hotter than air, which is naturally hot (AR^2 97).

We should dwell for a moment on the role that the earth's "density" plays in this explanation. It is this density that allows earth to be heated more easily, just as, in *Blue Color*, density allows earthy particles to be illuminated (so that earthy vapor can explain the sky's color). But this makes no sense in terms of the explanation of heat found in *Proximate Agent Cause*, where the celestial bodies heat by friction. Rather, in explaining why the earth's density matters, al-Kindī refers to the sun's rays.[38] The earth is more affected by the sun because it is dense enough to intercept, and thus be heated by, the sun's rays. Similarly, al-Kindī points out that shadowy places on the earth's surface are colder than illuminated places, even when two such places are adjacent. This can only be explained by saying that the sun causes both light and heat by means of rays, which are propagated along straight lines (*Higher Atmosphere* AR^2 96, *Blue Color* AR^2 104). Yet *Higher Atmosphere* has not abandoned the idea of heat by friction, but still says heat is caused by the motion of the heavens over the sublunary realm (AR^2 95).[39]

I believe therefore that in both *Higher Atmosphere* and *Blue Color*, al-Kindī is groping towards a theory in which the celestial bodies produce their effects (both heat and light) by means of rays. He has not yet given up the "friction" account of *Proximate Agent Cause*, which shows that he has not yet thought of using rays as his sole explanatory principle. But he sees that an account including rays will be required to deal with such problems as why the upper atmosphere is colder. The theory of *visual* rays is already implicit in *On the Body That Is the Bearer of Color* and in *Blue Color*, but will be fully developed only in *On Perspectives*.[40] In the same way, it makes perfect sense that al-Kindī should try to explain the illuminating and heating effects of the sun by appealing to solar rays and not to friction. It would then have been natural to extend that idea to other celestial bodies. We see this development in *On Rays*, which indeed takes the idea even further to explain interaction within the sublunary world. This, I think, is another good reason to accept the authenticity of *On Rays*.

In any case, we now have plenty of evidence for the importance of al-Kindī's cosmology in explaining certain sublunary phenomena. Yet these meteorological treatises don't look as though they could have anything to do with astrology. This impression is misleading, however, as we can see from two letters on astrological weather prediction, preserved only in Hebrew and Latin, which have recently been edited and translated.[41] These two letters build on the theory we find in the Istanbul manuscript. So far, we have seen al-Kindī trying to explain the mechanisms that cause rain, fog, wind, and so on only at a fairly general level. Occasionally, in the Istanbul manuscript's treatises on meteorology, he explains why we tend to see more rain in certain seasons or regions. But what if we want to predict exactly when and where it will rain? For that we need a much more detailed science of heavenly motions and why they produce their effects. For al-Kindī this detailed science is astrology.

The two letters on weather prediction consist mostly of technical astrological claims—for example, that "when the sun is in the fifteenth degree of Scorpio, it is in the end of the second degree of heat, dryness, coldness and moisture" *Letter 1*, §V.19).[42] But they also set out philosophical principles that justify the use of astrology in this context. In fact, *Letter 1* chastises would-be "astrologers" who try to practice this craft without a solid philosophical foundation: "someone can only achieve this knowledge after he has acquired profound knowledge of the four mathematical sciences—which are the introduction to philosophy—and after he has acquired knowledge of the words of the philosophers about the science of the elements and their qualities" (*Letter* 1, Prologue, §7, cf. *Letter 2*, §§3–16). One must, that is, know the properties of the four elements, the fact that the heavenly bodies are made of an incorruptible fifth element, and that they heat our world (by means of friction: *Letter 1*, §1.13) in accordance with their speed, size, and proximity. In short, to understand this application of astrology, one needs to understand first the account of *Proximate Agent Cause*, and then its ramifications, as explored in the other meteorological treatises. Thus al-Kindī begins this letter with the same sorts of methodological remarks and theoretical principles as we find in, for instance, *Higher Atmosphere*. (These introductory sections are similar in purpose and content to Aristotle's *Meteorology*, II.1.)

Let me give two examples of how specifically astrological principles are supported by al-Kindī's philosophical cosmology. According to al-Kindī's astrological theory planets have different effects when they are "retrograde" from those they have while "direct" (*Letter 1*, §§49–53). This refers to the fact that the planets seem sometimes to move backwards in their supposed orbits around the earth. Ancient astronomers solved this problem by positing "epicycles": small additional spheres inside the concentric celestial spheres which carry the planets in a subsidiary rotation. Motion around an epicycle causes a planet to seem to slow down and then move backward. Now, when it is apparently moving backward, the planet is closer to the earth, because it is somewhere on the lower half of the circumference of a sphere that is inside the larger sphere. This explains why a "retrograde" planet (one seeming to move backward) will have a stronger heating effect than one that is "direct" (one seeming to move forward).

Another, even more fundamental astrological idea is that the different heavenly bodies have different "natures" or "properties"—as we have seen, this is an idea that also appears in *On Rays*. Thus astrologers are wont to say, for instance, that the moon is "moist" or "watery." As Burnett and Bos have pointed out,[43] this cannot be taken literally, given that the heavens are neither hot nor cold, moist nor dry. (Indeed al-Kindī is able to insist that the heavens lack the contraries hot, moist, etc. and in the same breath to ascribe to them the special natures of being fiery, watery, etc. [*Letter 1*, §5.45–7].) Worse, according to the theory of *Proximate Agent Cause*, heavenly motions are said to produce heat, not moisture; cold and moisture can only be produced by the *absence* of the heavenly bodies over a given place on the earth. In the letters on weather forecasting, al-Kindī does not really resolve this problem, but he does make the suggestive remark, "we have established the relation of their spheres to the spheres of the four elements" (*Letter 1* §5.47). I think we can guess what he has in mind, in light of a remark made at the beginning of *Letter 2* (§10): "One who lacks [knowledge of] the art of music, by means of which can be found the harmonious and the non-harmonious, i.e. the fitting and the unfitting, will not understand which sphere is more similar to the lower things." This recalls the theory of *Five Figures* (see above, chapter 7), where al-Kindī argues that there are mathematical proportions that govern the arrangement and behavior of the heavens and the elements. Perhaps when al-Kindī says that the moon is "moist," he means not that it is literally moist, but that it has a close *mathematical* relation to the moist elements, and thus a greater influence on moist elements and moist bodies.

This is confirmed by a passage in *On Tides* (AR^2 120), where al-Kindī says, regarding the moon, that "the harmony of [*i'tilāf*] its ratio [*nisba*] to that of the sphere of water and earth—as we have explained in our discussions of harmony [*fī aqāwīlinā al-ta'līfiyya*]" is such that the moon has a greater effect on water and earth, the moist elements. He goes on to add, "hence what some of [the wise] said, in their proof of the indications for rain: that the moon is watery, whereas others said that it is earthy, in their proof of the indications for generation in cultivation and reproduction" (AR^2 121). This shows how al-Kindī's ideas about the harmonic relations between the parts of the cosmos could explain why certain celestial bodies have a greater effect on certain sublunary bodies. Again, he provides a rational foundation for astrological principles, this time using mathematics rather than physics.

Al-Kindī thus sees astrology as intimately related to, and as dependent on, the philosophical curriculum he describes in *On the Quantity of Aristotle's Books*. Most obviously, astrology draws on the findings of astronomy, the fourth mathematical science. In many of the texts mentioned in this chapter, we find al-Kindī providing calculations for the size of the earth and for various heavenly bodies, as well as comparing the speeds of different celestial revolutions.[44] On the other hand, the successful astrologer requires much more than a grasp of astronomy. In *Letter 2* on weather prediction, al-Kindī says that his account will draw not only on mathematics and physics, but also on metaphysics, since astrology is a study of causal relations between higher and lower bodies (§§14–16). This rather surprising remark is echoed in *Letter 1*, which calls astral prediction a "spiritual science" (Prol. §8), and also in *On Rays*, which stipulates that physics studies the sublunary world, whereas metaphysics studies the celestial world (§IV, 229). Nowhere does al-Kindī fully explain why he associates astrology with metaphysics, which in a Kindian context usually implies theology. Two relevant considerations do suggest themselves, however. First, book Λ of Aristotle's *Metaphysics* has a lot to say about the causes of celestial motion, and the prime mover (i.e. God) as the cause of this motion. Second, al-Kindī believes that the heavenly motions are an instrument by which God brings about whatever He wills in the sublunary realm. This means that when we practice astrology, we are in fact predicting the workings of divine providence.[45]

The Scope of Celestial Influence

How far does al-Kindī want to press these bold claims about astrology's predictive power? Could an astrologer use his observations of the heavens to predict *any* sublunary event, no matter how trivial? Obviously this question is closely related to a question I posed above: if all sublunary events are brought about by heavenly causes, then is al-Kindī committed to a thoroughly deterministic picture of the physical cosmos? Had al-Kindī wanted to limit the scope of the stars' influence, he would have had a model in the work of Alexander. As mentioned above, al-Kindī's account of the heavens' influence is based closely on Alexander's *On Providence*, a work extant only in Arabic. In fact there are two Arabic versions, one from the Kindī circle, and a later version, more complete and almost certainly more accurate, by Abū Bishr Mattā.[46] Tellingly, the Kindī-circle version has the title *On the Governances of the Heavenly Spheres* (*Fī Tadbīrāt al-Falakiyya*) instead of the *On Providence* (*Fī 'l-'Ināya*) of the later translation.

The fuller translation of Abū Bishr Mattā begins with a lengthy refutation of two views on providence: that of the Epicureans, who deny divine providence altogether, and that of the Stoics, who say that divine providence extends to and causes all things. Alexander defends what he claims to be the Aristotelian view, a sort of compromise according to which divine providence, brought about through heavenly motion, is realized only at the level of species, not particulars (*al-juz'iyyāt*).[47] For example the sun brings it about that crops and animals reproduce and nourish themselves in regular cycles. But the heavens do not bring it about that there be particular horses, like Secretariat, or particular humans, like Socrates (to say nothing of bringing it about that Secretariat wins a given race, or that Socrates decides to go down to the *agora* today for some philosophical disputation). This has many welcome consequences, from Alexander's point of view. For example, it allows him to explain why there are evils in a providentially ordered cosmos: evils are departures from the order of nature. They are therefore accidental, and proper to particulars. Since God's providence only extends to species, He is not to blame for evils.[48] Also, since divine providence does not necessitate any events at the level of particulars, Alexander is able to reject the determinism of the Stoics. That this would have been a key requirement for Alexander is clear from a different work, *On Fate*, which argues at length against determinism on the basis that it would make all events necessary, leaving no room for chance, accident, free will, or possibility.[49]

The Kindī-circle version of *On Providence* differs from Abū Bishr Mattā's in several respects. Most obviously, it omits the opening sections on the rival theories of providence, and concentrates on the latter parts of the treatise, which give details of how the heavens influence the sublunary world. Also striking is the emphasis on the heavens as providential: in several passages, references to the gods are replaced with references to the heavens.[50] These and other changes suggest that the early translation was produced specifically in order to support the practice of astrology. Al-Kindī duly incorporated passages and ideas from *On Providence* into his *Proximate Agent Cause* when he was giving his own theoretical basis for astrological science.[51] However, the Kindī-circle translation is more faithful to Alexander than al-Kindī himself would be, in at least one respect. In the translation, Alexander's restriction of God's providence to species comes through fairly clearly.[52] But al-Kindī adopts a position that marries the determinism of the Stoics to Alexander's Aristotelian account of providence, by acknowledging that this providence does extend to particulars after all. (This makes *On Providence* a particularly good example of the way al-Kindī's circle worked: the predilections and interests of al-Kindī and his patrons were reflected in the choice of texts to translate, and in modifications made in the process of translation. But al-Kindī's own works often stray yet further from the original sources, rather than simply reproducing the already modified doctrines of the translations.)

It must be said that al-Kindī is far from forthcoming in this departure from Alexander. In fact he only once explicitly raises the question of whether providence extends to particulars, in one of the letters on weather forecasting. He says that according to Aristotle "the planets only approximately indicate particulars," and then adds, noncommittally, "he may be correct."[53] However this is already different from Alexander's view, since Alexander does not think the heavens indicate or cause particulars at all, whether exactly or approximately. And in fact I suspect that what al-Kindī means is only that it may not be *practically* possible for astrologers to predict any and all particular events: the necessary calculations might be too complicated. We find him making this sort of caveat in *Higher Atmosphere*. There he admits that there are so many variables governing the height at which particular exhalations will congeal into cloud and precipitation that one can give no general rule about the altitude at which this occurs. Nor can one necessarily determine the precise location of the clouds that do form, for example, whether they are over a given city or not (AR^2 98). But of course, the philosophically pressing issue here is whether astrology could *in principle* predict any event, which amounts to asking whether every sublunary event, no matter how minor or "accidental," is in fact caused by the heavens.

In any case, the whole point of the letters on weather forecasting is that one can predict rainfall at particular times, in particular places, on the basis of celestial observation. Similarly, as we have seen, *Proximate Agent Cause* goes to great lengths to explain why the heavens bring about a variety of particular effects. Al-Kindī is not content to say simply that they give rise to the continued existence of natural species. By the same token, Alexander denies that the heavens are responsible for the accidental features of particulars. But in *On Tides* (AR^2 127), al-Kindī says instead that every place on the earth's surface is the same "by nature" but differs "accidentally" precisely insofar as it is differently influenced by the heavenly bodies. All of this indicates that al-Kindī's cosmological and meteorological works are committed to the idea that divine providence, by means of heavenly influence, determines events even at the level of particulars. And of course it is clearer still that such a view is presupposed by al-Kindī's astrological works, which deal almost exclusively with the prediction of events concerning particulars (e.g. how long the Arabs will rule, or on what day a given patient will reach the point of crisis in a disease).

This raises a further question: do the heavens cause *all* sublunary events, or are some events exempted from the scope of celestial influence? There is an obvious type of event one might wish to exclude, namely human actions. With the exception of *On Rays*, there is unfortunately no Kindian treatise that deals directly with this question. However there are scattered passages that give hints as to his view. Given the aforementioned difficulties surrounding *On Rays*, it will be worth examining these passages first. We should begin by noting that al-Kindī consistently speaks of humans as possessing a power of "choice [*ikhtiyār*]" and "volition [*irāda*]." But it would be too quick to conclude from this that he makes human actions exempt from celestial causation. Perhaps the stars causally determine the choices we make, even though we are still choosing in a meaningful sense. If this is right, then al-Kindī would hold something like a modern-day compatibilist view, or like the view that had been held by the Stoics. According to such a view, actions can be voluntarily chosen (they can be "up to us [*eph' hêmin*]") even though they are caused by external factors.[54]

That al-Kindī does hold this view is suggested by his saying, in *Proximate Agent Cause*, that "the actions of the soul" and "the soul's customs and its volitions [*irādāt*]" follow on the mixtures of bodies, which are of course brought about by the heavens; "for this reason there occur designs distinct from the first designs, and volitions distinct from the first volitions" (§VII.1, AR 224; §XII.7, AR 236). In *On Definitions* we get a bit more insight into the process by which humans make choices. A sequence of definitions stipulate that an action (*isti'māl*) is caused by a volition (*irāda*), which is in turn caused by an inclination (*khāṭir*), which itself is caused by an impulse (*sāniḥ*) (§§75–77, AR 175). Al-Kindī then adds:

> *On Definitions* §77 (AR 175): [An action] may also be the cause for further inclinations. It is a circle that makes all of these causes necessary [*yulzimu jamī' hādhihī 'l-'ilal*], [which] are the act of the Creator. We say, therefore, that the Creator, may He be exalted, lets some things He created be impulses for others, some actualize others, and some move others.

Here we have not only the notion that choices and volitions can be causally necessitated, but also that God is the ultimate cause of these choices and volitions.

Rather surprisingly, a still more useful passage on this topic is found in one of al-Kindī's musical treatises. The passage is a digression which explains how sounds, including musical sounds, are produced by humans.[55] It is worth quoting at some length, especially since as far as I know no one has noted its importance until now:

> Articulations [*makhārij*] of melody begin from the point of possibility [*ḥadd al-imkān*]. Possibility is not outward [*ẓāhir*], but inward [*bāṭin*], and is innate [*gharīzī*] within nature. It may be classified into three types: for the most part, half the time, and rarely [*'alā 'l-akthar, al-istiwā', wa-'l-aqall*]. For the most part is for instance what happens in nature, half the time is for instance what happens by choice, and rarely is, for instance, when someone digs and finds treasure, since one does not always find treasure when one digs. The innate is of all three types: it is what can move breath and propel it such that instruments are sounded, and when this happens there is a tone. But this is not by necessity [*bi-'l-iḍṭirār*], because the necessary [*al-iḍṭirār*] is of two kinds: necessary [*iḍ_ṭirār*] and necessitated [*bi-'l-iḍṭirār*]. "Necessary" is a connection [*la'm*] to the element [*'unṣur*]. "Necessitated" is when something belongs to the element at the point of possibility. This possibility is the incitement [*muhayyij*] of the motion; the motion is the incitement of the breath from the lung, and propelling it [sc. the breath] such that it goes to the outside and thereby sounds the instrument, and then there is a sound.

After some further comments about the types of motion, he adds that "the production [*kaynūn*] of motion is from the soul," and that the soul brings about action by means of the brain and the nerves, which then affect the muscles and the rest of the body.[56] He calls this "substantial motion." But then he continues:

> Motion may be accidental—in which case it is voluntary (*irādiyya*), for example saying of a man that he is standing or not, or awake or not. The motion of standing or sitting is voluntary, and is accidental; the engendering of this motion is from the psychic spirit (*min al-rūḥ al-nafsānī*).

This passage is difficult, but extremely interesting. For one thing, it shows al-Kindī's awareness of Aristotelian discussions of modality, even giving the classic example of chance (digging in the garden and finding treasure, which is from *Metaphysics,* Δ. 30) and Aristotle's example of sitting and standing as possibilities (*On the Heavens* I.12). Also following the Aristotelian tradition, he classifies possibilities into three types: what happens "for the most part" but not necessarily always, namely natural possibilities (fire will go up for the most part, though it can be hindered); what happens "half the time," namely human choice; and what happens rarely, namely chance. Al-Kindī then introduces a distinction of his own, namely that between the "necessary" and the "necessitated." Unfortunately this is explained so quickly that it is difficult to understand. I believe he means that the "necessary" is what is always true of a thing in terms of its own nature, for instance fire's being hot.[57] The "necessitated" is that which a thing might be or might not be, for example a person's making a sound; this will then be a possibility that becomes necessary only by virtue of something else. He goes on to say that human actions are initiated by the soul, which effects the action through a causal sequence in the body. These actions can be of two types, substantial (which may mean actions we always perform simply by virtue of being alive, like breathing) or voluntary.

As helpful as this passage is, it is not clear what it tells us about al-Kindī's views on determinism. There are some hints here that the soul is an uncaused cause of motion, and determines which of two genuine possibilities will be realized. The claim that choices are made "half the time" or between "equals" (*'alā 'l-istiwā'*) must mean that two mutually exclusive choices are equally live possibilities for the chooser. On the other hand, the "psychic spirit [*rūḥ nafsānī*]" mentioned at the end of the passage seems to refer to *pneuma*. The "soul" being presented here is not the immaterial, intellective soul of al-Kindī's psychological works, but a particularly fine, hot air which causes bodily motion.[58] Elsewhere, al-Kindī is happy to think of *pneuma* as being affected by external causes.[59] In light of this we should be hesitant to say that al-Kindī is claiming that our actions must be uncaused. More significant for our question may be the distinction drawn between the necessary and necessitated. Al-Kindī seems to tell us that every possibility that is realized is in fact *necessitated*, and that if it is a possibility that is not realized simply due to the thing's physical nature, then it will require a causal explanation—hence the elaborate causal story he then gives for the case of human action. Notice that this account would allow him to maintain that human actions fall within the domain of the possible, even though the choice that is made is somehow necessitated.[60]

From these merely suggestive passages, we can now turn to the much more explicit discussion of determinism in *On Rays*. The fourth chapter of this work, titled *De possibili*, boldly affirms that all sublunary events, including human actions, are indeed caused by the stars.[61] An objection is then considered: if our actions are caused by the stars, why does it seem to us that we exercise free will (*liberum arbitrium*)? The reason is our incomplete knowledge of the cosmos. If someone knew everything about the world, "he would have knowledge of the causality between things, and would hence know that all things which occur and happen in the world of the elements are caused by the celestial harmony, and would know that the things of this world come about necessarily [*ex necessitate*], being related to that [harmony]." So it is only out of ignorance that we believe in the "contingency of things." One might object to this (as for instance Aristotle did in chapter 9 of *On Interpretation*, his most famous discussion of determinism) that if determinism is true then our deliberation, hopes, and fears are groundless, because the stars have already determined what will happen. *On Rays* is happy to bite this bullet, and admit that desire, hope, and fear too are only the result of our ignorance, just like our frequently erroneous beliefs about the future ("Est ergo ignorantia hominis causa opinionis eventuum futurorum et per hoc medium est ignorantia causa desderii et spei et timoris"). On the other hand, *On Rays* has the wit to point out that human choice is itself part of the causal nexus that leads to action. Thus it is not the case that, without my choosing, my actions and the ensuing results would have been the same. Rather, my choosing is efficacious, but is itself brought about by astral radiation. In keeping with this, *On Rays* continues to speak in subsequent chapters about human volitions, despite its affirmation of determinism. One such passage, interestingly, is reminiscent of the text we examined from al-Kindī's musical treatise: "the *pneuma* [*spiritus*] of man or other animals, affected in this way [sc. by words], brings about a choice [*voluntatem*] in its subject, moving the limbs to another place or in some other way that would not otherwise have occurred."[62]

This chapter is certainly the fullest and most sophisticated discussion of determinism in the Kindian corpus, so much so that I would sympathize with readers who felt he could not possibly have written it. Still, the doctrine set forth here is broadly consonant with the drift of the other passages just examined: the stars are the causes of all sublunary events, including human actions, but this does not rule out the efficacy and reality of voluntary choice. Given al-Kindī's intense interest in astrology, it is clear enough why he might have consistently held this view. He would want to make sure that an astrologer could, at least in principle, predict events that are affected by human decisions. Indeed, astrology would be of fairly limited use otherwise. Since al-Kindī's version of astrology includes the claim that the stars actually *cause*, rather than merely symbolize or indicate, the events the astrologer predicts, he has good reason to claim that causal necessitation is compatible with voluntary choice. One might think that he would have at least as good a reason to reject astral determinism of human actions: his dualist account of the soul. How can the stars affect the immaterial soul, if all they do is heat the sublunary elements? Here, perhaps, we should remember that al-Kindī's immaterial soul is essentially a theoretical, not practical, intellect. Though the soul does project activities into the body, it would not be obviously inconsistent for al-Kindī to consider our worldly actions as belonging more to the material realm than to the psychic and intellective realm.[63] And this would allow the heavens to play a role, perhaps a determining role, in bringing about those actions.

In closing, let us consider more closely God's role in dispensing providence by means of the heavens. We have already seen that in *Prostration*, al-Kindī says that the heavens voluntarily move out of obedience to God's command. Thus, even though God does not directly bring about sublunary events, those events can be traced back to a divine command. This raises three problems, only one of which al-Kindī addresses. The first problem is that God would therefore seem to be ultimately responsible for evils in the sublunary world.[64] A second, related problem is whether the stars actually intend or will the events they cause in the sublunary world; if so, the stars might be thought to intend evils in our world, even if God does not. Alexander says explicitly that the stars do not intend their sublunary effects, and cause them only "accidentally." (He also considers it absurd that the stars should move for the sake of what is inferior to them.) This view is echoed at the beginning of the sixth chapter of the *Theology of Aristotle*,[65] but not mentioned by al-Kindī himself.

The third problem, which al-Kindī does discuss in the extant corpus, is why God dispenses providence in the first place. Must He do so, or could He have done otherwise? As we might expect, al-Kindī is keen to stress that God is not compelled by some distinct cause to show benevolence towards His creation. He emphasizes God's independence in an astrological work on predicting the time at which God will answer prayers.[66]

Al-Kindī wants to deny that the stars are the true causes for answered prayers; rather, the stars only "indicate" God's decisions. So although "one may learn from effects [i.e. the heavens] something of the will of the causes [i.e. God]," one should not fall into the error of directing prayers to the stars themselves. Al-Kindī associates this error with "philosophers not of our religion," and mentions as an example Socrates' instructing that a cock be sacrificed at the temple of Venus.[67] He may also have in mind the Sabeans, a group of pagan Neoplatonists at Ḥarrān in whom al-Kindī seems to have had an abiding interest.[68] There is in fact a report of their views preserved in the *Fihrist*, handed down from al-Kindī by his student al-Sarakhsī.[69]

One last text useful for the current question is a passage which is probably from the lost sections of *On First Philosophy*, preserved by Ibn 'Abd Rabbih al-Andalusī.[70] This is worth quoting in its entirety:

> Al-Kindī said, in the ninth part of the *Tawḥīd*: "know that the whole world is ruled by judgment [*qaḍā'*] and predestination [*qadar*]. By 'judgment' I mean that what is best, wisest, and most perfect in the construction of the cosmos [*al-kull*] is apportioned to all caused things [*li-kull maf'ūl*]. For He, the exalted, created and originated both necessarily and by choice [*muḍṭarran wa mukhtāran*] with complete power [*qudra*]. Because what is chosen is from perfect wisdom[71] (for the originator of the cosmos has complete wisdom), had His choice been unconstrained [*aṭlaqa*], He would have chosen many things that would have resulted in the corruption of the cosmos. So He, the exalted, predestined a construction of the universe in keeping with wisdom, and let some things be impulses [*sawāniḥ*] for others,[72] and chose through His volition [*irāda*] and desire, without being forced [*ghayr maqhūr*], what was best and wisest in the construction of the cosmos. So the determination [*taqdīr*] of these impulses is predestination [*qadar*]. Through judgment and predestination, then, He, the exalted, rules all that He originated, and this rule is perfectly wise, and no lapse or deficiency enters into it. So it is clear that everything caused is in a state which its Lord apportioned to it, from which it does not depart, and that some of these are necessitated while others are by choice, and that what is chosen is the result of the impulses of His predestination, and He does it through His volition, not by compulsion [*bi-'l-kurh*]."

Here, if the quotation is accurate, al-Kindī explicates two standard terms from Muslim theology, *qaḍā'* and *qadar*. As we would expect, he says that events within the created cosmos are all necessitated by God. God is said to act using "volition and choice," but also "necessarily."[73] The reason for this, apparently, is that God's wisdom ensures that He will choose what is best. Al-Kindī says that "unconstrained" choice would lead to worse results. I take this to mean that God's choice is necessarily guided by His own wisdom, and therefore must yield the best outcome. However God is not "forced" so to choose, since nothing distinct from God makes Him choose as He does. If this interpretation is correct, then we find al-Kindī here applying to God Himself the broadly compatibilist account we find him giving for human agents. Choice is not excluded by necessity, whether that necessity results from external causes, as in the human case, or from inevitable goodness and wisdom, in God's case.

This passage certainly makes one rue the loss of the latter sections of *On First Philosophy*, suggesting as it does that in those sections al-Kindī gave a still fuller account of divine providence than what we have in the extant corpus. Yet the evidence we do possess gives us a fairly complete account, and one that ties together many aspects of his thought. Al-Kindī uses principles of psychology to explain why the heavens move as they do. His Aristotelian physics explains why things under the heavens are affected by this celestial motion. This in turn undergirds a major part of Kindian science, the use of astronomical observation to predict future events here on earth. The entire theory, finally, provides the basis for al-Kindī's theory of providence. This chapter thus serves as a fitting conclusion to this study of al-Kindī's philosophy. Indeed, there is a sense in which al-Kindī could have considered the study of the heavens to be the culmination of his philosophical system. For our highest aim in philosophy is to grasp God, and we grasp God's creative activity most directly by discovering how, in Dante's words, God is "the love that moves the sun and the other stars."

NOTES

CHAPTER I

1. There are four main sources: the *Fihrist* of Ibn al-Nadīm, ed. Tajaddud (1971), 315–20 (there is also an older edition which is often cited, Flügel (1871–2)); Ṣā'id al-Andalusī, *Kitāb Ṭabaqāt al-Umum,* ed. Mu'nis (1998), 70–2; Ibn Abī Uṣaybi'a, *'Uyūn al-Anbā' fī Ṭabaqāt al-Aṭibbā'*, ed. Müller (1882), I.206–214; and Ibn al-Qifṭī, *Ta'rīkh al-Ḥukamā'*, ed. Lippert (1903), 376–8.

2. See Loth (1875).

3. *Letter to al-Ma'mūn on Cause and Effect*: see McCarthy (1962), §260.

4. Less encouraging is the detail that Sind knew they would get away with deceiving the caliph because the astrologers had accurately predicted his imminent death.

5. See especially Endress (1966, 1973, 1997, 1987/1992); Gutas (1998, 2000); and the work of Cristina D'Ancona listed in the bibliography.

6. See Gutas (1998).

7. Particularly Endress (1973).

8. On developments in many fields under the 'Abbāsids, see Young et al. (1990). For an astonishingly complete overview of developments in philosophy and other scientific fields see Endress (1987/1992).

9. On *kalām* during this period see the magisterial van Ess (1991–5).

10. Here it is worth noting that some Kindian treatises are addressed to named individuals other than members of the royal family: for example 'Alī b. al-Jahm, a poet, and Ibn Māsawayh, a physician.

11. See Ritter (1932). The manuscript is Aya Sofia 4832. I am very grateful to Charles Burnett and Dimitri Gutas for their help in obtaining copies of it.

12. Ed. Tajaddud (1971), 315–20; trans. Dodge (1970), 615–26. This list and other testimony about the titles of al-Kindī's books are collected in McCarthy (1962).

13. And of these some are clearly not about philosophy, for example *On Writing Missives to Caliphs and Viziers*.

14. Al-Kindī is also credited with what may be the earliest extant treatise on the use of statistical analysis to break codes. See Mrayati et al. (1987).

15. See Gutas (1998), 108–15.

16. See Rosenthal (1942), 268.

17. On this genre in the philosophical tradition see Endress (1987/1992), vol. 2, 465–6.

18. He does occasionally make cross-references to other works, but as often as not these titles do not match exactly to titles in the bibliographical tradition. See Rosenthal (1956a), 440–4. Rosenthal concludes that al-Kindī may have "preferred a loose form of citation." Some confirmation for this may be had from the fact that two meteorological works of al-Kindī's refer back to his work on why rain happens in some places more than in other places. But al-Kindī does not use the same title in these two cross-references (see AR^2 76.10 and 80.11–12).

19. The section on astronomy has more than one work whose title involves "rays [*shuʿūʿāt*]" while the optical work *De Aspectibus* may be represented here by the *Kitāb Ikhtilāf al-Manāẓir* (*On Different Perspectives*); this title appears under works on geometry, but *De Aspectibus* is a work of geometrical optics and thus could be grouped into this category.

20. For a very useful list of the extant works, with indications of manuscripts, editions, and translations, see Travaglia (1999), 103–146.

21. Abū Rīda (1950/1953).

22. A work preserved only in Latin, *On the Art of Demonstration*, is ascribed to "Muḥammad, a disciple of al-Kindī [*Mahometh discipulo Alquindi*]," but this work seems in fact to have nothing to do with al-Kindī. See Farmer (1934) and Baffioni (1994).

23. See Rashed (1997).

24. Ed. D'Alverny and Hudry (1974).

25. See Celentano (1979) for those in the Istanbul manuscript, and also Bos (1990).

26. Arabic ed. and trans. in Gauthier (1939). Latin ed. in McVaugh (1975).

27. Levey (1966).

28. For an edition of several musical works see Zakariyyā' (1962). For astrology see Burnett (1993) and Veccia Vaglieri and Celentano (1974).

29. For example his two most important cosmological works, *Proximate Efficient Cause* and *Prostration of the Outermost Sphere*, refer back to *On First Philosophy*. Some cross-references in a work on Ptolemy are mentioned in Rosenthal (1956a), 442–3, an article which also discusses the problem of titles mentioned above.

30. See Adamson (2006b) and Arnzen (1998).

31. For the *Rectification* see Rashed (1997). Al-Kindi does stress that he corrects Euclid in a spirit of charity. See *De Aspectibus*, Prop. 11, ll.79–81, which says that we should not delight in ascribing errors to Euclid, but instead "think well of him and shift what he says to the right path [convertamus eius sermonem ad semitam bonam]."

32. Here it is worth recalling that the scientifically and mathematically oriented Banū Mūsa made an enemy of al-Kindī, apparently out of professional jealousy, very late in al-Kindī's life.

33. For another discussion of this tradition, focusing especially on their eclecticism and their classifications of the sciences, see Adamson (forthcoming). The best general study of most of the philosophers in question is Rowson (1990).

34. On al-Sarakhsī see Rosenthal (1943). On Abū Zayd see Rowson (1990); the most important report is contained in Yāqūt's *Irshād*, ed. Margoliouth (1907), vol. 1, 141ff.

35. See Rosenthal (1943), 42ff.

36. On him see Rowson (1988).

37. See Biesterfeldt (1985). I am very grateful to Dr. Biesterfeldt for making available to me a copy of this study. A brief earlier study is Dunlop (1950–55). One manuscript of the *Compendium* has appeared in a facsimile edition, Ibn Farīghūn (1985).

38. See Adamson (2002a).

39. See Altmann and Stern (1958).

40. See the general study of Arkoun (1970). For the quotation from al-Kindī see Miskawayh, *Tahdhīb al-Akhlāq*, ed. Zurayk (1966), 156–7. In a forthcoming publication on Miskawayh, I show that he also knew and made use of *On First Philosophy*.

41. For example the "Brethren of Purity [*Ikhwān al-Safā'*]" and the circle of Abū Sulaymān al-Sijistānī, on whom see respectively Netton (1982) and Kraemer (1986).

42. See Rowson (1990), 63. Al-Kīndī was well respected for his astrological writings in the Arabic tradition; see Burnett (1993).

43. Less well-known Baghdad Peripatetics include 'Abū 'Alī b. al-Samḥ, a student of Yaḥyā b. 'Adī's, and Abū al-Farāj b. al-Ṭayyib, author of extant commentaries on the *Isagoge* and *Categories*.

44. See Biesterfeldt (1985), vol. 1, 166ff.

45. Edited, with other texts, in Khalifat (1996).

46. It might thus be a better approximation to say that the Kindians are in the tradition of Athenian Neoplatonism, while the Baghdad philosophers follow the Alexandrians. But even this needs qualification; for instance, as we'll see al-Kīndī was deeply influenced by John Philoponus, who was a student of Ammonius in Alexandria.

47. On this see Gutas (1998a), 248–9.

48. Here our understanding of al-Kīndī himself may admittedly be distorted by the loss of several works on politics mentioned in the *Fihrist*.

49. See his *Kitāb al-I'lām bi-Manāqib al-Islām*, ed. Ghurab (1967). On this work see Biesterfeldt (1977).

50. This irenic attitude finds an expression in al-Kīndī's claim that the Greek and Arab peoples could be traced to two brothers, Yūnān and Qaḥṭān. See al-Mas'ūdī, *Murūj al-Dhahab*, ed. Pellat (1965–79), §666; cf. Gutas (1998), 88. For citations and evidence supporting the generalizations made in the previous several paragraphs, see Adamson (forthcoming).

51. For the Arabic text see al-Jāḥiẓ, *Kitāb al-Bukhalā'*, ed. al-Hājirī (1948), 70–81, and for an English translation Serjeant (1997), 67–78. Al-Jaḥiẓ also wrote a work, now lost, called *On the Surpassing Ignorance of Ya'qūb ibn Isḥāq al-Kindī*, according to the *Fihrist* (see Tajaddud, 1971, 210).

52. My thanks to Robert Wisnovsky for suggesting this point to me. An example could be the strategy suggested for resisting one's desire to eat dates (80.11–81.2 in the Arabic); the passage is not so far removed from the practical asceticism of *On Dispelling Sadness*.

53. The report is preserved in al-Tawḥīdī, *Kitāb al-Imtā' wa 'l-Muwānasa*, ed. Amin and Zayn (1939–44), with the passage about al-Kīndī at vol. 1, 127.5–128.8. For an English translation of the report see Margoliouth (1905), with the passage about al-Kīndī at 127–8.

54. The passage includes such standard technical terms, familiar from al-Kīndī's works, as *istiṭā 'a* ("capacity"), *ghāya* ("final end") and *istiḥāla* ("change").

55. Mu'nis (1998), 72.

56. For *taḥlīl* to mean the acquisition of premises as starting-points for demonstration, see also Mallet (1994).

57. To which we can add the verse refutation, by al-Nāshi' al-Akbar, of al-Kīndī's fanciful genealogical story about the founders of the Greeks and the Arabs; see note 50.

58. See Périer (1920–21).

59. See al-Mas'ūdī, *Murūj al-Dhahab*, ed. Pellat (1965–79), §3312.

60. See Daiber (1986).

61. See Langermann (2003).

62. Giles of Rome, *Errores Philosophorum*, in Koch and Riedl (1944), chap. 10.

63. The translator Hermann of Carinthia extolled al-Kīndī as "the most suitable and true judge amongst astrologers." See Burnett (1993), 107.

64. For the Latin works see Nagy (1897).

65. See Cortabarria Beitia (1977).

66. See Burnett (1999).

CHAPTER 2

1. See Bosworth (1963).

2. Recently Robert Wisnovsky has usefully distinguished between the ancientcommentators' attempt to reconcile Aristotelian texts with each other—the "lesser harmony"—and their attempt to reconcile Aristotle with Platonism, to yield a single body of coherent Greek thought—the "greater harmony." Put in these terms, the burden of this chapter will be to show that al-Kindī not only inherited these projects, but also attempted a still greater harmony between Greek thought and his own culture and religion.

3. This would make much more sense in the context of a work addressed to the caliph al-Mu'taṣim, who followed his predecessor al-Ma'mūn in persecuting traditionalists in the *miḥna* (see chapter 4) and who himself installed broadly Mu'tazilite thinkers into seats of power. Though the traditionalists did not have caliphal support during this period, al-Kindī could well have seen them as having won renown amongst the people (the "crowns of truth"). Indeed al-Ma'mūn himself complains in his letter instituting the *miḥna* (see al-Ṭabarī, ed. de Goeje (1897), III, 1114) about the "glory and leadership [*ri'āsa*]" the traditionalists had accrued to themselves. Interestingly, in a later epistle he makes remarks much like al-Kindī's, to the effect that the traditionalists trade their faith for monetary gain (see al-Tabarī, ed. de Goeje [1897], III, 1127–8). I should add that there is no evidence that al-Kindī objected to the *miḥna* (contrast Ivry (1974), 32). Indeed as we will see (chapter 4), *On First Philosophy* itself supports principles like those that spawned the doctrine of the Koran's createdness.

4. On the relation between al-Kindī and the Mu'tazila see Adamson (2003).

5. For an example, see Endress (1966), 106–7.

6. Al-Jāḥiẓ later complained about the Arabic of the translations: see Endress (1997), 43–4.

7. Whether it might include more than that is disputed. For example, D'Ancona (2001) holds that the aforementioned original sections of the Arabic Plotinus may have been composed by al-Kindi himself, but I have denied

this in the conclusion to Adamson (2002b). (I do agree with D'Ancona that al-Kindi most likely wrote the Prologue to the translation.) See further D'Ancona (1995a) for her views on his role in the composition of the *Liber de Causis*.

8. Ed. Bouyges (1973). On the reception of the *Metaphysics* in Arabic see Martin (1989) and now Bertolacci (2005).

9. The text is preserved in a medieval Hebrew translation. See Freudenthal and Lévy (2004), and more generally on the Hebrew reception of Nicomachus, see Langermann (2001).

10. See Rosenthal (1956a).

11. On him see Endress (1966), 91ff, Endress (1997) 55–8, and Dunlop (1959).

12. He certainly knew something of the *Timaeus*, as is clear from his *The Reason Why the Ancients Related the Five Figures to the Elements*. See chapter 7.

13. For instance *On Dispelling Sadness*; see chapter 6.

14. Thus I would make so bold as to dissent from the opinion of the great Franz Rosenthal, who writes: "Al-Kindī shows no indication of true creative originality. His dependence on his sources, not always admitted with complete candor, is such as to preclude the thought that we are dealing here with a fundamentally creative mind. The few changes and additions in the work may be his own; that is, he may have expanded his source on his own, or he may have gathered further information from other translated Greek works himself. They should be considered as such until evidence to the contrary shows up. However, it is very well possible that the material reached him through his informants or translations exactly in the form in which he presented it" (Rosenthal (1956a), 455).

15. For divisions and classifications of the philosophical sciences in Greek and Arabic see Hein (1985).

16. For example in *On Definitions* "wisdom [*ḥikma*]" is defined as "the knowledge of universal things in their true natures, and putting truths into action as one ought" (§91, AR 177). *On the Five Essences* begins by stating, "Aristotle the wise, at the beginning of his discussion on dialectic, says that the knowledge [*scientia*, presumably translating *'ilm*] of anything that is sought falls under philosophy, which is the knowledge of all things. . . . Philosophy is divided into theoretical and practical [*scientiam et operationem, id est theoricam et practicam*]" (AR^2 9).

17. The first list mentions three works, the second list only two. The title "*Politics*" is only mentioned in the second list, and there seems to be some confusion on al-Kindī's part between the *Politics* and the *Eudemian Ethics*. However, there may be a textual corruption in this passage.

18. This is at least the implication of *On the Five Essences*, AR^2 11.

19. See the brief remarks on this work at §X.1 (AR 381), in contrast to the handling of the previous three books of the *Organon*. The *Posterior Analytics* seems to have been rendered into Arabic only by Abū Bishr Mattā, too late for al-Kindī to have read it.

20. Consider for instance the following passages from his meteorological works. In *On Tides* (*Fī'l'illa'lfā 'ila li-'l-madd wa-'l-jazr*): "every art [(*ṣinā'a*] has principles, and its principles are made manifest through [the principles] proper to another science" (AR^2 133.2–3). And in his *On Why the Higher Atmosphere Is Cold* (*Fī al-'illa allatī la-hā yabrudu a'lā al-jaww* . . .): "the sciences . . . are ordered [*murattaban*]: the first, then the second, then the third, until the last of the sciences is reached. For the second cannot be grasped until one already knows the first [*ba'd 'ilm al-awwal*], and the third cannot be grasped until one already knows the second. Thus the science of philosophy, which is the 'art of arts and the wisdom of wisdoms,' is ordered: the first, then the second, then the third. And it is ordered like this until the utmost [*aqṣā*] of its sciences, namely the science of divinity [*'ilm al-rubūbiyya*]. So no one achieves knowledge [*'ilm*] who proceeds to it directly and does not know that [sc. the prior science] first, contrary to what many people think: that anyone can achieve any knowledge he wants, whenever he wants to, before all other knowledge" (AR^2 92.10–16). These passages show that al-Kindī knows that the Aristotelian sciences should be interrelated and depend upon one another, but equally they fail to explain how this dependency works.

21. All of this is based on ideas taken from the opening chapters of Nicomachus of Gerasa's *Introduction to Arithmetic*; see Freudenthal and Lévy (2004).

22. See Hein (1985), 165–6.

23. Zakariyyā' (1962), 70.13ff., on which see Endress (2003), 130–1 and Rosenthal (1956b), 27. Rosenthal remarks that al-Kindī may have taken this classification from the beginning of Ptolemy's *Almagest*.

24. For this work, *Finiteness*, see chapter 4; in §9, al-Kindī remarks that he has used "mathematical proofs, which are intermediate between sensation and intellect."

25. For al-Kindī's use of mathematical methodology see Endress (2003) and Gutas (2004). I am grateful to Prof. Gutas for showing me an advance copy of this important paper, on which I depend in what follows.

26. Though as O'Meara (1989), 196–8, has pointed out, the method is not identical to that used in geometry.

27. Of course Aristotle too engages in dichotomous arguments and *reductio* arguments. What I mean is not that an Aristotelian theory of demonstration rules out the use of such arguments. Rather it rules this out as the primary or preferred method, which it seems to be in al-Kindī. On the other

hand, it is a notorious fact that the Aristotelian corpus rarely gives arguments that seem to fulfill Aristotle's own requirements for demonstration as set out in the *Posterior Analytics*. And in fact, al-Kindī may have used Aristotle as a model in his use of dichotomous arguments.

28. Here I agree with the assessment of Endress (1987/1992), vol. 2, 419: for al-Kindī "die Philosophie zeigt den Weg und das Ziel der Wissenschaften in einer islamischen Gesellschaft."

29. For this text see Rudolph (1989), which includes an edition, German translation and commentary.

30. On which see especially Gutas (1975, 1981).

31. For example al-Kindī uses numerous terms to refer to "being" or "existence," as we will see in chapter 3. Most of these are not taken over by later authors and one of them, *huwiyya*, is given a wholly different sense by Avicenna and others (see further in chapter 3).

32. As mentioned above it was used extensively by Isaac Israeli in his own *Book of Definitions*; see Altmann and Stern (1958).

33. On this definition see Riad (1973).

34. See Adamson (2003), 75 n. 87, and the introductory remarks to our translation in Adamson and Pormann (forthcoming).

35. Namely that the poet's use of a *maṣdar* or verbal noun indicates that the "prostration" he refers to is ongoing or continuous, and must therefore be taken figuratively, as "obedience," rather than as literal prostration.

36. The same point is made in al-Kindī's treatise *On Why the Higher Atmosphere Is Cold*, at AR^2 92–3: normal people must exert themselves by studying the philosophical sciences in order (*'alā tartīb*) until the last of the sciences, which is theology (*'ilm al-rubūbiyya*). But prophets receive knowledge through revelation (*ilhām*) without any effort and without recourse to prior principles (*bi-lā awā'il*).

37. As Walzer (1962), 181 notes, this conforms to the Muslim belief in the inimitable perfection of the Koran (*i'jāz*).

38. The poet he quotes here addresses the poem to the night, and anthropomorphizes night as having various body parts. Al-Kindī explains that one must take this reference to body parts figuratively, which may be intended to remind us of figurative readings of Koranic passages that anthropomorphize God. But the more immediate reason to quote this poem is the fact that the poet is speaking to the night; this is no less appropriate, says al-Kindī, than God's speaking to what does not yet exist, and commanding that it be.

39. The only passage in the Kindian corpus that might suggest this comes at the beginning of *On Lisping*, which contrasts "exoteric and esoteric knowledge [*'ilm al-ẓāhir wa 'l-bāṭin*]" and says that "exoteric knowledge is the knowledge of Socrates and Plato, whereas esoteric knowledge is the knowledge of Moses

and Solomon, the son of David" (ed. Celentano (1979), 47.12–15). Unfortunately al-Kindī makes no comment as to what distinguishes the two sorts of knowledge.

CHAPTER 3

1. These are found in Ibn Ḥazm and Ibn 'Abd Rabbih, and are edited in RJ. Both authors refer to it as al-Kindī's book *On Oneness* (*Tawḥīd*), which we know to be identical with *On First Philosophy* because Ibn Ḥazm gives numerous quotations, all but one of which are from the extant part of the work. (See my discussion of the title in chapter 1.) The report in Ibn 'Abd Rabbih is labelled as being drawn from the "ninth section [*fann*]," which suggests that we have at best only about half of the original treatise.

2. Both Ivry (1974), 165 *ad* 123.3, and Rashed and Jolivet (1998), 105–6 *ad* n. 36, draw attention to this ambiguity in the present context.

3. It is the ambiguity of the term *dhāt* that allows al-Kindī to shift so easily from the conceptual distinction between a thing and its *dhāt* to their real identity. If we translate *dhāt* as "essence" it is easier to set out the conceptual distinction, but it is hard to understand the claim that "a thing is the same as its essence." By contrast, if we translate *dhāt* as "self" it is easy to see why it must be that "a thing is the same as itself" but it is hard to understand the original conceptual distinction.

4. This is sometimes called the principle of the indiscernibility of identicals. It should not be confused with the much more controversial thesis of the identity of indiscernibles.

5. It seems to me that al-Kindī's argument does assume that causation is asymmetric, that is, that if a thing causes its *dhāt*, then its *dhāt* does not cause it. This assumption may be problematic, since it comes very close to implicitly denying that something can be its own cause and thus begging the question.

6. The issue is complicated by the fact that these terms are, according to al-Kindī, the subject of Aristotle's *Categories*. In *Quantity* he says that the *Categories* "deals with terms [*maqūlāt*], I mean the subject and the predicate. The subject is what is called 'substance,' whereas the predicate is what is called an 'accident' predicated of the substance, from which the substance takes neither its name nor its definition" (§III.1, AR 365). Notice that here *maqūlāt* explicitly include both predicates and the subject of predication.

7. These are technical terms, also defined in *On Definitions*: an "all [*kull*]" is a sum made up of different kinds of parts, like a car, whereas a "whole [*jamī'*]" is a sum of similar parts, like water, each of whose parts is also water. Al-Kindī further stipulates that a portion of an "all" is called a "part [*juz'*]" whereas the portion of a "whole" is "some [*ba'ḍ*]" of that whole. However we can ignore

these terminological distinctions for the sake of setting out the main thrust of his argument. (It may be worth noting though that there are similar distinctions in Aristotle at *Metaphysics* bk. Δ, 25–26; cf. *De Caelo* 268a20.)

8. Some readers may wonder whether there might not be some individuals that cannot be further divided into parts, like the indivisible "atoms" of the ancient atomist school, whose existence was also asserted by some theologians in al-Kindī's day. We know, however, that al-Kindī denied the existence of indivisible atoms, because of the title of a lost work named in the *Fihrist*: *On the Falsehood of the Statement of One Who Claims That There Is an Indivisible Part* (ed. Tajaddud, 1971, 319.1).

9. See Jolivet (1979).

10. The only exception is the argument at §XIV.9 (AR 135, RJ 57), that on (M) there would be no knowledge, which is refuted with the factive claim that there is indeed knowledge.

11. The only possible exception is a sub-argument having to do with parts and whole. Al-Kindī admits that one could eliminate multiplicity by supposing that there is nothing at all, but of course then there would be no unity either.

12. This is especially true for al-Kindī, who holds that the world is neither eternal nor necessary, and therefore that God can exist without the world's existing. So he is committed to the claim that pure unity can exist in the absence of multiplicity.

13. This passage raises the question of what al-Kindī would say about created things that are not sensible, such as the human soul. It may be that the phrase "and all that is concomitant to the sensible things" in the quotation given here is intended to refer to things like the soul. But in any case al-Kindī will show that the soul is multiple in the fourth section of *On First Philosophy*; see below.

14. Here one might worry that al-Kindī has not, in fact, shown it is strictly impossible for there to be only unity. As we saw his arguments against this all rely on a factive premise. But al-Kindī is here talking only about what was possible for the *created* world: it cannot be pure multiplicity, as shown by the refutation of (M). But nor can it be pure unity, because if the world is one pure unity and God is a second pure unity, then there will be multiplicity after all. This leaves open the possibility that there is only one pure unity, God, with no created world at all—ensuring that the created world remains contingent. (My thanks to Jon McGinnis for discussion of this point.)

15. As he repeats elsewhere: see *On Why the Higher Atmosphere is Cold*, AR^2 99.9–10 ("2 is the first number"). This follows Aristotle: *Physics* III.7, 207b7; *Metaphysics* A.1, 1053a30 and M.9, 1085b22.

16. Al-Kindī makes the same point at the end of *On Why the Ancients Related the Five Figures to the Elements* (AR^2 54–63), on which see further in

chapter 7), beginning at AR^2 60.13. Here the mathematical analogy is to the sphere, not the number 1. The sphere is said to be the "cause" of the other figures, insofar as it is a more perfect instance of "equality" than any polyhedron. Furthermore: "through the existence [*wujdān*] of the sphere exists every one of the remaining [figures], and the sphere is not similar to anything that has surfaces, for it is not multiple whereas those are" (60.16–17). However, as has been shown in *On First Philosophy* (to which al-Kindī refers explicitly at 62.13), all things other than God are to some extent multiple. This holds even of the sphere, since it is extended in three dimensions (62.14–16). One remarkable feature of this passage is that al-Kindī includes the abstract objects of mathematics among things that have both multiplicity and unity. The Platonic flavor of the argument is accentuated by his discussion of these abstract objects. He says that, for instance, sensible circles have accidents such as "color, position, motion, and generation," but "the cause and genus of all these [sensible circles] is the one circle, which has no matter, no accidents, and no motion with respect to size, because the great and small are only by relation [*iḍāfa*], and occur along with the extension of matter, and its being more and less. Likewise every other kind of figure has one figure that is unmoved and not multiple, which is the cause of its being [*kawn*]" (61.20–62.4).

17. As al-Kindī says himself, with a similar example, at *On First Philosophy* §VI.7 (AR 116, RJ 31).

18. For this terminology see Heinrichs (1984).

19. He even remarks, "someone might think that it [sc. the intellect] is the first multiple, and that it is unified in some way, since it is a whole, as we have said. For 'one' is said of the whole. But unity in truth is not intellect." This would seem to allude to the Neoplatonic doctrine of intellect as God's first effect, and the beginning of multiplicity. This is found throughout the Arabic Plotinus (e.g. at Badawī, 1947, 112, faithfully translating *Enneads* V.1.4) and also the *Liber de Causis*, for instance at §4, which states explicitly that the first created thing is intellect. Of course al-Kindī may not have been aware that Plotinus' contrast between the One and *nous* is an explicit attack on Aristotle. In fact his own account follows Aristotle in portraying God as an unmoved mover, as we will see.

20. In these texts we find the same concerns with divine simplicity and transcendence that appear in al-Kindī. For instance, in the *Theology of Aristotle*, at Badawī (1947), 148: "Necessarily, the oneness of the originated is not like [*mithl*] the oneness of the originator, otherwise the originator and the originated and the cause and the effect would be one thing." See also *Liber de Causis*, §5.

21. See Adamson (2003), 49ff.

22. See the text and translation at RJ 129–31, and chapter 8.

23. "Not-F" is therefore the contrary of F, not the privation of F. For instance, if we were discussing colors, "not-black" would mean "white," rather than just lacking the color black. Even what has no color at all could be "not-black" in the latter sense. This supports my claim that al-Kindī's calling God "one" in *On First Philosophy* does not merely mean denying multiplicity of God.

24. See especially Badawī (1947), 189. I have discussed this parallel in Adamson (2002b), app. sec. 2.

25. This is also strongly suggested by a parallel passage in the Kindī-circle version of a short treatise on the heavens by Alexander of Aphrodisias; it says that the heavens come "from the first agent without intermediary," and other things are produced through the intermediary of the heavens. See Fazzo and Wiesner (1993), 152.

26. *Liber de Causis* §4, Bardenhewer (1882), 65ff. The proposition first states that the "first created thing" is "being [*anniyya*]," which is "above sensation, soul, and intellect" (65.4–5). But it then goes on to say that "the first created being" is "entirely intellect" (66.5). For this theme in the *De Causis* see D'Ancona (1995b). In the Pseudo-Ammonian *Opinions of the Philosophers*, we find a passage that closely mirrors *De Causis* §4: "[God] created the simple thing, that is, the first, intelligible simple, which is first matter [*al-'unṣur al-awwal*]. Then He multiplied simple things from this simple, one, first created thing. And then, He generated the composed things from the simple things" (Rudolph, 1989, V.4–6). Here matter takes the place of intellect, but we have the same idea of God's act being mediated by a simple first effect.

27. It is suggestive that in *On Definitions*, the opening sequence of entries runs as follows: §1: the first cause; §2: intellect; §3: nature; §4 soul; §5 body. As Klein-Franke (1982) has remarked, this looks like a reflection of the Plotinian hierarchy found not only in the Arabic Plotinus but also in the streamlined metaphysics of the Arabic Proclus. It is strange that "nature" appears before and not after soul, but that may be an idiosyncrasy of the textual transmission. The Prologue to the *Theology of Aristotle*, which I have elsewhere argued was written by al-Kindī (see Adamson, 2002b, §2.1.2), includes nature as a hypostasis between soul and the physical world. The same scheme appears in al-Kindī's *Sayings of Socrates*; see chapter 6.

28. See *Prostration* §II.5 (AR 247, RJ 181). The distinction made in *On the True Agent* is also found in Aristotle's *Metaphysics*, Θ.8.

29. *Aysa* is probably a learned borrowing from Syriac *'īth*, a noun which expresses something like the force of the infinitive "to be." *Laysa* is probably just a nominalization of the Arabic verb *laysa* ("is not"), though it is clearly also meant to contrast with *aysa*. For a passage using the two terms extensively, see the proof against self-causation in section 3 of *On First Philosophy*

(§IX, AR 123–4, RJ 41–3), discussed above. See further Endress (1973), 80, and 101–5 for further discussion of al-Kindī's terminology for "being" and "non-being."

30. Another manuscript has *'an lā shay'*, literally "from not-thing."

31. See Frank (1956), D'Alverny (1959).

32. The origin of *anniyya* is contested: it may have a Syriac basis, or it may be an abstract form of the Arabic word *anna*, meaning "that"—thus *anniyya* could literally mean something like "that-ness." *Huwiyya* is clearly an abstract form of *huwa*, which means simply "it," yielding for *huwiyya* a literal meaning along the lines of "it-ness." It should be noted that al-Kindī coins similar words elsewhere. For example, he speaks in *On First Philosophy* of "which-ness," *ayyiyya* (§XII.4, AR 129, RJ 49). For the range of terms used for "being" see further Adamson (2002b), §5.2.1, and Adamson (2002c), 299–300.

33. I have already pointed this out in Adamson (2003). I will cite Philoponus' *Against Aristotle* by referencing the fragment numbers in Wildberg (1987). Despite the importance of Philoponus for the passage, al-Kindī also seems to be in dialogue with contempoary *kalām* authors. Compare for example the following passage from the slightly earlier Abū 'l-Hudhayl (d. 849 at an advanced age): "The creation of a thing, [which is] its being-brought-to-be [*takwīn*] after it was not, is distinct from it [sc. the created thing]. It [sc. the creation] is God's willing it and saying to it, "Be!"... God's originating something [*al-shay'*] after it was not is its creation" (cited by al-Ash'arī, *Maqālāt*, ed. Ritter (1929), 363.10–11, 363.15–364.1). For further details see Adamson (2003), 57–66.

34. Philoponus argued that Aristotle is committed to *ex nihilo* generation in the case of forms, if not matter-form composites: when a man is generated, his form does not come from a pre-existing substrate, even if the man as a whole does so. His arguments to this effect were known to the Kindī circle, as shown by Hasnawi (1994).

35. The word for "generation," *kawn*, is used by al-Kindī indiscriminately to refer both to creation and the production of substances from pre-existing matter. In the argument against self-causation at the beginning of section 3 of *On First Philosophy*, he says he intends to show that nothing can bring about the generation (*kawn*) of itself "either from a thing, or not from a thing." I take this to refer to the difference between "generation" in the narrow sense, which involves pre-existing matter, and "generation" in the sense of bringing something to be *ex nihilo*. It is interesting to notice, on the other hand, that in section 2 of *On First Philosophy* (§VI.9, AR 117, RJ 33), he says that "generation and corruption" constitute change in respect of "substance [*jawhar*]," which seems to refer to the more restricted sense of "generation" I have contrasted to creation. It is unsurprising that *kawn* is used in this ambiguous

sense. As we saw, Aristotle already used the corresponding term *genesis* in a strict or absolute sense, to refer to substantial generation (the change results in coming-to-be: *haplôs gignesthai*), but also in a broader sense to refer to a change that yields a new property (the result is coming-to-be something or other: *ti gignesthai*). Furthermore, *kawn* serves not only to translate the technical term *genesis*, but also as a common Arabic word meaning simply "existence": it is derived from the same root as the verb *kāna*, which is the closest that Arabic has for the verb "to be." Cf. RJ 34 n.32.

36. On which see Altmann and Stern (1958), 12–23, and Hein (1985), 57–63.

37. Indeed Ivry (1974), 145, takes *aysa* here simply as a way of referring to prime matter. One might alternatively suppose, given the phrase "primary bearer of predication," that "being" here means *substance*, e.g. a particular man or horse. In *Quantity* al-Kindī explicitly follows Aristotle's *Categories* by calling sense-particulars "primary substances," and identifying substance as the subject of predication (§III.1, AR 365). And as will be mentioned below, he sometimes uses the word *aysa* with a meaning close to "substance." However this does not seem to be what he means here, because if *aysa* here meant "substance" then he would be saying that primary substances are immune to corruption. And unfortunately for all of us primary substances, this is not the case.

38. Thus this passage should be contrasted to the very similar *Prostration* §II.4 (AR 246, RJ 179): "By 'change' I mean only alteration in predicates, whereas by 'generation' I mean alteration in the bearer of predication." Here the "bearer of predication" is obviously substance, and the "predications" are only accidents. The *On First Philosophy* passage, by contrast, speaks of the *first* bearer of predication, "being," which underlies also substantial predicates and thus subsists through substantial corruption.

39. For the identification of God with "being alone" in Kindī-circle texts, especially the Arabic Plotinus, see Adamson (2002b), chap. 5. See also Taylor (1998) and several of the studies in D'Ancona (1995d).

40. For the plural *anniyyāt* see e.g. Badawī (1947), 87.5 and *On First Philosophy* §I.2 (AR 97.14, RJ 9.13). For *huwiyyāt* see Badawī (1947), 196.21.

41. The Arabic version of Aristotle's *Metaphysics* produced in al-Kindī's circle uses the word *anniyya* in the same ambiguous way. We find it there as a translation for both the infinitive *einai* ("to be") and the expression *to ti ên einai* ("essence"). See D'Alverny (1959), 72–3. This ambiguity does not, incidentally, affect the term *wujūd*: that which has *wujūd*, "existence," is *al-mawjūd*, "the existent." Hence there is less room for confusion in later Arabic metaphysical works, where this becomes the dominant word for existence or being.

42. Particularly striking is a passage in *On the Prostration of the Outermost Sphere*, which describes the exercise of (divine) power as "bringing all concepts into existence [*ikhrāj al-ma'ānī ilā 'l-kawn*]." This is almost impossible to interpret because of the use of the notoriously untranslatable word *ma'ānī*; Rashed and Jolivet suggest translating it here as "forms." One might be tempted to think of the *ma'ānī* as purely mental existents (in God's mind) which are then granted existence. Be that as it may, I do not think that even the aspect of al-Kindī's thought that contrasts being with attributes should be assimilated to Avicenna's distinction. This is not only because al-Kindī is ambiguous about whether "being" means existence or substance. It is also because being seems, especially in the Arabic Plotinus and Proclus, to receive determination when it manifests itself as a particular substance. Thus we do not have here the idea of an act of existence being united to an essence. Rather we have the idea of an essence serving to delimit or contract being, which in itself is simple and without the determination that yields multiplicity. Here it is revealing that Avicenna sees the relationship of form to matter as analogous to the relation of existence to essence. By contrast, the Kindī texts are more likely to speak of being as analogous to matter, as that which receives determination. See further Adamson (2002c).

43. In the *Physics* Aristotle sometimes uses *kinêsis* interchangably with *metabolê*, and similarly here al-Kindī uses *ḥaraka* as a synonym for *tabaddul*. He also follows Aristotle in identifying the three kinds of change as locomotion, quantitative change, and qualitative change; see *Physics* V.1, 225b7–9; V.2, 226a24–25; VII.2, 243a35–39.

44. See §IV.15 (AR 111, RJ 25), §XIX.4 (AR 154, RJ 85). Al-Kindī also mentions this in passing in a work based on Ptolemy's astronomy: see Rosenthal (1956a), 449. Jolivet (1984), 319–20, has also stressed the fact that al-Kindī's assimilation of creation to motion allows him to incorporate Aristotle's theology into his own theology.

45. A remarkable passage in the *Theology of Aristotle*, at Badawī (1947), 51–52, could have helped to support this interpretation. On the basis of the good Aristotelian principle that God is pure actuality, the *Theology* claims that God "acts" by "gazing upon Himself"—the self-regard of God being another Aristotelian theme—and thereby originates all beings (*anniyyāt*).

CHAPTER 4

1. Ed. Najjar and Mallet (1999), 55.4–5.

2. Bear in mind that Aristotle is using "motion" here in a wider sense that includes not only motion in place, but also change in quality or quantity. It does not, however, include what he called "absolute" generation and corruption in

Physics V.1; as we have already seen he denies that this should be called a *kinêsis*. So *Physics* VIII.1 does not have to do even with the generation of the world as a whole from some pre-existing substrate, never mind the generation of the world *ex nihilo*.

3. Thus Aristotle gives short shrift, in this context, to the Heraclitean or Eleatic views that all things are always in motion, or always at rest. He feels free to do so in part because he is doing natural philosophy or physics, which is primarily the study of both motion and rest; these theories are not properly engaged within physics because they deny the very principles of the science.

4. On the history of these interpretations see Dillon (1996), especially 242–3 (on Taurus) and 286 (for the *Didaskalikos*), Baltes (1976/1978) and Phillips (1997).

5. I put "literal" in scare-quotes because those who interpreted Plato as holding that the cosmos is eternal did not see themselves as giving a figurative or metaphorical reading; rather they pointed to different senses of ambiguous terms, as we will see shortly.

6. The Greek text is included in Rabe (1899); for an English translation see Lang and Macro (2001).

7. For which see Philoponus, *Against Proclus* VI.8, ed. Rabe (1899), translated in Share (2005).

8. As pointed out by Phillips (1997), 184.

9. Ed. Diehl (1903–6), vol.2, 294.3–17.

10. Alexander of Aphrodisias, *Quaestiones* I.18, in Bruns (1887), 30–32, at 30.23–24. Cf. the translation in Sharples (1992), 66–70.

11. Compare for instance *Elements of Theology* §48.

12. *Against Proclus* §VI.29, ed. in Rabe (1899), 240.13–19. Translations of this work are from Share (2004, 2005).

13. *Against Proclus* VI.29, at Rabe (1899), 242.3–5.

14. See Hasnawi (1994).

15. On this see Judson (1987).

16. Simplicius sometimes casts doubt on whether Philoponus accepted the eternity of the world *ex parte post*. But the later books of *Against Aristotle*, which are mostly lost, seem to have argued that God will replace the current physical cosmos with something "more divine": see Fr. 132, where Simplicius admits as much, and also the Syriac Fr. 134.

17. *Against Proclus* VI.29, at Rabe (1899), 242.17–19.

18. Cf. his commentary on the *Timaeus*, ed. Diehl (1903–6), vol. 2, 288.28–289.5.

19. Whether or not this is a convincing claim is open to dispute; see further below on al-Kindī's version of the same point. One ingenious way of deriving an actual infinity from eternity *ex parte ante* is to say that if an

infinite number of humans have already died, there should now be an infinite number of immortal souls. On this see Marmura (1960).

20. Rabe (1899), 14.7–8. On the other hand Philoponus does speak in the same section of its being "absolutely necessary [*anangkê pantôs*] that the number of things be finite" (8.6–7, cf. 9.5–6). He also says it is "absolutely necessary [*dia to dein pantôs*]" that things created by the Demiurge are inferior to him (8.14–15); and from this it is supposed to follow that the created world must fall short of the Demiurge's eternity.

21. And to these we can add a passage from one of his meteorological works; see note 40.

22. *Oneness* overlaps very closely with *On First Philosophy* but still there are bits added in the latter text, for instance three lines at §VI.5–6 (AR 116.5–12, RJ 31.8–16), and, more important, the entire interpolation at §§VI.12–VII.1 (AR 118.14–120.6, RJ 33.25–35.23). Given how much of al-Kindī's writings we have lost it is not at all impossible that other parts of *On First Philosophy* were likewise copied from previous, shorter works, with or without additions and changes. But if so we have no evidence of this.

23. This is also suggested by the greater terminological precision of *Finiteness*. Al-Kindī explains here exactly what he means by "magnitude," for instance, which he does not do in the other three works.

24. He makes the same point at *Prostration* §IX.1 (AR 258, RJ 195), and in a fragment found in the Istanbul manuscript on fol. 35a, labelled "Al-Kindī's statement about composition," edited in Celentano (1979), 8. This fragment says that the elements are subject to contraries and hence generation and corruption, whereas this is not true of the celestial sphere. The latter is, however, composed in a different way, because it is three-dimensional and spherical, and thus subject to quantity and quality.

25. Indeed, those ideas that al-Kindī may have taken from *Against Aristotle* can all be found in the sixth book.

26. Ivry (1974), *ad* 109.6. Similarly, regarding the argument against plenum, Ivry writes, "al-Kindī offers no physical argument in support of this statement. . . . He concentrates rather upon the logical entailments of 'infinite body'" (139, *ad* 109.11).

27. That this is his point is also suggested by what follows (§IV.16, AR 112, RJ 25), where al-Kindī again raises mathematics as an example of a science with demonstrative, rather than persuasive, proofs.

28. On the other hand, in the conclusion to *Finiteness* (§9, AR 192, RJ 165) al-Kindī contrasts his method in this short treatise, which uses "mathematical proofs which are intermediate between sensation and intellect," to his method in previous works where he "furnished reliable evidence taken from natural things [*al-shahādāt al-ṣādiqa min al-umūr al-ṭabī'iyya*]." If the latter remark is

a reference to *On First Philosophy* then it is puzzling, since according to my interpretation at least al-Kindī expressly says that in *On First Philosophy* he is using a method that is *not* applicable to natural things. And in any case, *Finiteness* does little more than to provide a more solid (mathematical) grounding for the same premises used in the arguments of *On First Philosophy*. A related question is how "metaphysics" relates to "physics." If al-Kindī understands the latter as an intellectual, axiomatic enterprise rather than an empirical inquiry, perhaps he thinks physics and metaphysics share an "intellectual" methodology, despite the classificatory scheme of *Quantity*. He could have been encouraged in this by Aristotle's proving the existence of God in his *Physics*. The argument concerning void quoted above also indicates that al-Kindī was willing to treat topics covered in Aristotle's *Physics* in an "intellectual" way.

29. *Against Aristotle* Fr. 132, at Simplicius *in Phys.* 1178.9–15.

30. In *Finiteness* al-Kindī will specify that "magnitude" means a line, a plane, or a body, but in *On First Philosophy* he seems to want the conclusion to apply to anything quantitative, including especially time itself.

31. Actually this step is more complicated in al-Kindī's argument; he uses the idea that the supposedly smaller infinite would have to "measure," i.e. be equal to, a sub-part of the supposedly larger infinite. But there can only be equality between finite magnitudes, because equality means having similar limits.

32. To see this, just match up the members of the complete and incomplete set, as follows:

Complete set: 1, 2, 3, . . . , n

Incomplete set: 2, 3, 4, . . . , n + 1

So long as there is one distinct member of the incomplete set to match with each member of the complete set, the two sets must be equal. The same matching procedure would work with bodily parts, of course, so al-Kindī's argument does not prove the impossibility of an actually infinite magnitude. (If you still aren't convinced that the set of integers is the same size as the set of all the integers but 1, Michael Pelsmajer (conversation, May 2005) suggests to me the following argument. Beginning with the complete set of positive integers, add 0.5 to each integer, yielding the set {1.5, 2.5, 3.5, . . . }. This set is obviously the same size as the set of integers, so the operation does not change the size of the set. But performing the same operation again will yield the incomplete set, i.e. {2, 3, 4, . . . }. Thus the incomplete set must be the same size as the complete set.)

33. Aristotle also argues for this in *On the Heavens* I.5–7.

34. Cf. *On the Heavens* III.1, 299a19–24, which argues that bodies, being divisible, have properties that are also somehow divisible.

35. Which appears only in the version in *On First Philosophy*.

36. Ivry (1974), 159, *ad* 119.8. The arguments al-Kindī gives against eternal rest are based on those in *Physics* VIII.1, but there are some differences. In particular al-Kindī mentions the possibility that the world is brought to be from non-being (§VI.12; quoted in chapter 3 above). Of course on this assumption (which turns out to be true, according to al-Kindī), the universe will not have been at rest before it moves, but rather non-existent.

37. See Davidson (1969), 371. Al-Kindī also explicitly mentions finite power in *Quiddity*; see Davidson (1987), 115.

38. See Davidson (1969, 372; 1987, 111–2). It is also worth noting that the Kindī-circle translation of Alexander of Aphrodisias' *On Providence* does give a clear version of the infinite power argument against the world's eternity, even citing *On the Heavens*: "[The heavens'] being passes away, as the philosopher says convincingly in *On the Heavens*. For he says there that there is no body that is infinite or endless, whether it be rectilinear or circular. And if there is only finite body, then every body has a finite power. For a finite body cannot have an infinite power. If this is the case, and the heavens are a finite body, then they do not have an infinite power. And if it [sc. the heavens' power] is finite, then it will stop one day, and when it stops they will pass away" (see Ruland, 1976, 89.6–91.4, lower text). This is of course not in the original version by Alexander, but seems to have been added by the Kindī circle. A marginal note to one manuscript refutes the argument in the spirit of Proclus, arguing that an infinite power could still be imposed on the heavens from outside, i.e. by God.

39. Interestingly, al-Kindī does not add, as Philoponus did, that as time passes we would also have an actual infinity that is, absurdly, getting larger all the time. This would have been a natural point for him to make, since he has already objected to differently sized infinities in argument (2).

40. He makes the same point, explicitly relating it to numbers, in a meteorological work, *On Why the Higher Atmosphere Is Cold*. In a passage that is obviously related to his work on the eternity of the world, al-Kindī argues that it is misleading to speak of "infinite numbers." Rather any particular number will be finite; numbers are only potentially infinite in the sense that one can keep adding to them. As a result we should say that they are "limited [*maḥdūd*]" by nature, but infinite in an accidental sense (AR^2 99.5–12). He then goes on to apply this to the things created by God: though God can create whatever He wants, whatever He does create will be an actual thing and therefore limited (AR^2 99.17–19).

41. Ivry (1974), 151–2, believes that al-Kindī simply fails to take potential infinity seriously, since it is only infinite in the imagination. I disagree. I think

that al-Kindī does take potential infinity seriously, and accepts it wholeheartedly both for the spatial magnitude and temporal magnitude of the cosmos. With regard to spatial magnitude, the universe can be imagined as growing larger with no absurdity resulting (remember we are dealing here with "intellectual" considerations only). But of course it must be some finite size, as must any body that is merely *potentially* infinitely large. And the same goes for future time.

42. Or at least, al-Kindī shows this for created *magnitudes*. A conspicuous absence is any discussion of the status of immaterial existents, such as the human soul. Presumably they are created, yet nothing in the eternity arguments could show that an immaterial existent must have limited temporal duration. Indeed, since al-Kindī stresses that time is only the number of motion, and that only body moves, an immaterial existent should be atemporal.

43. In this passage al-Kindī says that God is "the first in time [*al-awwalī bi-'l-zamān*]." But this does not, I take it, require that God actually be *in* time, just that He is prior to all temporal things.

44. For the Arabic Plotinus see Adamson (2002b), 5.3.2. For the Arabic Proclus see D'Ancona (1995c).

45. For the history of the *miḥna* and its intellectual background, see Madelung (1974), and van Ess (1991–95), especially the discussion of the *miḥna* in vol.3, and vol.4, 625–30. Patton (1897) remains a useful survey of the primary sources, though overly influenced by sources sympathetic to Ibn Ḥanbal.

46. This at least was the position of a thinker like Abū 'l-Hudhayl; see e.g. Al-Ash'arī's *Maqālāt*, ed. Ritter (1929), 177.14–16, and on this theory Frank (1969). See further Adamson (2003).

47. On this claim see Patton (1897), 90, 101–2, 184.

48. An accusation some modern scholars have been happy to endorse; see for instance Tritton (1972), 8, and Wolfson (1976), chap. 3. Wolfson admits that there was some basis in the Koran itself for this development, however (Wolfson (1976), 238). For a contrary view see Watt (1998), 243.

49. Ed. de Goeje (1897), with the section on the imposition of the *miḥna* at III.1111–34. This part has been translated in Bosworth (1987).

50. As pointed out by van Ess (1991–95), vol. 3, 183. For texts concerning Bishr see vol.5, §XX.

51. See the remarks of van Ess (1991–95), 447ff.

52. Madelung (1974).

53. See al-Ṭabarī, *Tarīkh*, ed. de Goeje (1897), III.1113.

54. This is how al-Ash'arī puts it in his *Maqālāt*, ed. Ritter (1929), 582 (cited at Madelung (1974), 516). Notice the resonance with the passage on creation in al-Kindī's *Quantity*.

55. Al-Ṭabarī, *Tarīkh*, ed. de Goeje (1897), III.1113, 1118, 1120. Because the literalist view makes the Koran divine, he accuses them of "polytheism [*shirk*]," at III.1116, 1128–30, as well as "unbelief [*kufr*]."

56. Al-Ṭabarī, *Tarīkh*, ed. de Goeje (1897), III.1118.

57. Ibid., III.1119.

58. Thus the literalists needed to show why the Koran's eternity (or the eternity of any attribute) did not imply its being equal to God. On this point see the very useful overview in Wisnovsky (2003), chap. 13.

59. Al-Kindī's patron al-Mu'taṣim in fact seems to have pursued the *miḥna* much less zealously than al-Ma'mūn had planned to do. At the time *On First Philosophy* was written, the creation of the Koran may have seemed more vivid as a theological issue than a political one.

60. If this is right, it is natural to ask how well al-Kindī's arguments would apply to the case of the Koran. He deals solely with the question of whether a *body* can be eternal, and the Koran is not obviously a body. But in fact, the question of whether the Koran is a body was a central part of the debate. Traditionalists (Ibn Kullāb, for instance) distinguished between the primordial Koran, written on the "Preserved Tablet" by God, and the Koran as it is made manifest in a particular utterance (*lafẓ*) or written version. One might then admit that the latter is a body, and is created (those who took this view were called the *lafẓiyya*). The Koran in the Preserved Tablet, though, would be uncreated, being the word of God. (Here there would still be room for disagreement about the nature of this word, for instance whether it was already in Arabic, with discrete letters and words: Ibn Ḥanbal affirmed this, but Ibn Kullāb denied it.) Proponents of the Koran's createdness did claim that the Koran was a body (the view of al-Naẓẓām) or an accident created in a body (the view of Mu'ammar). Al-Kindī's sympathies in this debate would doubtless have been with the austere theologians, as is suggested by passages in his works on interpreting the Koran (see chapter 2). So he may, like some of these theologians, have thought that arguments about body and its attributes would apply to the case of the Koran. For further discussion of the *kalām* context, see Daiber (1975), Nader (1984), Watt (1998), Wolfson (1976).

61. Indeed, well before the *miḥna*, the early theologian Jahm b. Ṣafwān (d. 745) already claimed the Koran was created in the context of an anti-literalist, austere theology. See Madelung (1974), 505–6.

CHAPTER 5

1. So actually it would seem that for al-Kindī, the distinction of *Categories* chap. 1 (between univocal and equivocal predicates) and the distinction of

Categories chap. 2 (between essential and accidental predicates, or as Aristotle says, those that are "said of" their subject and those that are "present in" their subject) are in fact the same distinction. This has the awkward consequence that for al-Kindī accidents fall under the class of equivocal predicates.

2. As pointed out by Jolivet (1971), 120. He does follow this terminology in *Quantity* (§V.6, AR 372), however.

3. He even says in this very treatise (§7, AR 268) that individuals are many, whereas the species is one.

4. Formerly I followed Altmann and Stern (1958), 43, in understanding this phrase to mean, "one might think that Aristotle and Plato disagree [with each other]," and that al-Kindī wishes to deny this (see Adamson, 2005b, 50 n. 13). However I now think the context shows that it means the statements in §1 cohere with the philosophers' other writings.

5. It is not clear whether anything other than the celestial spheres would count as a *jism*; he says that "*jism* is *for instance* the celestial sphere [*wa-amma al-jism, fa-ka-'l-falak*]." Perhaps he would count the planets embedded within the spheres as distinct bodies?

6. If this is the correct reading of the Arabic; see AR 271 n. 3.

7. We might be encouraged to do so given that, in this section (at AR 271.13), he uses the phrase *al-ajsām wa 'l-ajrām*, as if these were distinct.

8. Encouraged by the claim at *Timaeus* 41d–e that the Demiurge associates souls with the stars.

9. On this see Finamore (1985).

10. Walzer (1962) sees this passage as an authentic fragment from Aristotle's lost dialogue *Eudemus*. Others are skeptical; see Genequand (1987–88), 10.

11. See Genequand (1987–88).

12. A bit later in the *Discourse* (§II.5), al-Kindī gives a modified version of Plato's analogy, from *Republic* 588, for the tripartite soul. Plato compares the soul to a chimera formed from a many-headed beast (desire), a lion (spirit), and a man (intellect). In al-Kindī we have instead a pig, a dog, and an angel. This has a parallel in Galen, *De moribus*. The skeleton of the third item, *m-l-ḳ*, could be vocalized either *maliḳ*, "king" or *malaḳ*, "angel"—see Genequand (1987–88), 4, who chastises Walzer for reading *maliḳ*.

13. Here al-Kindī uses the term *'araḍan*, which I take to mean "accidentally," that is, not essentially.

14. A slightly different impression is given by a work preserved only in Latin, *On the Five Essences*, which says that the soul "is divided into two parts [*partes*]: thought and sensation [*cogitatio vel ratio et sensus*]" (AR^2 9.9–10).

15. Whether this filtering was already present in al-Kindī's Greek source or sources is difficult to say. I believe that some of the filtering is al-Kindī's

own doing, however, as is clear from the terminological and doctrinal impact of the *Theology of Aristotle* on the *Discourse*. The *Theology* was not, that is, the direct source of the materials that make up the *Discourse*, but it affects the way these materials are presented, in the framing and transitional passages that are more likely to have been written entirely by al-Kindī (like §§I.2, II.4, III.1–2, V.1, and VII.1–3). For the impact of the *Theology* on the *Discourse* see Adamson (2000), D'Ancona (1996), and Jolivet (1996). For Hermetic influence see Genequand (1987–88).

16. For this text see Arnzen (1998).

17. The same section, incidentally, also has a more Platonic definition of the soul as an "intellectual substance" and "self-moving by means of number."

18. But see Adamson (2003), sec. 3.1, for the Arabic Plotinus' attempt to square the idea of soul as *entelechia* with Plotinian dualism. See also the Arabic *De Anima*, at Arnzen (1998), 321.

19. Arnzen (1998), e.g. at 135–6 and 349–50, finds convincing parallels between the Arabic *De Anima* and several Kindian works (especially the cosmological treatises), but not the *Discourse*. See Arnzen (1998), 375–6, for a comparison of al-Kindī's definition of "soul" in this context.

20. For example, at *On Definitions* §70E, which is a gloss on the saying that "philosophy is man's knowledge of himself [*nafs*]": "This statement is noble in the extreme and profound. For example, I say that things are either bodies or not. Things that are not bodies are either substances or accidents. Man is body, soul, and accidents. And his soul [*nafs*] is a non-bodily substance. Therefore, if someone knows all this [i.e. all the parts of man], then he knows everything. For this reason wise men call man a microcosm." *On Definitions* §71 compares the soul's relationship to the body to God's relationship to the cosmos.

21. Cf. *Theology of Aristotle* IX.12–3, Badawī (1947), 122, corresponding to Plotinus, *Enneads* IV.7.1.

22. Jolivet (1971).

23. *De Anima* III.6–7 also deal with intellect but do not seem to be considered in al-Kindī's interpretation. In particular, the famous statement in III.7 that "soul never thinks without an image [*phantasmatos*]" is, as we will see, not factored into the epistemology of *On the Intellect* and seems to be outright contradicted by a passage from *On First Philosophy* (§IV.5–8, RJ 19–21, AR 107–8). Here al-Kindī states that universals, which are the objects of human intellect, are not "represented by the soul's using an image." This does not actually rule out that an image was a necessary condition for the development of the image-less representation that is intellection. But al-Kindī does not say this, and puts all stress on the distinction between intellection and any process involving images.

24. Themistius dissents from this view, however, connecting it rather to the "common intellect" he thinks is mentioned at *De Anima* 408b25–29; see Themistius *in De an.*, ed. Heinze (1899), 105.22–28.

25. For the gradual emergence of these terms see Huby (1991).

26. I use this rather than "agent intellect," a term found in al-Fārābī and subsequent authors, but absent in al-Kindī (and, for that matter, in Aristotle).

27. See e.g. *On the Intellect* §4, AR 355.5, where al-Kindī equates the "sensible form [*al-ṣūra al-maḥsūsa*]" with the "object of sense [*al-maḥsūs*]."

28. Isaac Israeli uses the same terminology; see Altmann and Stern (1958), 35.

29. This, I take it, is the meaning of the disputed word *thānī* at §2, AR 354.1; it reappears with a similar meaning at §7, AR 357.4.

30. See Adamson (2004a). The role of "abstraction" in his epistemology is controversial; see recently Hasse (2001).

31. Endress (1980), 430.

32. This school produced three commentaries on the relevant sections of the *De Anima*: a genuine one by Philoponus (ed. Verbeke, 1966), one ascribed to Philoponus but probably to be attributed to Stephanus (ed. Hayduck, 1897), and one ascribed to Simplicius which may or may not be by Priscian (ed. Hayduck, 1882).

33. E.g. at Verbeke (1966), 91.44.

34. This last point is made particularly clearly by Pseudo-Philoponus, who follows the real Philoponus, at Hayduck (1897), 538–9.

35. I suspect Philoponus was here inspired by Aristotle's comparison of the weak-willed man to a drunk or sleeping person, at *Nicomachean Ethics* VII.3: the weak-willed or acratic man, too, has knowledge (in his case, of what he ought to do) without deploying this knowledge.

36. See Pseudo-Philoponus, ed. Hayduck (1897), 535.5–8. Philoponus describes a similar position, without naming its author, at Verbeke (1966), 44.25ff.

37. On this view in Aristotle and in later Arabic philosophy, see Adamson (2005a).

38. Cf. *Prostration* §V.2 (AR 254, RJ 190–1), which says that vision and hearing must belong to the heavens, since it is through sense and hearing that all knowledge is acquired.

39. Cf. *On First Philosophy* §X.1 (AR 124, RJ 43): "Philosophy does not study particulars, because particulars are unlimited, and knowledge does not encompass what is unlimited."

40. A source for al-Kindī's theory of flux, and identification of secondary substances as the objects of knowledge, is Nicomachus of Gerasa's *Introduc-*

tion to Arithmetic I.1. The version of the *Introduction* corrected by al-Kindī includes a gloss by al-Kindī himself, explaining that all physical things are subject to flux in some respect—even the heavenly spheres, which are in constant locomotion. See Freudenthal and Lévy (2004), 524–6 (see 528 for the claim that knowledge of the infinite is impossible). Interestingly, the Nicomachus text does mention abstraction of universals from particulars, immediately following the discussion of flux (526–8), but al-Kindī does not make use of this idea in *Quantity* or *On First Philosophy*.

41. See Endress (1986, 1994).

42. See Kutsch (1954), and for its dependence on the *Theology* Adamson (2002b), §3.2.2. The recollection theme also appears in a *Treatise on the Two Worlds* which, I have argued, is also based on the Arabic Plotinus materials. For this text see Rosenthal (1952–55).

43. The theory of recollection is also in the *Meno*, of course, but there is no sign here that al-Kindī has this dialogue in mind; unlike Philoponus, he does not allude to the role of the teacher in prompting recollection, but only to sensible particulars.

44. In fact this is not mentioned at all in the *Theology* or the *Treatise on the Soul*; it is mentioned however in *Treatise on the Two Worlds*, for which see note 42.

45. For al-Kindī's knowledge of the *Phaedo* in Arabic, see chapter 6.

46. Unless we should read this into the reference to the "world of the intellect" in the title, which echoes the Arabic Plotinus and thus might imply that al-Kindī has in mind a Plotinian universal *nous* above soul.

47. Tornero Poveda (1992), 221, also points out the presence of an abstraction doctrine in *On Rays*.

48. The same point is made in a fragment found in the Istanbul manuscript (fol. 35a), edited in Celentano (1979), 9. Here al-Kindī is asked whether one can imagine what one has not seen. After getting clear on the meaning of imagination (here *wahm* is said to be ambiguous, and *taṣawwur* is given as one of its meanings), al-Kindī says that one can only imagine what has not been seen insofar as one combines things one has seen. The same example of the feathered man is given.

49. What does this tell us about whether we might still have imagination once our souls are freed from the body? *On Recollection* says that we will have no memory of sensible forms after death precisely because we will no longer have a faculty of imagination. If this is al-Kindī's considered view then the lower faculties may in some sense "belong" to the soul—so that my soul is really the subject that engages in my acts of imagination—but bodily organs are necessary conditions for the use of all faculties apart from intellection. Nothing said in *On Sleep and Dream* rules out this interpretation.

50. This is made clear in *On the Intellect* §§3–4 (AR 354–5), when al-Kindī says that the soul is identical with the sense faculty and thus with the object of sensation; cf. *On Sleep and Dream* §VIII.1 (AR 301–2).

51. *De Anima* 427b17–18.

52. The *Fihrist* is not very helpful, since Ibn al-Nadīm does not know when or by whom these works were translated. We do know, thanks to Averroes' epitome, that in Arabic the whole collection went by the title of the first treatise, *On Sense and Sense-Objects*, and that it was divided into three parts, the second part including the works on sleep and dream. See further Peters (1968), 45–7.

53. See Daiber (1986). I am grateful for information about this manuscript from Rotraud Hansberger, who is currently at work on an edition and study of the translation. I have also benefitted greatly from reading an unpublished paper of hers on the topic. Making use of a draft translation and edition kindly provided by her, I have briefly compared the Arabic version of Aristotle's *On Dreams* in this manuscript with al-Kindī's *On Sleep and Dream*. I could not find any strong evidence that the former is the direct source for the latter, though some changes are the same (in particular the more central role given to the brain, and possibly the doctrine of internal senses which appears explicitly in the Arabic *On Dreams* and implicitly in al-Kindī; see further below). One striking difference is that the Arabic *On Dreams* says that prophetic dreams are sent by God, which is reflected in some later Arabic works (including one ascribed to Avicenna; see Pines, 1974) but not in al-Kindī.

54. Al-Kindī refers to the "common" or "universal" sense faculty at *On First Philosophy* §IV.6 (AR 108, RJ 21). In *On Sleep and Dream* he says simply that "the organs of sensation proceed and arise from the brain" (§X.1, AR 306).

55. Mentioned also at *De Anima* 428a8.

56. At 458b29–31 Aristotle skirts the question of whether *to phantastikon* and *to aisthêtikon* are the same or different, but he goes on to say at 459a21–22 that "dreaming belongs to the sensitive faculty, but *qua* imaginative [*tou aisthêtikou men esti to enupniazein, toutou d' hêi phantastikon*]." Al-Kindī's presentation is closer to, and presumably at least indirectly inspired by, the claim at *De Anima* 427b14–15 that "imagination is distinct from perception and thought [*dianoias*]." Cf. the Arabic paraphrase of *De Anima*, Arnzen (1998), 295–7, showing that imagination (here *wahm*) is distinct from both sensation and intellect.

57. It is interesting to note that in the *Fihrist*, the title of the present treatise is "On sleep, dream and *what the soul represents* in [dream] symbolically [*wa mā tarmuzu bi-hī al-nafs*]" (Tajaddud, 1971, 319.7). It should also be noted that there is a whole section of the *Fihrist*'s inventory (319–20) about his

treatises on prediction (*kutubuhū al-taqdumiyyāt*), and only one of these titles mentions the heavenly bodies. This may imply that al-Kindī believed some people could predict the future without recourse to either dreams or astrology. A possibly relevant passage is the story given at *Discourse on the Soul* §VI.1 (AR 279) of the Greek king who reports prophetic visions after hovering between life and death; it is not clear whether this is meant to involve the sort of dreams described in the present treatise.

58. Al-Kindī's description of the process bears some similarities to that of Synesius, *On Dreams*; see Sheppard (1997), 204–5. Synesius also thinks that the soul grasps forms of future things, and then projects these into the *phantasia*.

59. The term for "opinion" is *ẓann*, used in a definition of "belief [*ra'y*]" at *On Definitions* §27 (AR 168); as in *On Sleep and Dream* the connotation of *ẓann* is negative, since it involves a conviction that may be only temporary, and is susceptible of falsehood. Here we are in the presence of something like *doxa* as opposed to *epistêmê*. It is worth noting that Plato (*Sophist*, 264b) defines *phantasia* in terms of *doxa*, and Aristotle too sees a close relationship between *phantasia* and *doxa* (see especially *De Anima* 428b1–2), but distinguishes between them. The Arabic paraphrase of the *De Anima* thus contrasts imagination and belief: Arnzen (1998), 299. On the connection between *phantasia* and *doxa* in later Greek thought see Blumenthal (1977), 249–50, and Sheppard (1997), 209.

60. For this topic see Wolfson (1935), Harvey (1985).

61. A perplexing passage in *On Sleep and Dream* tells us that the brain is "a primary organ that partakes in sensation, intellect [*'aql*], this imaginative power, and the other powers of the soul" (§III.7, AR 297). Why is intellect included here, since al-Kindī is elsewhere so explicit that intellect is entirely immaterial? Unless he's just being sloppy, my guess is that he has in mind not *'aql* properly speaking, but *fikr*, a type of "intellection" located in the brain and distinct from genuine intellect in view of its objects and discursivity.

62. Ed. in Zakariyyā' (1962), 95–110.

63. Ibid., 96.12. The verb here may imply that they are "delegated" or "emitted" from the immaterial soul into the body.

64. Ibid., respectively at 100.21–101.1; 101.10; 101.20; 102.7–8. The same correspondences are given in his treatise *On Stringed Instruments*, 86–8.

65. The latter possibility is more or less confirmed later in the treatise (105.1), when we get another list of internal senses, which are provoked into motion by the mixture of colors: *al-muṣawwir*, *al-fikr*, *al-wahm*, *al-dhikr*. Here the first and third items seem to be synonyms for "imagination," and we have only one place for memory.

66. Ibid. 107.3.

CHAPTER 6

1. Gutas (1990).

2. See Gutas (1975, 1981), and several of the articles in Gutas (2000). For extensive bibliography and a discussion of a passage from *On First Philosophy* used in a later gnomological context, see D'Ancona (2005).

3. For Socrates in this tradition see Alon (1991, 1995), as well as Strohmaier (1974).

4. For an overview of related materials see Hein (1985), 234–7. An interesting feature of al-Kīndī's exposition here is the distinction between virtues that are proper to the soul (namely wisdom, courage, and temperance) and those that have to do with the effects of the soul on "what surrounds that which has the soul," i.e. what surrounds the body (such as justice).

5. Some of the lost works mentioned in the *Fihrist* would also have belonged here, including an epistle *On the Virtues* (ed. Tajaddud, 1971, 319.10).

6. Druart (1993), 349, suggests rather that the recipient is a "friend," which might perhaps be inferred from the fact that al-Kīndī twice addresses him as "praiseworthy brother [*akh maḥmūd*]." This is also how he addresses al-Khurāsānī, the recipient of *Finiteness*, and the anonymous recipients of other treatises (such as *Why the Ancients Related the Five Shapes to the Elements*, at AR^2 54.6 and 60.10).

7. The works discussed in this chapter have recently appeared in a French translation: Mestiri and Dye (2004).

8. Much of the following section is based on Adamson (2007).

9. Dodge (1970), 623 n. 235, proposes that this refers to Aeschines, a character in the *Phaedo*; if this is correct then both items (3) and (4) would be based on the *Phaedo*. (Al-Kīndī also quotes Socrates' dying words, as reported in the *Phaedo*, in an astrological work: see Mahdi, 1976, 66.7–9.) The Arabic looks more like a transliteration of Archigenes. For further discussion of this title see Gutas (1988a), 46, which points out that the work in question is preserved by Ibn Hindū, and consists of a series of symbolic Pythagorean utterances. Prof. Gutas has suggested to me that the original name may have been Antisthenes, in which case we will probably be dealing with a compilation from the late Cynic tradition.

10. Dodge (1970) and Tajaddud (1971) read *ḥurās*, "guards," but Gutas (1988b), 43–4, has argued that "Ḥarranians" here may simply mean "pagans," i.e. the citizens trying him in the *Apology*.

11. See Gutas (1988b).

12. For general studies of Plato's reception in Arabic see Rosenthal (1940) and Klein-Franke (1973).

13. Ed. Fakhry (1963), 28–31.

14. Ed. and tr. in Atiyeh (1966), app. 3. For an edition of the entire *Muntakhab* see Dunlop (1979), with al-Kīndī's sayings at 114.1–122.5. One reason I am optimistic about the authenticity of this collection is that 5 and 7 are genuine quotations from the *Discourse on the Soul*. Also we have other evidence that al-Kīndī composed aphorisms in the *'Uyūn al-Anbā' fī Ṭabaqāt al-Aṭibbā'* of Ibn Abī Uṣaybī'a.

15. See Druart (1993), 335, mentioning the view of Majid Fakhry; see also Butterworth (1992), 52ff.

16. See Strohmaier (1974), Gutas (1993). Socrates is also conflated with Solon at *Sayings of Socrates* §5.

17. This is also a running theme in al-Kīndī's own sayings, as I mention in Adamson (2007), 171.

18. Dimitri Gutas has suggested to me that the association between Socrates and Neoplatonic doctrines may have come from the Sabeans, in whom al-Kīndī was interested (see chapter 8).

19. See Mestiri and Dye (2004), 36–7, and Griffith (2002).

20. Druart (1993), 350.

21. See Ritter and Walzer (1938). I cite the work by their section numbers, which are reproduced in Adamson and Pormann (forthcoming).

22. See Pohlenz (1938).

23. A point made by Gutas (1988a), 168–70.

24. On this dimension of Epictetus' thought see Long (2002).

25. See Long and Sedley (1987), §58. It must be said that the doctrine of preferred indifferents does not come out strongly in Epictetus himself.

26. On the contrast between the Stoics and Cynics on this issue, see Long (1996).

27. *'ālam al-'aql*, a phrase found also in the Arabic Plotinus and al-Kīndī's *Discourse on the Soul*.

28. Notice here the echo of the argument of *On Incorporeal Substances*.

29. And notice here the echo of *Short Statement on the Soul* §I.1 (AR 281): "the soul is a simple substance that makes its acts manifest through bodies."

30. That it does come down to him from an Aristotelian source is shown by the discussion of Aristotle's theory of virtue as a mean, at *On Definitions* §91 (AR 177), which begins by calling virtue a "praiseworthy character [*khulq*]." The contrast made in this section between what is "by nature" and what is "by imposition [*waḍ'*]" is also a Greek inheritance: see Pohlenz (1938), 415–6.

31. Druart (1993), 336.

32. Druart (1993), 340. She later adds that "thoughtful readers" of *On Dispelling Sadness* will note "the faint but unmistakable call to serious philosophical studies" and turn to al-Kīndī's more theoretical works, which "will provide serious answers to their questions" (355).

33. Butterworth (1992), 34. Butterworth's interpretation is given in summary form as well in Butterworth (2005).

34. Butterworth (1992), 40, thus has to say that in these opening sections al-Kīndī speaks only "*momentarily* as though we can always acquire what we seek in the world of the intellect" (my emphasis). One does not need to survey al-Kīndī's epistemology and psychology, as I have set it out in chapter 5, to see that this is too pessimistic. In §I.2 of *On Dispelling Sadness* al-Kīndī says explicitly that it is possible for us to grasp the intelligibles (*'ālam al-'aql alladhī huwa mumkin li-nā mushāhadatuhū*), and he never says anything in what follows to put this in question.

35. Butterworth (1992), 58–60.

36. Druart (1993), 336–9.

37. However this qualification is absent in the parallel definitions found in the Kindian redaction of Nicomachus' *Introduction to Arithmetic*: see Freudenthal and Lévy (2004), 520.

38. Druart (1993), 337 and 339, has also pointed out these qualifications, following Gimaret (1976), 58.

39. *Discourse on the Soul* §II.3, AR 274; §§III.2–IV.1, AR 275; §V.1, AR 278. The phrase "world of the intellect" echoes the Arabic Plotinus; see Adamson (2000), 116. In the *Discourse* al-Kindī also calls this the "world of truth" and even the "world of the divine [*'ālam al-rubūbiyya*]."

40. Genequand (1987–88) connects this idea to the Hermetic tradition; it is also found in Neoplatonic authors. See Finamore (1985), 15–6, on Iamblichus' idea that the descending soul gradually acquires bodily shells and powers which it must cast off individually to return to its origin.

41. For example §II.6 (AR 274–5) follows on the heels of "Plato's" comparison in §II.5 of the three parts of the soul to a swine, a dog, and an angel. But it is not clear whether we are even intended to believe that Plato is also the source for the claim that the one who has "knowledge of the true natures [*ḥaqā'iq*] of things"—note the characteristically Kindian terminology—"is a virtuous man close in similarity to the Creator [*al-bāri'*]."

42. The most relevant passage is the one in *Short Statement on the Soul*, where al-Kīndī seems to accept some close relationship between souls and celestial bodies, but rejects the theory of the soul "vehicle." See above, chapter 5.

CHAPTER 7

1. Ed. and tr. Celentano (1979).

2. Ed. and tr. Klein-Franke (1975). Cf. Bos (1990) for a text about the signs of death.

3. For which see Levey (1966).

4. The Arabic title is *On Knowledge of the Powers of Compound Drugs*, but it is usually referred by the Latin title *De Gradibus*. For the Arabic text and a French translation see Gauthier (1938); for the Latin see McVaugh (1975), app. 1. I will cite by page number from the Arabic followed by the Latin in square brackets.

5. Here he is drawing on several works, including Galen's *On Compound Medicines* (*Peri suntheseôs pharmakôn*), mentioned at 24 [283].

6. Though moisture and dryness are subject to the same laws, for simplicity's sake al-Kindī speaks only of heat and cold through the theoretical part of *On Degrees*.

7. These are as follows (the value of n is 1 for the first member of the set, and for every member thereafter it is the previous member):

(1) "Doubling": 2n {2, 4, 8, 16,...}.
(2) "Adding a part": n + 1 {2, 3, 4, 5,...}.
(3) "Adding several parts": n + m, where m is greater than 1, e.g. {3, 5, 7, 9,...} if m = 2.
(4) "Doubling and adding a part": 2n + 1 {3, 7, 15, 31,...}.
(5) "Doubling and adding several parts": 2n + m, where m is greater than 1, e.g. {4, 10, 22, 46,...} where m = 2.

8. On Averroes' critique see the introduction in Gauthier (1938) and more recently Langermann (2003).

9. Why does al-Kindī prefer doubling to tripling, or some other simple multiplication? Though he does not address this explicitly, the technical answer would be that the tripling progression cannot be "reduced to equality" as simply as the doubling progression (9 minus 3 minus 1 does not equal 1.) The more intuitive answer would be that doubling is obviously the "first" relation of this kind and so prior to tripling, quadrupling, etc.

10. An equilibriate compound is 1/2 hot and 1/2 cold, a first-degree hot is 5/8 hot and 3/8 cold, a second-degree hot is 6/8 hot and 2/8 cold (i.e. 3/4 hot and 1/4 cold), and so on. Notice that something hot in the fourth degree, on this view, would be completely hot (8/8) and not cold (0/8) at all.

11. Gauthier (1938), 38.

12. See Langermann (2003), 359.

13. Celentano (1979), 21–7.

14. See Burnett (1993), 100–1. Both *On Coitus* (reading *adwiyya mujarraba* at Celentano, 1979, 21.7) and the title of the *Formulary* (see Levey, 1966, 29) say that the drugs described were actually used or tested by al-Kindī.

15. For a more detailed discussion of the issues raised in this section, see Adamson (2006).

16. Edited and translated into French in Rashed (1997). I will cite by proposition number.

17. A second emissionist view is a kind of halfway house between an effluence theory and a visual ray theory, in which the ray has to meet, and mingle with, an effluence from the object. This was the view of Plato in the *Timaeus*.

18. This "active" understanding of vision tends to undermine the close analogy that Aristotle tried to draw between vision and the other senses. Al-Kindī says that the physical structure of the different sense organs, providentially arranged by God, already shows that the other senses function passively. The nose and ears have cavities designed to "catch" or "hold" the impressions that come to them, whereas vision is active and thus has a round, mobile organ.

19. Lindberg (1971), 479, goes so far as to assume they are identical; Travaglia (1999), 53, agrees with me that they merely obey the same laws. Whereas al-Kindī normally just moves freely from one sort of ray to the other, he is at one point explicit that we apply to visual rays the laws demonstrated to hold of light rays: see the first sentence of §17.

20. Also edited and translated in Rashed (1997).

21. As emphasized by Kheirandish (1996), 232, and Smith (1994), 131.

22. Al-Kindi's importance in this regard has been highlighted by Lindberg (1971, 1976).

23. See further Adamson (2006).

24. One problem with al-Kindī's view is that, as he admits, heavenly bodies are also visible, but they are made of aether and contain no earth. His solution to this seems to be simply that aether is also dense. See *On the Bearer of Color* §8 (AR^2 66) and *On the Blue Color of the Sky* §9 (AR^2 107).

25. This does not emerge clearly from *On the Bearer of Color* but seems to be assumed in the closely related *On the Blue Color of the Sky*, at §6 (AR^2 106). Alternatively it may be just a matter of the ratio of earth to the other elements in a given body. This might also be inferred from the claim in *On the Blue Color of the Sky* §9 (AR^2 107) that blue results from the sky's having both "dark" air and colored earthy particles. See further chapter 8.

26. See again Adamson (2006).

27. The Greek text is edited in Hoche (1866) and translated in D'Ooge (1926). Al-Kindī corrected an Arabic translation which is now extant only in Hebrew. The beginning of this translation, which includes several glosses explicitly ascribed to al-Kindī, has been edited and translated in Freudenthal and Lévy (2004).

28. On this topic see the excellent O'Meara (1989).

29. See Freudenthal and Lévy (2004), 530.

30. *Introduction to Arithmetic*, I.17; cf. II.24. This was noticed by Langermann (2003), 352.

31. In bk. 2, chap. 21, Nicomachus says that "the nature of proportions is most essential for speculation about the nature of the universe" (D'Ooge translation). This is the start of the culminating section of the *Introduction*, which deals with proportion. In chap. 6 of bk. 1, Nicomachus has already said that God created all things in accordance with number and harmony.

32. For the edition see Zakariyyā' (1962); I will cite by page and line number from this edition. Shehadi (1995), chap. 1, gives an overview of some of the main ideas in these works. The fifth treatise edited by Zakariyyā' may be alluded to in *Quantity*, following the passage just cited.

33. Ed. Zakariyyā' (1962), 95–110. Partial translation in Farmer (1955–56); this unfortunately does not include the very interesting "sayings" on music in the last section of the treatise.

34. The *'ūd*, or short-necked lute, used in al-Kindī's region and time had four strings, but in highly theoretical discussions of music (for example his *Great Epistle on the Composition of Melodies*, the first text edited in Zakariyyā' (1962), al-Kindī refers to five strings. However this has been taken to be merely an expedient for clarifying the theory: see Lachmann and el-Hefai (1931), 4.

35. This last grouping falls into three categories: the just-mentioned internal senses; the "powers in the body," which look as though they all have to do with the nutritive faculty; and the "acts made manifest in the living thing." These are harder to classify, since they include "courage," "mind [*'aql*]," "cowardice," and "gentleness." The context here may be one of practical philosophy, with *'aql* corresponding to something like *phronêsis*; al-Kindī associates it with happiness, pleasure, and goodness (103.19–20). We find similar correspondences to the four *'ūd* strings in *On Stringed Instruments*, ed. Zakariyyā' (1962), 69–92, at 85–9.

36. This is a question raised, but not satisfactorily answered, in Shehadi (1995), 23–7.

37. Al-Kindī is also said to have quoted Orpheus saying that he could change his hearers' "ethical qualities," turning anger into calm, grief into joy, etc. See Rosenthal (1975), 228.

38. See Ibn al-Qifṭī, *Ta'rīkh al-ḥukamā'*, ed. Lippert (1903), 376.12–378.2.

39. This loose sense of "proportion" will be sufficient for our purposes here. The more technical sense is explained in Nicomachus (*Introduction* II.21): a proportion consists of two ratios or relations which share a term, for example 1, 2, 4. There are three kinds of proportions, namely arithmetic, geometric, and harmonic. Harmonic proportions, the kind studied in music, are the most complex; see *Introduction* II.25. Ultimately, al-Kindī would presumably like to show how *harmonic* proportions are replicated in natural

phenomena, in order to demonstrate that the universe is composed in a harmonious way. But as far as I can see he never attempts anything nearly this ambitious.

40. We find this move already in Xenocrates, according to the report of Simplicius. See Dillon (2003), 128 n. 112.

41. Baffioni (1984), 36–7.

42. Al-Kindī also invokes other, less obvious properties of numbers in order to explain the Platonic system. For instance, he follows Pythagorean numerological theory in saying that even numbers are "passive" or "feminine," because they can all be divided by 2, whereas odd numbers are indivisible and hence "masculine" (AR^2 55). As we will see in chapter 8, he considers the two moist elements, water and air, to be "active" and the two dry elements, fire and earth, to be "passive." Therefore polygons involving even numbers, like the cube, will be related to the dry elements like earth.

43. If so, he may have been convinced by Aristotle's attacks on the Platonic theory in bk. III of *On the Heavens*.

44. A concrete example appears in al-Kindī's *On Tides*, at AR^2 120.9–11: the ratio (*nisba*) or the sphere of the moon is in "harmony [*i'tilāf*] with the ratio of the sphere of water and earth, as we have explained in our discussions on harmony [*fī aqāwīlinā al-ta'līfiyya*]," and as a result the moon has a greater effect on earth and water than on air and fire, which are more strongly affected by the sun (120.14). (Cf. AR^2 125.3–7 for a similar discussion of Venus and Mercury.)

45. One striking doctrine mentioned in the sayings is not otherwise attested in al-Kindī: the unnamed philosophers mention a "universal, celestial soul [*al-nafs al-kulliyya al-falakiyya*]" (110.18–19), which is the cause of beautiful things in the physical world, and which seems to be distinguished from "particular souls [*al-nufūs al-juz'iyya*]" (110.21). This doctrine of the world soul is common in the sort of Neoplatonic texts that evidently stand behind these sayings, but nowhere else do we find al-Kindī explicitly speaking of a "universal soul." On the question of the world soul in al-Kindī's circle, see further D'Ancona (1999b).

46. Cf. 108.5–10; 109.6.

47. See Aristotle, *De Anima* 408b32–33.

48. Al-Kindī, modifying Nicomachus' distinction (*Introduction* I.3) between arithmetic and music on the one hand, and astronomy and geometry on the other, thinks that the latter pair of sciences study quality rather than quantity. See *Quantity* §VII.2 (AR 377). However al-Kindī also mentions the "quality [*kayfiyya*]" of musical notes, presumably meaning their audible pitch as opposed to their numerical values. See his *On the Art of Harmony*, ed. Zakariyyā' (1962), e.g. at 48.8–10.

49. This is why I would persist in contrasting al-Kindī's strictly intellectualist handling of the world's eternity (which is also highly mathematical, given its extensive discussion of the notion of infinity), in *On First Philosophy* section 2, with his procedure in scientific inquiries. Al-Kindī himself sometimes contrasts a "mathematical" and "physical" approach, but this usually sheds little light. For example, as mentioned above (chapter 4, note 28), *Finiteness* emphasizes that it has used a mathematical arguments instead of the arguments "taken from natural things" used in other treatises. But the premises demonstrated are the same as those used elsewhere; the main difference is the use of simple geometric diagrams to prove those premises. Another treatise, *That the Elements and the Outermost Body Are Spherical in Shape* (AR^2 48–53), is full of geometrical demonstrations but also invokes premises from observation of physical things (e.g. that fire and air go up, but water and earth go down). In conclusion al-Kindī says (AR^2 53): "it has been shown on the basis of physics [*min jiha al-ṭabīʿa*] that the surface of water is spherical, and also that all the elements and the outermost body are spherical." He then adds, rather cryptically, "but [or "and": *wa-*] it is possible to show that the body of the universe is spherical, using mathematics [*min al-ṣināʿa al-riyāḍiyya*]." In this case it is unclear to me whether he is contrasting, or assimilating, the physical and mathematical treatments of the question. To these ambiguous passages we can add the distinction al-Kindī elsewhere makes between physics as a study of the sublunary world, and metaphysics as the study of the heavens (see chapter 8).

50. *On First Philosophy* §IV.13–14 (AR 110–1, RJ 23–5), cited in chapter 2.

51. See chapter 3, note 16. Yet another example would be the allusion to al-Kindī's teaching on the finiteness of the created world towards the end of *On Why the Higher Atmosphere Is Cold*, at AR^2 99–100.

CHAPTER 8

1. For a good discussion of the philosophical implications of al-Kindī's cosmology, see Wiesner (1993).

2. On the reception of *On the Heavens* in Arabic, see Endress (1966). The closest thing we find to an explicit citation of *On the Heavens* in al-Kindī is a passage where he says that he himself tested Aristotle's claim (II.7) that the lead tip of an arrow melts during flight, due to friction with the air. Al-Kindī found that this was not the case, as he mentions in *On Tides* AR^2 117.11ff. and the first letter on weather prediction in Bos and Burnett (2000), §1.16–19.

3. This account is based on *Meteorology* 4, with the basic distinction made already at 4.1, 378b10ff.; cf. *On Generation and Corruption* 2.2. Al-Kindī sets it out most fully at *On Why the Higher Atmosphere Is Cold*, AR^2 93–4; cf. *On the*

Proximate Agent Cause §VI.5, AR^2 224, and *On the Nature of the Celestial Sphere* §4, AR^2 41.

4. Edited at AR^2 48–53, translated in Rescher and Khatchadourian (1965a). This treatise consists mainly of geometrical demonstrations. Al-Kindī shows that if the outermost body were not spherical it could not move, since it would have to move into a place where there is nothing, not even void. The elements, meanwhile, will automatically distribute themselves in concentric spherical regions because of their natural motions. The latter argument seems to be based on *On the Heavens* II.4, 287b4ff.

5. Al-Kindī makes this point at *Proximate Agent Cause* §V.3–6, AR 221–3, by means of an elaborate thought experiment designed to rule out the idea that the elements could transform one another just by touching at their borders.

6. We know that *Prostration* was written later, because he refers back to *Proximate Agent Cause* at §III.1 (AR 247, RJ 181) and §VI.2 (AR 255, RJ 191).

7. Here he is in agreement with Aristotle: see e.g. *On the Heavens* II.12, 292a20–1.

8. As Walzer (1962), 203, notes, this was also the view of Proclus, as reported in Olympiodorus' commentary on the *Phaedo*. Al-Kindī also discusses vision and hearing as the two most excellent senses in the "sayings" at the end of *On Stringed Instruments*, ed. Zakariyyā' (1962), 109–10.

9. Note that this argument should also show that the heavens are alive; al-Kindī comes close to making this point in the earlier section but does not quite do so.

10. Fazzo and Wiesner (1993). See also Wiesner (1993), 41ff. and 54ff.

11. See Ruland (1976), 75–7.

12. Aristotle goes on to compare this to the way motion produces sparks from wood, stone and metal. Also related is *Meteorology* 1.2, 339a20–22, which says that the sublunary world is "continuous [*sunechês*] with the higher motions, so that its entire potentiality is governed [*kubernasthai*] from there." In the Arabic version, the text says even more bluntly that the change and alteration of elemental bodies is "from the celestial things [*min al-umūr al-'alawiyya*], which are the agent for alterations in them" (Petraitis, 1967, 14.2–3).

13. Cf. his first letter on weather forecasting, ed. in Bos and Burnett (2000), §1.13: "The philosophers agreed that the heat and the light which come from the stars are caused by the striking and friction of the air which is caused by their movement; for it is in the nature of movement to get hot as [can be seen] in the striking of wood, stones and iron." See also *On Tides*, AR^2 116–7.

14. Cf. *On Tides*, AR^2 120. Though Aristotle had said (*Meteorology* 1.3, 341a18–22) that the sun is the only heavenly body that produces heat, al-Kindī generally gives this role to all the heavenly bodies, even the fixed stars (though

he does deny this once, in a letter on meteorology: see Bos and Burnett (2000), 330, discussing the first letter, §I.21). His preference here already shows up in the translation of Ibn al-Biṭrīq: see Petraitis (1967), 35 n. 2.

15. As pointed out by Fazzo and Wiesner (1993), 144 n. 61.

16. See particularly AR^2 124ff.

17. Ed. D'Alverny and Hudry (1974), French trans. in Ottaviani (2003). I will cite by chapter number and page number from the Latin edition.

18. See above, chapter 1. Al-Kindī is also probably the target in Aquinas' *Summa Contra Gentiles* III.104–5; see D'Alverny and Hudry (1974), 140.

19. Probably *On Rays* goes further than intended here, in order to ensure the centrality of astral causation. Even after the present passage it says that elemental matter is both active and passive ("hinc agente, illinc vero patiente," §VI, 244), and that this is brought about by the stars. I suspect then that what the passage in §IV means to say is that the elements exercise no causality that is *independent* of astral causality.

20. As pointed out by D'Alverny and Hudry (1974), 149. Other titles in this section also refer to "rays" (*shuʿāʿ*).

21. On the possible background of this phrase see D'Alverny and Hudry (1974), 160–1.

22. To give a couple of examples, *On Rays* says that desire and voluntary action begin in the heart (§VI, 243), whereas we know from *On Sleep and Dream* that al-Kindī wanted to transpose at least some faculties from the heart to the brain, following the Galenic model. *On Rays* also gives a more naturalistic explanation of prayer (§VI, 246) than that found in an astrological work by al-Kindī dealing with God's answering of prayers (see further below).

23. As discussed in Travaglia (1999).

24. For example, (a) *On Rays* calls the study of the sublunary realm "physics" and the study of celestial bodies and their influence "metaphysics" (§IV, 229), a claim found in his letters on weather prediction (see Bos and Burnett, 2000, 14–5, and further below). (b) In *On Rays* (§II, 220), there is an affirmation of flux in the physical world: "every thing in this world is constantly moved with some sort of motion" ("omnis res huius mundi continue moveatur aliqua specie motus"), which is parallel to *On First Philosophy* (§IV.2, AR 106, RJ 19), where al-Kindī says that any sense-object "flows and is in constant change, with some sort of motion [*bi-aḥad anwāʿ al-ḥarakāt*]." (c) *On Rays* displays the Kindian habit of confident, but vague, allusions to ancient authority (e.g. at §1, 218), and some of the ancient sources and themes used by *On Rays* are favorites of al-Kindī's, such as the *Isagoge* (§I, 216) and the idea of man as a microcosm (§§V, 230; VI, 243; VIII, 253). (d) *On Rays* (§VI, 240) mentions the three internal senses in passing, which as we have

seen were known to al-Kindī. (e) *On Rays* (§VI, 243) seems to allude to a pharmacological theory like that of *On Degrees*: "plants, when compounded [*confecte*], owing to the compounding have a resulting effect that they would not have when separate." (f) The constant reference to celestial "harmony" (*armonia*, presumably translating *ta'līf*, as noted by D'Alverny and Hudry, 1974, 220) resonates well with the texts I discussed at the end of chapter 7.

25. See Burnett (1993, 1999).

26. See Loth (1875).

27. See Klein-Franke (1975).

28. See Burnett et al. (1997).

29. See Burnett (1993).

30. See Mahdi (1976).

31. As recounted in the *Fihrist*, ed. Tajaddud (1971), 335.

32. See Adamson (2002a).

33. These are edited in AR². The contents of most of them are summarized briefly in various sections of Lettinck (1999). For a partial translation of the last work about tides (which actually details a wide range of phenomena having to do with the increase and decrease in volumes of water), see Wiedemann (1922). This translation does not include the sections most relevant for the question of celestial influence, however. For a translation of the short treatise on fog, see Cabanelas (1962).

34. The Arabic version is edited in Petraitis (1967), who mentions parallels with al-Kindī in his notes to the edition.

35. The reason that we can see watery exhalations is that they also contain an admixture of earth.

36. This contrast between smoky and vaporous exhalations is also from Aristotle: see e.g. *Meteorology* 1.4, 341b10, cf. Petraitis (1967), 30–1.

37. As Lettinck (1999), 110–1, points out, al-Kindī is inconsistent about the cause of wind. This "vertical" account matches what we find in Aristotle, but elsewhere al-Kindī says it is because of the horizontal "expansion" of the air in places heated by the heavens, which pushes the surrounding air away and causes wind (in *On Why Rain Falls in Certain Places*, AR² 71, cf. *On Tides*, AR² 123). Either way, though, the heating of the heavens is the main explanation.

38. Here he is following stray references to solar rays in Aristotle: see *Meteorology* 1.3, 340a22–31 (cf. Petraitis, 1967, 17.1, with the phrase *in'ikās al-shu'ā'*, also found in al-Kindī) and 346b23.

39. Indeed it must still accept this part of the account found in *Proximate Agent Cause* and elsewhere, since only on the friction view is the central puzzle of the treatise puzzling.

40. See above, chapter 7, and Adamson (2006).

41. In Bos and Burnett (2000). I will cite these as *Letter 1* and *Letter 2*, with section numbers from their edition.

42. Notice that al-Kindī here uses the same terminology of four degrees of heat, cold, etc. found in *On Degrees*, as also noted by Bos and Burnett (2000), 332–3.

43. Bos and Burnett (2000), 18.

44. Often he refers to the "mathematical discussions" in such contexts, for example at *Prostration* §VII.1 (AR 256, RJ 193) and *Proximate Agent Cause* VIII.2 (AR 227). These will be treatises of his own based on Ptolemy and others, or perhaps even the Greek works themselves. (See Rosenthal, 1965, for a work explicitly drawing on Ptolemy to give astronomical calculations.) In *On Tides* (AR^2 125) he refers to a work of his own called *On the Layers* [*naḍad*] *of the World and the Resemblance of Its Spheres*, which may have combined astronomical calculations with the sort of considerations presented in *Five Figures*.

45. Compare my remarks on Abū Ma'shar's praise of astrology as the highest science, in Adamson (2002a), 250–3.

46. These are edited in Ruland (1976), and discussed in Sharples (1982).

47. See Ruland (1976), especially at 13, 31.

48. Ruland (1976), 11.

49. For this work see Sharples (1983).

50. For example at Ruland (1976), 77, the Kindī version calls nature a "heavenly power" whereas the Abū Bishr Mattā version has "divine power."

51. All this is shown in Fazzo and Wiesner (1993).

52. See for instance Ruland (1976), 57, which says that the heavenly bodies operate through species (here *ṣuwar*, "forms"), and 91, lower text, which says that particulars are differentiated only by matter and not by nature.

53. *Letter 1* on weather forecasting, in Bos and Burnett (2000), §4.104. Al-Kindī cites *On Generation and Corruption* as the work where Aristotle expresses this opinion.

54. Here I will be extending the argument made in Adamson (2002a, 2003, 2004b).

55. This is found in *Epitome on Music, on the Harmony of Melody and the Art of the 'ūd*, ed. Zakariyyā' (1962), 113–22, at 116.3–117.14. I am grateful to Anna Akasoy for her help in translating the passage.

56. Cf. al-Kindī's *Sayings*, §8 at Atiyeh (1966), ed. at 200–1, trans. at 222.

57. Al-Kindī uses the term *'unṣur*, which usually means "material constituent," so he may be focusing on what is necessarily or possibly true of things in virtue of their physical composition.

58. That this is what al-Kindī has in mind is made clear at the end of the treatise (119–20); we also find here another reference to "substantial motion."

59. For example in the medical treatise *On Coitus*, discussed in chapter 7.

60. This would fit with the definition of "the possible" he gives in *On Definitions*: the possible is what is sometimes the case, as opposed to what is never the case or always the case (impossibility and necessity, respectively). For the relevance of this conception of modality to the determinism issue, and the way it was exploited by al-Kindī's associate Abū Maʿshar, see Adamson (2002a) and (2003).

61. Ed. D'Alverny and Hudry (1974), 226–9.

62. Ibid., 241.

63. On the other hand, in *Prostration* (§II.4, AR 246, RJ 179) al-Kindī stipulates that "choice [*ikhtiyār*]" belongs only to "complete souls, i.e. rational souls." This suggests that the power of choice operates above the level of the physical.

64. Towards the beginning of *Proximate Agent Cause* al-Kindī refers to God's "universal providence [*al-tadbīr al-kullī*]" (§III.5, AR 219). As Fazzo and Wiesner (1993), 137, point out, this echoes the Kindī version of Alexander's *On Providence*. There we find a contrast between "universal providence [*l-tadbīr al-kullī*]" and "particular providence [*al-tadbīr al-juzʾī*];" the former is said to be the subject of *On Providence*, whereas the latter is studied in astrology (or more specifically, a supposed Aristotelian work called *Astrologia*). Perhaps then al-Kindī hoped that God's being a "remote" or "universal" cause would absolve Him of blame for evils. But since universal providence necessitates particular providence, it still looks as though God indirectly causes every particular event. So al-Kindī has no obvious escape from the problem of evil. He would need to add that some features of the workings of celestial providence are not intended by God. This could be explained either by saying that the heavens are not perfect instruments, or that matter cannot perfectly receive the forms providence gives to it.

65. Ed. Badawī (1947), 74–5. The beginning of the chapter in fact reads "a discussion of the stars, and that we must not ascribe any of the particular things that arise from them to a volition [*irāda*] in them." The stars act by necessity, not volition, which according to the *Theology* means that the stars do not do evil. For "every agent that acts voluntarily [*bi-irạda*] performs [both] commendable and blameworthy actions, and does both good and evil. But every agent that performs its action without volition [*bi-ghayr irāda*] is above volition, and therefore does nothing but the good, and all its actions are satisfactory and praiseworthy."

66. Ed. Mahdi (1976).

67. Al-Kindī's view of these philosophers is, as one might expect, rather tolerant; their mistake is a natural one, since the heavens do in fact indicate God's will. Worse are those who actually made idols to the heavens.

68. As pointed out by Wiesner (1993), 115.

69. Tajaddud (1971), 383–5.

70. Edited at RJ 129.

71. Rejecting RJ's insertion of *'ājizan*.

72. Cf. *On Definitions* §77 (AR 175).

73. The idea of "voluntary necessity [*al-iḍṭirār al-irādī*]" appears also in the Kindī-circle translation of Plotinus; see Adamson (2004b).

BIBLIOGRAPHY

EDITIONS AND TRANSLATIONS OF AL-KINDĪ'S WORKS

Abū Rīda, M. 'A. H., ed. (1950/1953). al-Kindī, *Rasā'il al-Falsafiyya*, 2 vols. (Cairo; Dār al-Fikr al-'Arabī).

Allard, M. (1972). "L'épître de Kindī sur les definitions." *Bulletin d'études orientales de l'Institut français de Damas* 25, 47–83.

Atiyeh, G. N. (1966). *Al-Kindī: The Philosopher of the Arabs* (Rawalpindi; Islamic Research Institute).

Bos, G. (1990). "A Recovered Fragment on the Signs of Death from al-Kindī's Medical Summaries." *Zeitschrift für Geschichte der arabisch-islamischen Wissenschaften* 6, 190–4.

Bos, G., and Burnett, C. (2000). *Scientific Weather Forecasting in the Middle Ages: The Writings of al-Kindī* (London; Kegan Paul).

Burnett, C., Yamamoto, K., and Yano, M. (1997). "Al-Kindī on Finding Buried Treasure." *Arabic Sciences and Philosophy* 7, 57–90.

Celentano, G. (1979). *Due scritti medici di al-Kindi,* Annali del'I.U.O. supp. 18, vol. 39.1 (Naples; I.U.O.).

D'Alverny, M.-T., and Hudry, F., (1974). "Al-Kindī, *De Radiis.*" *Archives d'histoire doctrinale et littéraire du moyen âge* 61, 139–260.

Endress, G. (1994). "Al-Kindī über die Wiedererinnerung der Seele." *Oriens* 34, 174–221.

Fakhry, M. (1963). "Al-Kindī wa 'l-Suqrāṭ." *al-Abḥāth* 16, 23–34.

Farmer, H. G. (1955–56). "Al-Kindī on the 'êthos' of Rhythm, Color and Perfume." *Glasgow Oriental Society Transactions* 16, 29–38.

Frank, T. (1975). "*Al-Kindī's Book of Definitions:* Its Place in Arabic Definition Literature." PhD. diss., Yale University.

Furlani, G. (1922). "Una risālah di al-Kindī sull'anima." *Rivista Trimestale di Studi Filosofici e Religiosi* 3, 50–63.

Gauthier, L. (1938). *Antécédents gréco-arabes de la psycho-physique* (Beirut; Imprimerie Catholique).

Guidi, M., and Walzer, R. (1940). *Uno Scritto Introduttivo allo Studio di Aristotele* (Rome; Reale Accademia Nazionale dei Lincei).

Ivry, A. (1974). *Al-Kindi's Metaphysics* (Albany; SUNY Press).

Jolivet, J. (1971). *L'Intellect selon Kindī* (Leiden; Brill).

Gimaret, D. (1976). *Al-Kindī: Cinq Épîtres* (Paris; CNRS).

Klein-Franke, F. (1975). "Die Ursachen der Krisen bei akuten Krankheiten: eine wiederentdeckte Schrift al-Kindī's." *Israel Oriental Studies* 5, 161–88.

———. (1982). "Al-Kindī's 'On Definitions and Descriptions of Things.'" *Le Muséon* 95, 191–216.

Lachmann, R., and el-Hefai, M., eds. (1931). *Ja'qūb Ibn Isḥāq al-Kindī: Risāla fī khubr ta'līf al-alḥān. Über die Kompositionen der Melodien*, Veröffentlungen der Gesellschaft zur Erforschung der Musik des Orients 1 (Leipzig; Kistner and Siegel).

Levey, M. (1966). *The Medical Formulary or Aqrābādhīn of al-Kindī* (Madison; University of Wisconsin Press).

Loth, O. (1875). "Al-Kindī als Astrolog." *Morgenländische Forschungen*, 261–309.

Mahdi, M. (1976). "Unedited Texts of al-Kindī and al-Fārābī" [in Arabic]. In U. 'Amīn (ed.), *Nuṣūs falsafiyya* (Cairo; al-Hay'a al-Miṣriyya al-'āmma al-Kitāb), 53–78.

McCarthy, R. (1964). "Al-Kindī's Treatise on the Intellect." *Islamic Studies* 3, 119–49.

McVaugh, M. (1975). Arnaldi de Villanova, *Opera medica omnia II* (Grenada-Barcelona; University of Barcelona).

Mestiri, S., and Dye, G. (2004). *Al-Kindī: Le moyen de chasser les tristesses et autres textes éthiques* (Paris; Fayard).

Mrayati, M., Alam, Y. M., and al-Tayyan, H. (1987). *Origins of Arab Cryptography and Cryptanalysis* (Damascus; Arab Academy of Damascus).

Nagy, A. (1897). *Die philosophische Abhandlungen des Ja'qūb ben Isḥāq al-Kindī* (Münster; Aschendorff).

Ottaviani, D. (2003). *Al-Kindi, "De radiis": Théorie des arts magiques* (Paris; Allia).

Périer, A. (1920–1). "Un traité de Yahyā ben 'Adī: Défense du dogme de la Trinité contre les objections d'al-Kindī." *Revue de l'orient christian,* 3rd ser., 22, 3–21.

Rashed, R. (1997). *Oeuvres Philosophiques et Scientifiques d'al-Kindi.* Vol. 1. *L'Optique et la Catoptrique* (Leiden; Brill).

Rashed, R., and Jolivet, J., eds. and trans. (1998). *Oeuvres Philosophiques et Scientifiques d'al-Kindī.* Vol. 2. *Métaphysique et cosmologie* (Leiden; Brill).

Rescher, N., and Khatchadourian, H. (1965a). "Al-Kindī's Epistle on the Concentric Structure of the Universe." *Isis* 56, 190–5.

———. (1965b). "Al-Kindī's Epistle on the Finitude of the Universe." *Isis* 56, 426–33.

Rescher, N. (1963). "Al-Kindī's Sketch of Aristotle's Organon." *New Scholasticism* 37, 44–58.

———. (1968). "Al-Kindī's Treatise on the Platonic Solids." In *Studies in Arabic Philosophy* (Pittsburgh; Pittsburgh University Press), 15–37.

Ritter, H., and Walzer, R. (1938). *Uno Scritto Morale Inedito di al-Kindī* (Rome; Reale Accademia Nazionale dei Lincei).

Ruffinengo, P. P. (1997). "Al-Kindī, *Trattato sull'intelletto. Trattato sul sogno e la visione.*" *Medioevo* 23, 337–94.

Spies, O. (1937). "Al-Kindī's Treatise on the Cause of the Blue Colour of the Sky." *Journal of the Bombay Branch of the Royal Asiatic Society* 13, 7–19.

Veccia Vaglieri, L., and Celentano, G. (1974). *Trois épîtres d'al-Kindī.* Annali del'I.U.O. 34.4 (new ser. 24). (Naples; I.U.O), 536–62.

Wiedemann, E. (1922). "Über al-Kindī's Schrift über Ebbe und Flut." *Annalen der Physik* 67, 374–87.

Zakariyyā', Y. (1962). *Mu'allafāt al-Kindī al-mūsīqiyya* (Baghdad; Maṭba'a Shafīq).

OTHER PRIMARY SOURCES AND TRANSLATIONS

Amin, A., and Zayn, A., eds. (1939–44). al-Tawḥīdī, *Kitāb al-Imtā' wa 'l-Muwānasa* (Cairo; Dār al-Maktaba al-Ḥayā).

Arnzen, R. (1998). *Aristoteles' De Anima, eine verlorene spätantike Paraphrase in arabischer und persischer Überlieferung* (Leiden; Brill).

Badawī, A., ed. (1947). *Aflūṭīn 'inda 'l-'Arab* (Cairo; Dirāsa Islāmiyya).

Bardenhewer, O. (1881). *Die pseudo-aristotelische Schrift über das reine Gute bekannt unter dem Namen Liber de Causis* (Freiburg; Harder).

Blumenthal, H. J., trans. (2000). "Simplicius," *On Aristotle On the Soul 3.1–5* (London; Duckworth).

Bosworth, C. E., trans. (1987). *The History of al-Ṭabarī,* vol. 32 (Albany; SUNY Press).

Bouyges, M., ed. (1973). Averroes, *Tafsīr mā ba'd al-ṭabī'a* (Beirut: Dar el-Machreq).

Bruns, I., ed. (1887). *Commentaria in Aristotelis Graeca,* supp. 2.2 (Berlin; Teubner).

Charlton, W., trans. (1991). Philoponus, *On Aristotle on the Intellect* (London; Duckworth).

———. (2000). "Philoponus," *On Aristotle On the Soul 3.1–8* (London; Duckworth).

de Goeje, M. J., ed. (1897). al-Ṭabarī, *Tarīkh al-Rusūl wa'l-Mulūk* (Leiden; Brill).

Diehl, E., ed. (1903–1906). Proclus, *In Platonis Timaeum Commentaria* (Leipzig; Teubner).

Dodge, B., trans. (1970). *The Fihrist of al-Nadīm* (New York; Columbia University Press).

D'Ooge, M. L., trans. (1926). Nicomachus of Gerasa, *Introduction to Arithmetic* (New York; Macmillan).

Dunlop, D. M., ed. (1979). *Muntakhab Ṣiwān al-Ḥikma* (Hague; Mouton).

Fazzo, S., and Zonta, M. (1998). Alessandro di Afrodisia, *La Provvidenza* (Milan; Bilbioteca Universale Rizzoli).

Flügel, G., ed. (1871–72). Ibn al-Nadīm, *al-Fihrist* (Leipzig; F.C.W. Vögel).

Ghurāb, A., ed. (1967). al-'Āmirī, *Kitāb al-I 'lām bi-Manāqib al-Islām* (Cairo; Dār al-Kātib al-'Arabī).

al-Hājirī, Ṭ., ed. (1948). al-Jāḥiẓ, *Kitāb al-Bukhalā'* (Cairo; Dār al-Kātib al-Miṣrī). (English translation: Serjeant [1997]).

Hayduck, M., ed. (1882). [Pseudo] Simplicius, *Commentaria in Aristotelis de Anima libros* (Berlin; Reimer). (Commentaria in Aristotelem Graeca, English translation: Blumenthal [2000]).

———. (1897). [Pseudo] Philoponus, *Commentaria in Aristotelis de Anima libros* (Berlin; Reimer) (Commentaria in Aristotelem Graeca, English translation: Charlton [1991]).

Heinze, R., ed. (1866). *Nichomachi Geraseni Pythagorei Introductionis Arithmeticae Libri II* (Leipzig; Teubner).

———. (1899). *Themistii in Libros Aristotelis De Anima Paraphrasis* (Berlin; Reimer). (Commentaria in Aristotelem Graeca, English translation: Todd [1996]).

Ibn Farīghūn (1985). *Jawāmi' al-'ulūm* (Frankfurt am Main; Institute for the History of Arabic-Islamic Science).

Khalifat, S., ed. (1996). *Rasā'il Abū al-Ḥasan 'Āmirī* (Tehran; Nashr-i Danisgahi).

Koch, J., ed., and Riedl, J. O., trans. (1944). Giles of Rome, *Errores Philosophorum* (Milwaukee: Marquette University Press).

Kutsch, W. (1954). "Ein arabisches Bruchstück aus Porphyrios (?) *Peri Psykhês*, und die Frage des Verfassers der 'Theologie des Aristoteles,'" *Melanges de l'Université Saint Joseph* 31, 265–86.

Lang, H. S., and Macro, A. D. (2001). Proclus, *On the Eternity of the World* (Berkeley; University of California Press).

Lippert, J., ed. (1903). Al-Qifṭī, *Ta'rīkh al-Ḥukamā'* (Leipzig; Dieterich'sche Verlagbuchhandlung).

Margoliouth, D. S., ed. (1907). Yāqūt b. 'Abd Allāh al-Hamawī, *Irshād al-'arīb ilā Ma'rifa al-'adib* (London; Luzac).

Müller, A., ed. (1882). Ibn Abī Uṣaybi'a, *'Uyūn al-Anbā' fī Ṭabaqāt al-Aṭibbā'* (Cairo; no pub.).

Mu'nis, H., ed. (1998). Ṣā'id al-Andalusī, *Ṭabaqāt al-Umam* (Cairo; Dār al-Ma'ārif). (English translation: Salem and Kumar [1991]).

Najjar, F. M., and Mallet, D., eds. and trs. (1999). al-Fārābī, *L'Harmonie entre les opinions de Platon at d'Aristote* (Damascus; Institute Français de Damas).

Pellat, C., trans. (1962–97). al-Mas'ūdī, *Les Prairies d'Or*. 5 vols. (Paris; Société Asiatique).

———, ed. (1965–79). al-Mas'ūdī, *Muruj al-Dhahab wa Ma'ādin al-Jawhar*. 7 vols. (Beirut; al-Jāmi'a al-Lubnāniyya). (French translation: Pellat [1962–97]).

Petraitis, C., ed. (1967). *The Arabic Version of Aristotle's Meteorology* (Beirut; Dar el-Machreq).

Rabe, H., ed. (1899). Philoponus, *De Aeternitate Mundi Contra Proclum* (Leipzig; Teubner; reprint, Hildesheim; Olms, 1984).

Ritter, H., ed. (1929). al-Ash'arī, *Maqālāt al-Islāmiyyīn wa-Ikhtilāf al-Muṣallīn*, *Bibliotheca Islamica* 1.

Rosenthal, F. (1952–55). "Ash-Shayh al-Yūnānī and the Arabic Plotinus Source." *Orientalia* 21 (1952), 461–92; 22 (1953), 370–400; 24 (1955), 42–66.

Ruland, H.-J. (1976). "Die arabische Fassungen von zwei Schriften des Alexander von Aphrodisias: Über die Vorsehung und Über das liberum arbitrium." Diss. Universität Saarbrücken.

Salem, S. I., and Kumar, A., eds. and trans. (1991). Ṣā'id al-Andalusī, *Science in the Medieval World: Book of the Categories of Nations* (Austin; University of Texas Press).

Sayyid, F., ed. (1955). Ibn Juljul al-Andalusī, *K. Ṭabaqāt al- Aṭibbā' wa 'l-Ḥukama'* (Cairo; Institut français d'archéologie orientale).

Serjeant, R. B., trans. (1997). al-Jāḥiẓ, *The Book of Misers* (Reading; Garnet).

Share, M., trans. (2004). Philoponus, *Against Proclus on the Eternity of the World 1–5* (London; Duckworth).

———. (2005). Philoponus, *Against Proclus on the Eternity of the World 6–8* (London; Duckworth).

Sharples, R. W. (1983). Alexander of Aphrodisias, *On Fate* (London; Duckworth).

———, trans. (1992). Alexander of Aphrodisias, *Quaestiones* 1.1–2.15 (London; Duckworth).

Tajaddud, M. R., ed. (1971). Ibn al-Nadīm, *al-Fihrist* (Tehran; Marvi).

Thillet, P. (2003). Alexandre d'Aphrodise, *Traité de la providence* (Lagrasse; Verdier).

Todd, R. B., trans. (1996). Themistius, *On Aristotle on the Soul* (London; Duckworth).

Verbeke, G., ed. (1966). Jean Philopon, *Commentaire sur le De anima d'Aristote* (Louvain; Publications universitaires de Louvain). (English translation: Charlton [1991]).

Wildberg, C. (1987). Philoponus, *Against Aristotle on the Eternity of the World* (London; Duckworth).

Zurayk, C., ed. (1966). Miskawayh, *Tahdhīb al-Akhlāq*, ed. C. Zurayk (Beirut; al-Nadin al-Lubnāniyya) (English translation: Zurayk [1968]).

———, trans. (1968). Miskawayh, *The Refinement of Character* (Beirut; American University of Beirut).

SECONDARY SOURCES

Note: publications focusing specifically on al-Kindī are marked with an asterisk.

*Adamson, P., and Pormann, P. E., trans. (forthcoming). *The Philosophical Works of al-Kindī* (New York; Oxford University Press).

*Adamson, P. (2000). "Two Early Arabic Doxographies on the Soul: Al-Kindī and the 'Theology of Aristotle.'" *Modern Schoolman* 77, 105–25.

*———. (2002a). "Abū Ma'shar, al-Kindī and the Philosophical Defense of Astrology." *Recherches de philosophie et théologie médiévales* 69, 245–70.

———. (2002b). *The Arabic Plotinus: A Philosophical Study of the "Theology of Aristotle"* (London; Duckworth).

*———. (2002c) "Before Essence and Existence: Al-Kindī's Conception of Being." *Journal of the History of Philosophy 40, 297–312.*

*———. (2003). "Al-Kindī and the Mu'tazila: Divine Attributes, Creation and Freedom." *Arabic Sciences and Philosophy 13.1, 45–77.*

———. (2004a). "Correcting Plotinus: Soul's Relationship to Body in Avicenna's Commentary on the *Theology of Aristotle*." In P. Adamson, H. Baltussen, and M. W. F. Stone (eds.), *Philosophy, Science and Exegesis in Greek, Arabic and Latin Commentaries* (London; Institute of Classical Studies), 59–75.

———. (2004b). "A Note on Freedom in the Circle of al-Kindī." In J. E. Montgomery (ed.), *'Abbasid Studies* (Leuven; Peeters), 199–207.

———. (2005a). "On Knowledge of Particulars." *Proceedings of the Aristotelian Society* 105, 273–94.

*———. (2005b). "Al-Kindī and the Reception of Greek Philosophy." In P. Adamson and R. C. Taylor (eds.), *The Cambridge Companion to Arabic Philosophy* (Cambridge: Cambridge University Press, 2005), 32–51.

*———. (2006). "Vision, Light and Color in al-Kindi, Ptolemy and the Ancient Commentators." *Arabic Sciences and Philosophy* 16, 207–36.

*———. (2007). "Stoic, Cynic, Platonic: al-Kindī's Version of Socrates." In M. B. Trapp (ed.), *Socrates, from Antiquity to the Enlightenment* (Aldershot: Ashgate), 161–78.

*———. (forthcoming). "The Kindian Tradition: The Structure of Philosophy in Arabic Neoplatonism." In C. D'Ancona (ed.), *Proceedings of the European Science Foundation Meeting, "The Libraries of the Neoplatonists."*

Alon, I. (1991). *Socrates in Mediaeval Arabic Literature* (Leiden; Brill).

———. (1995). *Socrates Arabus* (Jerusalem; Hebrew University).

Altmann, A., and Stern, S. M. (1958). *Isaac Israeli: A Neoplatonic Philosopher of the Early Tenth Century* (Oxford; Oxford University Press).

Arkoun, M. (1970). *L'humanisme arabe au IVe/Xe siècle: Miskawayh, philosophe et historien* (Paris; J. Vrin).

*Atiyeh, G. N. (1966). *Al-Kindī: The Philosopher of the Arabs* (Rawalpindi; Islamic Research Institute).

*Baffioni, C. (1984). "La scala Pitagorica in al-Kindi." In R. Traini (ed.), *Studi in onore di Francesco Gabrieli nel suo ottantesimo compleanno*, vol. 1 (Rome; Università di Roma), 35–41.

———. (1994). "Il Liber Introductorius in Artem Logicae Demonstrationis: Problemi storici e filologici." *Studi Filologici* 1, 69–90.

Baltes, M. (1976/1978). *Die Weltentstehung des platonischen Timaios nach den antiken Interpreten*. 2 vols. (Leiden; Brill).

Bertolacci, A. (2005). "On the Arabic Translations of Aristotle's *Metaphysics*." *Arabic Sciences and Philosophy* 15, 241–75.

Biesterfeldt, H. H. (1977). "Abu l-Hasan al-'Amiri und die Wissenschaften." *Zeitschrift der Deutschen Morgenländischen Gesellschaft,* supp. 3.1, 335–41.

———. (1985). *Die Zweige des Wissens: Theorie und Klassifikation der Wissenschaften in der Darstellung des Ibn Farīghūn*. Habilitationsschrift (Universität Bochum).

Bosworth, C. E. (1963). "A Pioneer Arabic Encyclopedia of the Sciences: al-Khwārizmī's Keys of the Sciences." *Isis* 54, 97–111.

Blumenthal, H. J. (1977). "Neoplatonic Interpretations of Aristotle on *Phantasia*." *Review of Metaphysics* 31, 242–57.

———. (1991). "*Nous Pathêtikos* in Later Greek Philosophy." In H. J. Blumenthal and H. Robinson (eds.), *Oxford Studies in Ancient Philosophy*, supp. (Oxford; Oxford University Press), 191–205.

*Burnett, C. (1993). "Al-Kindī on Judicial Astrology: 'The Forty Chapters.'" *Arabic Sciences and Philosophy* 3, 77–117.

*———. (1999). "Al-Kindī in the Renaissance." In P. R. Blum (ed.), *Sapientiam Amemus: Humanismus und Aristotelismus in der Renaissance* (Munich; Fink), 13–30.

*Butterworth, C. (1992). "Al-Kindi and the Beginnings of Islamic Political Philosophy." In C. Butterworth (ed.), *The Political Aspects of Islamic Philosophy* (Cambridge, Mass.; Harvard University Press), 14–32.

———. (2005). "Ethics and Politics." In P. Adamson and R. C. Taylor (eds.), *The Cambridge Companion to Arabic Philosophy* (Cambridge; Cambridge University Press), 266–86.

*Cabanelas, C. (1962). "Nuevos documentos sobre la filosofia de al-Kindī." *Miscelanea de Estudios Arabes y Hebraicos* 11, 16–19.

*Cortabarria Beitia, A. (1970). "A partir de quelles sources étudier al-Kindī?" *MIDEO* 10, 83–108.

*———. (1972). "La classification des sciences chez al-Kindī." *MIDEO* 11, 49–76.

*———. (1974). "Un traite philosophique d'al-Kindī." *MIDEO* 12, 5–12.

*———. (1977). "Al-Kindī vu par Albert le Grand." *MIDEO* 13, 117–46.

Daiber, H. (1975). *Das theologisch-philosophische System des Mu'ammar Ibn 'Abbād as-Sulamī* (Beirut; Steiner).

———. (1985). "New Manuscript Findings from Indian Libraries." *Manuscripts of the Middle East* 1, 26–84.

*———. (1986). "Die Kritik des Ibn Ḥazm an Kindī's Metaphysik." *Der Islam* 63, 284–302.

———. (1990). "Qosṭā ibn Lūqā (9. Jh.) über die Einteilung der Wissenschaften." *Zeitschrift für Geschichte der arabisch-islamischen Wissenschaften* 6, 93–129.

D'Alverny, M.-T. (1959). "Anniyya-Anitas." In *Mélanges offerts a Étienne Gilson* (Toronto: Pontifical Institute), 59–91.

*D'Ancona, C. (1992). "Aristotele e Plotino nella dottrina di al-Kindī sul primo principio." *Documenti e Studi Sulla Tradizione Filosofica Medievale* 3.2, 363–422.

*——— (1995a). "Al-Kindī et l'auteur du *Liber de Causis*." In D'Ancona (1995d), 155–94.

———. (1995b). "La doctrine de la création 'mediante intelligentia' dans le *Liber de Causis* et dans ses sources." In D'Ancona (1995d), 73–96.

———. (1995c). "*Esse quod est supra eternitatem*: La Cause primière, l'être, et l'eternité dans le *Liber de Causis* et dans ses sources." In D'Ancona (1995d), 53–72.

———. (1995d). *Recherches sur le Liber de Causis* (Paris; Vrin).

*———. (1996). "La dottrina Neoplatonica dell'anima nella filosofia Islamica: Un esempio in al-Kindī." In *Actes del Simposi Internacional de Filosofia de l'Edat Mitjana* (Vic; Patronat d'Estudis Osonencs), 91–6.

*———. (1998). "Al-Kindī on the Subject Matter of the First Philosophy: Direct and Indirect Sources of 'Falsafa-l-ūlā,' Chapter One." In J. A. Aertsen and A. Speer (eds.), *Was ist Philosophie im Mittelalter* (Berlin; de Gruyter), 841–55.

*———. (1999a). "Aristotelian and Neoplatonic Elements in Kindī's Doctrine of Knowledge." *American Catholic Philosophical Quarterly* 73, 9–35.

———. (1999b). "Porphyry, Universal Soul and the Arabic Plotinus." *Arabic Sciences and Philosophy* 9, 47–88.

———. (2001). "Pseudo-*Theology of Aristotle*, Chapter I: Structure and Composition." *Oriens* 36, 78–112.

*———. (2005). "Fonti greche e rielaborazione arabe nella dossografie filosofiche: Una citazione della *Filosofia Prima* di al-Kindī nel *Quartetto Filosofico*." In M.S. Funghi (ed.), *Aspetti di Letteratura Gnomica nel Mondo Antico* (Florence; Olschki), 305–37.

Davidson, H. A. (1969). "John Philoponus as a Source of Medieval Islamic and Jewish Proofs of Creation." *Journal of the American Oriental Society* 89, 357–91.

———. (1987). *Proofs for Eternity, Creation and the Existence of God in Medieval Islamic and Jewish Philosophy* (New York; Oxford University Press).

Dillon, J. M. (1996). *The Middle Platonists: A Study of Platonism, 80 B.C. to A.D. 220* (London; Duckworth).

———. (2003). *The Heirs of Plato: A Study of the Old Academy, 347–274 B.C.* (Oxford; Clarendon).

*Druart, T.-A. (1993). "Al-Kindī's Ethics." *Review of Metaphysics* 47, 329–57.

Dunlop, D. M. (1950–55). "The *Jawāmi' al-'ulūm* of Ibn Farīghūn." *Zedi Velidi Togan'a armagan*, 348–53.

*———. (1957). "Biographical Material from the *Siwān al-Ḥikma*." *Journal of the Royal Asiatic Society*, 81–9.

———. (1959). "The Translations of al-Biṭrīq and Yaḥyā (Yūḥanna) b. al-Biṭrīq." *Journal of the Royal Asiatic Society*, 140–50.

Endress, G. (1966). "Die arabischen Übersetzungen von Aristoteles' Schrift *De Caelo*." Ph.D. diss., Universität Frankfurt.

———. (1973). *Proclus Arabus: zwanzig Abschnitte aus der Institutio Theologica in arabischer Übersetzung* (Beirut; Steiner).

*———. (1980). Review of *L'Intellect selon Kindī*, by J. Jolivet (1971). *Zeitschrift der deutschen morgenländischen Gesellschaft* 130, 422–35.

*———. (1986). "Al-Kindī's Theory of Anamnesis: A New Text and Its Implications." In *Islão e arabismo na Península Ibérica: Actas do XI Congreso da União Europaeia de Arabistas e Islamólogos* (Évora; Universidade de Évora), 393–402.

———. (1987/1992). "Die wissenschaftliche Literatur." In H. Gätje (ed.), *Grundriß der arabischen Philologie* (Wiesbaden; Reichert), vol. 2, 400–506, vol. 3, supp., 3–152.

———. (1990). "The Defense of Reason: The Plea for Philosophy in the Religious Community." *Zeitschrift für Geschichte der arabisch-islamischen Wissenschaften* 6, 1–49.

*———. (1997). "The Circle of al-Kindī." In G. Endress and R. Kruk (eds.), *The Ancient Tradition in Christian and Islamic Hellenism* (Leiden; Research School CNWS), 43–76.

———. (2003). "Mathematics and Philosophy in Medieval Islam." In J. P. Hogendijk and A. I. Sabra (eds.), *The Enterprise of Science in Islam* (Cambridge, Mass.; MIT Press), 121–76.

Farmer, H. G. (1934). "Who Was the Author of the *Liber Introductorius in Artem Logicae Demonstrationis*?" *Journal of the Royal Asiatic Society*, 553–56.

*Fazzo, S., and Wiesner, H. (1993). "Alexander of Aphrodisias in the Kindī Circle and in al-Kindī's Cosmology." *Arabic Sciences and Philosophy* 3, 119–53.

Finamore, J. F. (1985). *Iamblichus and the Theory of the Vehicle of the Soul* (Chico, Calif.; Scholars Press).

*Flügel, V. G. (1857). "Al-Kindī genannt des Philosoph der Araber." *Abhandlungen für die Kunde des Morgenlandes* 1.2 (Leipzig; Brockhaus).

Frank, R. M. (1956). "The Origin of the Arabic Philosophical Term *Anniyya*." *Cahiers de Byrsa* 6, 181–201.

———. (1969). "The Divine Attributes According to the Teaching of Abū 'l-Hudhayl al-'Allāf." *Le Muséon* 82, 451–506.

*Freudenthal, G., and Lévy, T. (2004). "De Gérase à Bagdad: Ibn Bahrīz, al-Kindī, et leur recension arabe de l'*Introduction Arithmétique* de Nicomaque, d'après la version hébraïque de Qalonymos ben Qalonymos d'Arles." In R. Morelon and A. Hasnawi (eds.), *De Zénon d'Élée à Poincaré: Recueil d'études en hommage à Roshdi Rashed* (Louvain; Peeters), 479–544.

*Genequand, C. (1987—88). "Platonism and Hermetism in al-Kindī's *fī al-Nafs*." *Zeitschrift für Geschichte der arabisch-islamischen Wissenschaften* 4, 1–18.

*Griffith, S. H. (2002), "The Muslim Philosopher al-Kindī and His Christian Readers: Three Arab Christian Texts on 'The Dissipation of Sorrows.' " In *The Beginnings of Christian Theology in Arabic: Muslim-Christian Encounters in the Early Islamic Period* (Aldershot, England: Ashgate, 2002), chap. 9.

*Guerrero, R. R. (1982). "La tradición Griega en la filosofía Árabe: El tema del alma en al-Kindi." *Al-Qanṭara* 3, 1–26.

Gutas, D. (1975). *Greek Wisdom Literature in Arabic Translation: a Study of the Graeco-Arabic Gnomologia* (New Haven; American Oriental Society).

———. (1981). "Classical Arabic Wisdom Literature: Nature and Scope." *Journal of the American Oriental Society* 101, 49–86.

———. (1988a). *Avicenna and the Aristotelian Tradition* (Leiden; Brill).

———. (1988b). "Plato's Symposion in the Arabic Tradition." *Oriens* 31, 36–60. (Reprinted in Gutas [2000]).

———. (1990). "Ethische Schriften im Islam." In W. Heinrichs (ed.), *Orientalisches Mittelalter*; *Neues Handbuch der Literatur Wissenschaft*, vol. 5 (Wiesbaden; AULA-Verlag), 346–65.

———. (1993). "Sayings by Diogenes Preserved in Arabic." In M.-O. Goulet-Cazé and R. Goulet (eds.), *Le Cynisme ancien et ses prolongements* (Paris; Presses Universitaires de France), 475–518.

———. (1998). *Greek Thought, Arabic Culture: The Graeco-Arabic Translation Movement in Baghdad and Early Society (Second–Fourth/Eighth–Tenth Centuries)* (London; Routledge).

———. (2000). *Greek Philosophers in the Arabic Tradition* (Aldershot; Ashgate Variorum).

*———. (2004). "Geometry and the Rebirth of Philosophy in Arabic with al-Kindī." In R. Arnzen and J. Thielmann (eds.), *Words, Texts and Concepts Cruising the Mediterranean Sea: Studies on the Sources, Contents and Influences of Islamic Civilization and Arabic Philosophy and Science* (Leuven; Peeters), 195–209.

*Hamarneh, S. (1963). "The Life and Ideas of al-Kindī." *Middle East Forum* 39, 35–8.

*———. (1965). "Al-Kindī, a Ninth-Century Physician, Philosopher, and Scholar." *Medical History* 9, 328–42.

Hasnawi, A. (1994). "Alexandre d'Aphrodise vs. Jean Philopon: Notes sur quelques traités d'Alexandre 'perdus' en grec, conservés en arabe." *Arabic Sciences and Philosophy* 4, 53–109.

Harvey, E. R. (1985). *The Inward Wits: Psychological Theory in the Middle Ages and the Renaissance* (London; Warburg Institute).

Hasse, D. (2001). "Avicenna on Abstraction." In R. Wisnovksy (ed.), *Aspects of Avicenna* (Princeton; Markus Wiener), 39–72.

Hein, C. (1985). *Definition und Einteilung der Philosophie* (Frankfurt; Lang).

Heinrichs, W. (1984). "On the Genesis of the *Ḥaqīqa-Majāz* Dichotomy." *Studia Islamica* 59 (1984), 111–40.

Huby, P. (1991). "Stages in the Development of Language about Aristotle's *Nous*." In H. J. Blumenthal and H. Robinson (eds.), *Oxford Studies in Ancient Philosophy*, supp. (Oxford; Oxford University Press), 129–43.

*Ivry, A. (1972). "Al-Kindī as Philosopher: The Aristotelian and Neoplatonic Dimensions." In *Oriental Studies 5: Islamic Philosophy and the Classical Tradition* (Columbia; University of South Carolina Press), 117–39.

*Janssens, J. (1994). "Al-Kindī's Concept of God." *Ultimate Reality and Meaning* 17, 4–16.

*Jolivet, J. (1979). "Pour le dossier du Proclus arabe: Al-Kindī et la *Théologie Platonicienne*." *Studia Islamica* 49, 55–75.

*———. (1984). "L'Action divine selon al-Kindī." *Mélanges de l'Université Saint-Joseph*, 313–29.

*———. (1993). "Al-Kindī, vues sur le temps." *Arabic Sciences and Philosophy* 3, 55–75.

*———. (1996). "La topographie du salut d'après le *Discours sur l'Âme* d'al-Kindī." In M. A. Amir-Moezzi (ed.), *La voyage initiatique en terre d'Islam* (Louvain; Peeters, 1996), 149–58.

*———. (2004). "*L'Épître sur la quantité des livres d'Aristote* par al-Kindī (une lecture)." In R. Morelon and A. Hasnawi (eds.), *De Zénon d'Élée à Poincaré: Recueil d'études en hommage à Roshdi Rashed* (Louvain; Peeters), 665–83.

Judson, L. (1987). "God or Nature? Philoponus on Generability and Perishability." In R. Sorabji (ed.), *Philoponus and the Rejection of Aristotelian Science* (Ithaca; Cornell University Press), 179–96.

Kheirandish, E. (1996). "The Arabic 'Version' of Euclidean Optics: Transformations as Linguistic Problems in Transmission." In F. J. Ragep and S. P. Ragep (eds.), *Tradition, Transmission, Transformation* (Leiden; Brill), 227–43.

Klein-Franke, F. (1973). "Zur Überlieferung der platonischen Schriften im Islam." *Israel Oriental Studies* 3, 120–39.

Kraemer, J. (1986). *Philosophy in the Renaissance of Islam: Abū Sulaymān al-Sijistānī and his Circle* (Leiden; Brill).

Langermann, Y. T. (2001). "Studies in Medieval Hebrew Pythagoreanism: Translations and Notes to Nichomachus' Arithmological Texts." *Micrologus* 9, 219–36.

*———. (2003). "Another Andalusian Revolt? Ibn Rushd's Critique of al-Kindī's *Pharmacological Computus*." In J. P. Hogendijk and A. I. Sabra (eds.), *The Enterprise of Science in Islam* (Cambridge, Mass.; MIT Press), 351–72.

Lettinck, P. (1999). *Aristotle's Meteorology and Its Reception in the Arab World* (Leiden; Brill).

*Lindberg, D. C. (1971). "Alkindi's Critique of Euclid's Theory of Vision." *Isis* 62, 469–89.

———. (1976). *Theories of Vision from al-Kindi to Kepler* (Chicago; University of Chicago Press).

Long, A. A. (1996). "The Socratic Tradition: Diogenes, Crates, and Hellenistic Ethics." In R. B. Branham and M.-O. Goulet-Cazé (eds.), *The Cynics: The Cynic Movement in Antiquity and Its Legacy* (Berkeley; University of California), 28–46.

———. (2002). *Epictetus: A Stoic and Socratic Guide to Life* (Oxford; Clarendon Press).

Long, A. A., and Sedley, D. (1987). *The Hellenistic Philosophers*. 2 vols. (Cambridge; Cambridge University Press).

Madelung, W. (1974). "The Origins of the Controversy Concerning the Creation of the Koran." In J. M. Barral (ed.), *Orientalia Hispanica*, vol. 1 (Leiden; Brill), 504–25.

Mallet, D. (1994). "Le *Kitāb al-taḥlīl* d'al-Fārābī," *Arabic Sciences and Philosophy* 4, 317–35.

Margoliouth, D. S. (1905). "The Discussion between Abu Bishr Matta and Abu Sa'id al-Sirafi on the Merits of Logic and Grammar." *Journal of the Royal Asiatic Society*, 79–129.

Marmura, M. E. (1960). "Avicenna and the Problem of Infinite Number of Souls." *Mediaeval Studies* 22, 232–9. (Reprinted in Marmura [2005]).

———. (2005). *Probing in Islamic Philosophy* (Binghamton; Global Academic).

*Marmura, M. E., and Rist, J. M. (1963). "Al-Kindi's Discussion of Divine Existence and Oneness." *Mediaeval Studies* 25, 338–54. (Reprinted in Marmura [2005]).

Martin, A. (1989). "La *Métaphysique:* Tradition Syriaque et Arabe." In R. Goulet (ed.), *Dictionnaire des philosophes antiques* 1 (Paris; CNRS), 528–34.

McCarthy, R. J. (1962), *Al-Taṣānīf al-Mansuba ilā Faylasūf al-'arab* (Baghdad; Matba'a al-'ānī).

*Moosa, M. I. (1967). "Al-Kindī's Role in the Transmission of Greek Knowledge to the Arabs." *Journal of the Paḳistan Historical Society* 15, 3–14.

Nader, A. (1984). *Le système philosophique des Mu'tazila* (Beirut; Dar el-Machreq Sarl).

Netton, I. R. (1982). *Muslim Neoplatonists: An Introduction to the Thought of the Brethren of Purity, Ikhwān al-Ṣafā'* (London; Allen and Unwin).

O'Meara, D. J. (1989). *Pythagoras Revived* (Oxford; Oxford University Press).

Patton, W. M. (1897). *Aḥmed ibn Ḥanbal and the Miḥna* (Leiden; Brill, 1897).

Peters, F. E. (1968). *Aristoteles Arabus: The Oriental Translations and Commentaries on the Aristotelian Corpus* (Leiden; Brill).

Phillips, J. F. (1997). "Neoplatonic Exegeses of Plato's Cosmogony (*Timaeus* 27C–28C)." *Journal of the History of Philosophy* 35, 173–96.

Pines, S. (1974). "The Arabic Recension of *Parva Naturalia* and the Philosophical Doctrine Concerning Veridical Dreams According to *al-Risāla al-Manāmiyya* and Other Sources." *Israel Oriental Studies* 4, 104–53.

*Pohlenz, M. (1938). Review of *Uno Scritto Morale Inedito di al-Kindi,* by H. Ritter and R. Walzer (1938). *Göttingische Gelehrte Anzeigen* 10, 409–16.

*Riad, E. (1973). "A propos d'une définition de la colère chez al-Kindī." *Orientalia Suecana* 22, 62–5.

Ritter, H. (1932). "Schriften Ja'qūb ibn Isḥāq al-Kindī's in Stambuler Bibliotheken," *Archiv Orientální* 4, 363–72.

Rosenthal, F. (1940). "On the Knowledge of Plato's Philosophy in the Islamic World." *Islamic Culture* 14, 387–422.

*———. (1942). "Al-Kindī als Literat." *Orientalia* 11, 262–88.

———. (1943). *Aḥmad b. aṭ-Ṭayyib as-Sarakhsī* (New Haven; American Oriental Society).

*———. (1956a). "Al-Kindī and Ptolemy." In *Studi orientalistici in onore di Giorgio Levi della Vida* (Rome; Istituto per l'Oriente), 436–56.

*———. (1956b). "From Arabic Books and Manuscripts VI: Istanbul Materials for al-Kindī and as-Sarakhsī." *Journal of the American Oriental Society* 76, 27–31.

———. (1975). *The Classical Heritage in Islam*. Trans. E. Marmorstein and J. Marmorstein (London; Routledge).

Rowson, E. (1988). *A Muslim Philosopher on the Soul and Its Fate* (New Haven; American Oriental Society).

———. (1990). "The Philosopher as Littérateur: Al-Tawḥīdī and His Predecessors." *Zeitschrift für Geschichte der arabisch-islamischen Wissenschaften* 6, 50–92.

Rudolph, U. (1989). *Die Doxographie des Pseudo-Ammonios: ein Beitrag zur neuplatonischen Überlieferung im Islam* (Stuttgart; Steiner).

Sharples, R. W. (1982). "Alexander of Aphrodisias on Divine Providence: Two Problems." *Classical Quarterly* 32, 198–211.

Shehadi, F. (1995). *Philosophies of Music in Medieval Islam* (Leiden; Brill).

Sheppard, A. (1997). "Phantasia and Imagination in Neoplatonism." In M. Joyal (ed.), *Studies in Plato and the Platonic Tradition* (Aldershot; Ashgate), 201–10.

Smith, A. M. (1994). "Extremal Principles in Ancient and Medieval Optics." *Physis* 31, 113–40.

*Staley, K. (1989). "Al-Kindi on Creation: Aristotle's Challenge to Islam." *Journal of the History of Ideas* 50, 355–70.

Strohmaier, G. (1974). "Die arabische Sokrateslegende und ihre Ursprünge." In P. Nagel (ed.), *Studia Coptica* (Berlin: Akademie Verlag), 121–36.

Taylor, R. C. (1998). "Aquinas, the *Plotiniana Arabica* and the Metaphysics of Being and Actuality." *Journal of the History of Ideas* 59, 241–64.

*Tornero Poveda, E. (1992). *Al-Kindī: La transformacion de un pensamiento religioso en un pensamiento racional* (Madrid; Consejo Superior de Investigaciones Científicas).

*Travaglia, P. (1999). *Magic, Causality, and Intentionality: The Doctrine of Rays in al-Kind*i (Turnhout; Micrologus).

Tritton, A. S. (1972). "The Speech of God." *Studia Islamica* 36, 5–22.

van Ess, J. (1991–95). *Theologie und Gesellschaft im 2. und 3. Jahrhundert Hidschra: eine Geschichte des religiösen Denkens im frühen Islam*. 6 vols. (Berlin; de Gruyter).

*Van Riet, S. (1963). "Joie et bonheur dans le traité d'al-Kindi sur l'art de combattre la tristesse." *Revue philosophique de Louvain* 61, 13–23.

*Walzer, R. (1962). "New Studies on al-Kindī" and "Un frammento nuovo in Aristotele." In *Greek into Arabic* (Oxford; Cassirer), 175–205.

Watt, W. M. (1998). *The Formative Period of Islamic Thought* (Oxford; Oneworld).

*Wiesner, H. (1993). "The *Cosmology of al-Kindi*." Ph.D. diss., Harvard University.

Wisnovsky, R. (2003). *Avicenna's Metaphysics in Context* (London; Duckworth).

Wolfson, H. A. (1935). "The Internal Senses in Latin, Arabic, and Hebrew Philosophic Texts." *Harvard Theological Review* 28, 69–133.

———. (1976). *The Philosophy of the Kalām* (Cambridge, Mass.; Harvard University Press).

Young, M. J. L., Latham, J. D., and Serjeant, R. B., eds. (1990). *Religion, Learning and Science in the 'Abbāsid Period* (Cambridge; Cambridge University Press).

INDEX

Abū Bishr Mattā, 14, 17, 185, 197–8, 213 n.19
Abū 'l-Hudhayl, 219 n.33, 226 n.46
Abū Ma'shar al-Balkhī, 5, 13–14, 192, 245 n.45, 246 n.60
Abū Rīda, Muḥammad, 9
Abū Zayd al-Balkhī, 12–14
adab, 6, 16, 147
aether, 78, 83, 86–8, 112, 177, 181, 195, 238 n.24
Aḥmad b. al-Mu'taṣim, 4, 8, 42
Albert the Great, 19
alchemy, 7, 19
Alexander of Aphrodisas, 6, 81, 92, 170–1, 185–8, 197–9, 204, 218 n.25, 225 n.38, 246 n.64
Alexander the Great, 145, 147, 154
al-'Āmirī, 13, 15–16
Ammonius, 73, 125, 210 n.46. *See also* Pseudo-Ammonius
Arabic Plotinus. See *Theology of Aristotle*
Arabic Proclus. See *Liber de Causis*
Aristotle, 6, 8, 15, 29, 54, 72–8, 87, 95–7, 111–3, 154–5, 158, 167–8, 170–1, 177, 185–5, 199
works
Categories, 15, 26, 28, 31, 107–9, 111, 116, 215 n.6, 220 n.37, 227 n.1
De Anima, 11, 26, 32, 109, 113, 116–22, 125–6, 133, 137, 170–1, 229 n.19, 23, 232 n.55–6, 233 n.59, 240 n.47
Eudemian Ethics, 212 n.17
Eudemus, 228 n.10
Metaphysics, 15, 27, 30, 32, 34, 72–3, 77–8, 109, 130, 184, 197, 202, 216 n.7, 216 n.15, 218 n.27, 220 n.41
Meteorology, 27–8, 31, 181, 192, 195, 241 n.3, 242 n.12, 14, 244 n.38